ENGLAND IN AMERICA

SIR WALTER RALEIGH
(1552-1618)

From an engraving by Robinson after a painting by
Zucchero

ENGLAND
IN
AMERICA
1580–1652

By
Lyon Gardiner Tyler, LL.D.

J. & J. Harper Editions
Harper & Row, Publishers
New York and Evanston

CONTENTS

xii   CONTENTS

MAPS

EDITOR'S INTRODUCTION

SOME space has already been given in this series to the English and their relation to the New World, especially the latter half of Cheyney's *European Background of American History*, which deals with the religious, social, and political institutions which the English colonists brought with them; and chapter v. of Bourne's *Spain in America*, describing the Cabot voyages. This volume begins a detailed story of the English settlement, and its title indicates the conception of the author that during the first half-century the American colonies were simply outlying portions of the English nation, but that owing to disturbances culminating in civil war they had the opportunity to develop on lines not suggested by the home government.

The first two chapters deal with the unsuccessful attempts to plant English colonies, especially by Gilbert and Raleigh. These beginnings are important because they proved the difficulty of planting colonies through individual enterprise. At the same time the author brings out clearly the various motives for colonization—the spirit of adventure, the desire to enjoy a new life, and the intent to harm the commerce of the colonies of Spain.

In chapters iii. to vi. the author describes the final founding of the first successful colony, Virginia, and emphasizes four notable characteristics of that movement. The first is the creation of colonizing companies (a part of the movement described in its more general features by Cheyney in his chapters vii. and viii.). The second is the great waste of money and the awful sacrifice of human life caused by the failure of the colonizers to adapt themselves to the conditions of life in America. That the people of Virginia should be fed on grain brought from England, should build their houses in a swamp, should spend their feeble energies in military executions of one another is an unhappy story made none the pleasanter by the knowledge that the founders of the company in England were spending freely of their substance and their effort on the colony. The third element in the growth of Virginia is the introduction of the staple crop, always in demand, and adapted to the soil of Virginia. Tobacco, after 1616, speedily became the main interest of Virginia, and without tobacco it must have gone down. A fourth characteristic is the early evidence of an unconquerable desire for self-government, brought out in the movements of the first assembly of 1619 and the later colonial government: here we have the germ of the later American system of government.

The founding of the neighboring colony of Maryland (chapters vii. and viii.) marks the first of the proprietary colonies; it followed by twenty-five years and had the advantage of the unhappy experience of Virginia and of very capable management. The author shows how little Maryland deserves the name of a Catholic colony, and he develops the Kent Island episode, the first serious boundary controversy between two English commonwealths in America.

To the two earliest New England colonies are devoted five chapters (ix. to xiii.), which are treated not as a separate episode but as part of the general spirit of colonization. Especial attention is paid to the development of popular government in Massachusetts, where the relation between governor, council, and freemen had an opportunity to work itself out. Through the transfer of the charter to New England, America had its first experience of a plantation with a written constitution for internal affairs. The fathers of the Puritan republics are further relieved of the halo which generations of venerating descendants have bestowed upon them, and appear as human characters. Though engaging in a great and difficult task, and while solving many problems, they nevertheless denied their own fundamental precept of the right of a man to worship God according to the dictates of his own conscience.

Chapters xiv. to xvi. describe the foundation of the little settlements in Connecticut, Rhode Island,

New Haven, New Hampshire, and Maine; and here we have an interesting picture of little towns for a time standing quite independent, and gradually consolidating into commonwealths, or coalescing with more powerful neighbors. Then follow (chapters xvii. and xviii.) the international and inter-colonial relations of the colonies, and especially the New England Confederation, the first form of American federal government.

A brief sketch of the conditions of social life in New England (chapter xix.) brings out the strong commercial spirit of the people as well as their intense religious life and the narrowness of their social and intellectual status. The bibliographical essay is necessarily a selection from the great literature of early English colonization, but is a conspectus of the most important secondary works and collections of sources.

The aim of the volume is to show the reasons for as well as the progress of English colonization. Hence for the illustration Sir Walter Raleigh has been chosen, as the most conspicuous colonizer of his time. The freshness of the story is in its clear exposition of the terrible difficulties in the way of founding self-sustaining colonies — the unfamiliar soil and climate, Indian enemies, internal dissensions, interference by the English government, vague and conflicting territorial grants. Yet out of these difficulties, in forty-five years of actual settlement, two southern and six or seven northern communities were permanently established, in the face of the opposition and rivalry of Spain, France, and Holland. For this task the editor has thought that President Tyler is especially qualified, as an author whose descent and historical interest connect him both with the northern and the southern groups of settlements.

AUTHOR'S PREFACE

THIS book covers a period of a little more than three-quarters of a century. It begins with the first attempt at English colonization in America, in 1576, and ends with the year 1652, when the supremacy of Parliament was recognized throughout the English colonies. The original motive of colonization is found in English rivalry with the Spanish power; and the first chapter of this work tells how this motive influenced Gilbert and Raleigh in their endeavors to plant colonies in Newfoundland and North Carolina. Though unfortunate in permanent result, these expeditions familiarized the people of England with the country of Virginia — a name given by Queen Elizabeth to all the region from Canada to Florida—and stimulated the successful settlement at Jamestown in the early part of the seventeenth century. With the charter of 1609 Virginia was severed from North Virginia, to which Captain Smith soon gave the name of "New England"; and the story thereafter is of two streams of English emigration—one to Virginia and the other to New England. Thence arose the Southern and Northern colonies of English America, which, more than a century beyond the period of this book, united to form the great republic of the United States.

The most interesting period in the history of any country is the formative period; and through the mass of recently published original material on America the opportunity to tell its story well has been of late years greatly increased. In the preparation of this work I have endeavored to consult the original sources, and to admit secondary testimony only in matters of detail. I beg to express my indebtedness to the authorities of the Harvard College Library and the Virginia Library for their courtesy in giving me special facilities for the verification of my authorities.

LYON GARDINER TYLER.

ENGLAND IN AMERICA

ENGLAND IN AMERICA

CHAPTER I

GENESIS OF ENGLISH COLONIZATION

(1492–1579)

UP to the last third of the sixteenth century
American history was the history of Spanish
conquest, settlement, and exploration. Except for
the feeble Portuguese settlements in Brazil and at
the mouth of the La Plata, from Florida and the
Gulf of Mexico, around the eastern and western
coasts of South America, and northward to the Gulf
of California, all was Spanish—main-land and islands
alike. The subject of this volume is the bold assertion of England to a rivalry in European waters
and on American coasts.

How came England, with four millions of people,
to enter into a quarter of a century of war with
the greatest power in Europe? The answer is that
Spain was already decaying, while England was
instinct with the spirit of progress and development.
The contrast grew principally out of the different
attitude of the two nations towards the wealth

introduced into Europe from America, and towards
the hitherto established religion of the Christian
world.   While the treasure from Mexico and Peru
enabled Charles V. and Philip II. to carry on great
wars and to establish an immense prestige at the
different courts of Europe, it created a speculative
spirit which drew their subjects away from sober
employment.   For this reason manufacturing and
agriculture, for which Spain was once so distinguished, were neglected; and the kingdom, thinned of
people and decreasing in industry, grew dependent
for supplies upon the neighboring countries.[1]

On the other hand, the treasures which destroyed
the manufactures of Spain indirectly stimulated
those of England.   Without manufactures, Spain
had to employ her funds in buying from other
countries her clothing, furniture, and all that was
necessary for the comfort of her citizens at home
or in her colonies in America.   In 1560 not above
a twentieth part of the commodities exported to
America consisted of Spanish-manufactured fabrics:
all the rest came through the foreign merchants
resident in Spain.[2]

Similar differences arose from the attitude of the
two kingdoms to religion.   Philip loved to regard
himself as the champion of the Catholic church,
and he encouraged it to extend its authority in

[1] Cf. Bourne, *Spain in America*, chap. xvi.
[2] Cf. Cheyney, *European Background of American History*,
chap. v.

Spain in the most absolute manner. Spain became the favored home of the Inquisition, and through its terrors the church acquired complete sovereignty over the minds of the people. Since free thought was impossible, private enterprise gave way to mendicancy and indolence. It was not long before one-half of the real estate of the realm fell into the hands of the clergy and monastic orders.[1]

In England, on the other hand, Henry VIII.'s quarrel with the pope in 1534 gave Protestantism a foothold; and the suppression of the convents and monasteries in 1537–1539 put the possibility of the re-establishment of papal power out of question. Thus, while the body of the people remained attached to the Catholic church under Edward VI. and Queen Mary, the clergy had no great power, and there was plenty of room for free speech. Under Elizabeth various causes promoted the growth of Protestantism till it became a permanent ruling principle. Since its spirit was one of inquiry, private enterprise, instead of being suppressed as in Spain, spread the wings of manufacture and commerce.[2]

Thus, collision between the two nations was unavoidable, and their rivalry enlisted all the forces of religion and interest. Under such influences thousands of young Englishmen crossed the channel to fight with William of Orange against the Span-

---

[1] Prescott, *Hist. of the Reign of Philip II.*, III., 443.
[2] *Ibid.*, chaps. xi., xii.

iards or with the Huguenots against the Guises, the allies of Spain. The same motives led to the dazzling exploits of Hawkins, Drake, and Cavendish, and sent to the sea scores of English privateers; and it was the same motives which stimulated Gilbert in 1576, eighty-four years after the Spaniards had taken possession, in his grand design of planting a colony in America. The purpose of Gilbert was to cut into Spanish colonial power, as was explained by Richard Hakluyt in his *Discourse on Western Planting*, written in 1584: "If you touche him [the king of Spain] in the Indies, you touche the apple of his eye; for take away his treasure, which is *neruus belli*, and which he hath almoste oute of his West Indies, his olde bandes of souldiers will soone be dissolved, his purposes defeated, his power and strengthe diminished, his pride abated, and his tyranie utterly suppressed."[1]

Still, while English colonization at first sprang out of rivalry with Spain and was late in beginning, England's claims in America were hardly later than Spain's. Christopher Columbus at first hoped, in his search for the East Indies, to sail under the auspices of Henry VII. Only five years later, in 1497, John Cabot, under an English charter, reached the continent of North America in seeking a shorter route by the northwest; and in 1498, with his son Sebastian Cabot, he repeated his visit. But nothing important resulted from these

---

[1] Maine Hist. Soc., *Collections*, 2d series, II., 59.

voyages, and after long neglect their memory was revived by Hakluyt,[1] only to support a claim for England to priority in discovery.

Indeed, England was not yet prepared for the work of colonization. Her commerce was still in its infancy, and did not compare with that of either Italy, Spain, or Portugal. Neither Columbus nor the Cabots were Englishmen, and the advantages of commerce were so little understood in England about this period that the taking of interest for the use of money was prohibited.[2] A voyage to some mart "within two days' distance" was counted a matter of great moment by merchant adventurers.[3]

During the next half-century, only two noteworthy attempts were made by the English to accomplish the purposes of the Cabots: De Prado visited Newfoundland in 1527 and Hore in 1535,[4] but neither of the voyages was productive of any important result. Notwithstanding, England's commerce made some advancement during this period. A substantial connection between England and America was England's fisheries on the banks of Newfoundland; though used by other European states, over fifty English ships spent two months in every year in those distant waters, and gained,

---

[1] Hakluyt, *Discourse on Western Planting.*
[2] Robertson, *Works* (ed. 1818), XI., 136.
[3] *Nova Britannia* (Force, *Tracts,* I., No. vi.).
[4] Purchas, *Pilgrimes* (ed. 1625), III., 809; Hakluyt, *Voyages* (ed. 1809), III., 167–174.

in the pursuit, valuable maritime experience. Probably, however, the development of trade in a different quarter had a more direct connection with American colonization, for about 1530 William Hawkins visited the coast of Guinea and engaged in the slave-trade with Brazil.[1]

Suddenly, about the middle of the century, English commerce struck out boldly; conscious rivalry with Spain had begun. The new era opens fitly with the return of Sebastian Cabot to England from Spain, where since the death of Henry VII. he had served Charles V. In 1549, during the third year of Edward VI., he was made grand pilot of England with an annual stipend of £166 13s. 4d.[2] He formed a company for the discovery of the northeast and the northwest passages, and in 1553 an expedition under Sir Hugh Willoughby and Richard Chancellor penetrated the White Sea and made known the wonders of the Russian Empire.[3] The company obtained, in 1554, a charter of incorporation under the title of the "Merchant Adventurers for the Discovery of Lands, Territories, Isles, Dominions, and Seignories Unknown or Frequented by Any English." To Russia frequent voyages were thereafter made. A few days after the departure of Willoughby's expedition Richard Eden published his *Treatyse of the Newe India;* and

---

[1] Hakluyt, *Voyages*, III., 171; IV., 198.
[2] Purchas, *Pilgrimes*, III., 808; Hakluyt, *Voyages*, III., 31.
[3] Hakluyt, *Voyages*, I., 270.

two years later appeared his *Decades of the New World*, a book which was very popular among all classes of people in England. Cabot died not many years later, and Eden, translator and compiler, attended at his bedside, and "beckons us with something of awe to see him die." [1]

During Mary's reign (1553–1558) the Catholic church was restored in England, and by the influence of the queen, who was married to King Philip, the expanding commerce of England was directed away from the Spanish colonial possessions eastward to Russia, Barbary, Turkey, and Persia. After her death the barriers against free commerce were thrown down. With the incoming of Elizabeth, the Protestant church was re-established and the Protestant refugees returned from the continent; and three years after her succession occurred the first of those great voyages which exposed the weakness of Spain by showing that her rich possessions in America were practically unguarded and unprotected.

In 1562 Sir John Hawkins, following in the track of his father William Hawkins, visited Guinea, and, having loaded his ship with negroes, carried them to Hispaniola, where, despite the Spanish law restricting the trade to the mother-country, he sold his slaves to the planters, and returned to England with a rich freight of ginger, hides, and pearls. In 1564 Hawkins repeated the experiment with

[1] Winsor, *Narrative and Critical History*, III., 7.

greater success; and on his way home, in 1565, he stopped in Florida and relieved the struggling French colony of Laudonnière, planted there by Admiral Coligny the year before, and barbarously destroyed by the Spaniards soon after Hawkins's departure.[1] The difference between our age and Queen Elizabeth's is illustrated by the fact that Hawkins, instead of being put to death as a pirate for engaging in the slave-trade, was rewarded by the queen on his return with a patent for a coat of arms.

In 1567 Hawkins with nine ships revisited the West Indies, but this time ill-fortune overtook him. Driven by bad weather into the harbor of San Juan de Ulloa, he was attacked by the Spaniards, several of his ships were sunk, and some of his men were captured and later put to torture by the Inquisition. Hawkins escaped with two of his ships, and after a long and stormy passage arrived safe in England (January 25, 1569).[2] Queen Elizabeth was greatly offended at this conduct of the Spaniards, and in reprisal detained a squadron of Spanish treasure ships which had sought safety in the port of London from some Huguenot cruisers.

In this expedition one of the two ships which escaped was commanded by a young man named Francis Drake, who came to be regarded as the greatest seaman of his age. He was the son of a clergyman, and was born in Devonshire, where

---

[1] Hakluyt, *Voyages*, III., 593, 618.   [2] *Ibid.*, 618–623.

centred for two centuries the maritime skill of
England. While a lad he followed the sea, and
acquired reputation for his courage and sagacity.
Three years after the affair at San Juan, Drake
fitted out a little squadron, and in 1572 sailed, as
he himself specially states, to inflict vengeance upon
the Spaniards. He had no commission, and on his
own private account attacked a power with which
his country was at peace.[1]

Drake attacked Nombre de Dios and Cartagena,
and, as the historian relates, got together "a pretty
store of money," an evidence that his purpose
was not wholly revenge. He marched across the
Isthmus of Panama and obtained his first view of
the Pacific Ocean. "Vehemently transported with
desire to navigate that sea," he fell upon his knees,
and "implored the Divine Assistance, that he might
at some time or other sail thither and make a
perfect discovery of the same."[2] Drake reached
Plymouth on his return Sunday, August 9, 1573,
in sermon time; and his arrival created so much
excitement that the people left the preacher alone
in church so as to catch a glimpse of the famous
sailor.[3]

Drake contemplated greater deeds. He had now
plenty of friends who wished to engage with him,

[1] Hakluyt, *Voyages*, IV., 1; Winsor, *Narrative and Critical History*, III., 59–84.

[2] Camden, *Annals*, in Kennet, *England*, II., 478.

[3] Harris, *Voyages and Travels*, II., 15.

and he soon equipped a squadron of five ships. That he had saved something from the profits of his former voyage is shown by his equipment. The *Pelican*, in which he sailed, had "expert musicians and rich furniture," and "all the vessels for the table, yea, many even of the cook-room, were of pure silver." [1] Drake's object now was to harry the coast of the ocean which he had seen in 1573. Accordingly, he sailed from Plymouth (December 13, 1577), coasted along the shore of South America, and, passing through the Straits of Magellan, entered the Pacific in September, 1578.

The *Pelican* was now the only one of his vessels left, as all the rest had either returned home or been lost. Renaming the ship the *Golden Hind*, Drake swept up the western side of South America and took the ports of Chili and Peru by surprise. He captured galleons carrying quantities of gold, silver, and jewelry, and acquired plunder worth millions of dollars.[2] Drake did not think it prudent to go home by the way he had come, but struck boldly northward in search of a northeast passage into the Atlantic. He coasted along California as far as Oregon, repaired his ship in a harbor near San Francisco, took possession of the country in the name of Queen Elizabeth and called it Nova Albion. Finding no northeast passage, he turned his prow to the west, and circumnavigated the globe by the

[1] Harris, *Voyages and Travels*, II., 15.
[2] Camden, *Annals*, in Kennet, *England*, II., 478, 479.

Cape of Good Hope, arriving at Plymouth in November, 1580.[1]

The queen received him with undisguised favor, and met a request from Philip II. for Drake's surrender by knighting the freebooter and wearing in her crown the jewel he offered her as a present. When the Spanish ambassador threatened that matters should come to the cannon, she replied "quietly, in her most natural voice," writes Mendoza, "that if I used threats of that kind she would throw me into a dungeon." The revenge that Drake had taken for the affair at San Juan de Ulloa was so complete that for more than a hundred years he was spoken of in Spanish annals as "the Dragon."

His example stimulated adventure in all directions, and in 1586 Thomas Cavendish, of Ipswich, sailed to South America and made a rich plunder at Spanish expense. He returned home by the Cape of Good Hope, and was thus the second Englishman to circumnavigate the globe.[2]

In the mean time, another actor, hardly less adventurous but of a far grander purpose, had stepped upon the stage of this tremendous historic drama. Sir Humphrey Gilbert was born in Devonshire, schooled at Eton, and educated at Oxford. Between 1563 and 1576 he served in the wars of France, Ireland, and the Netherlands, and was

[1] Camden, *Annals*, in Kennet, *England*, II., 479, 480; Hakluyt, *Voyages*, IV., 232–246.   [2] *Ibid.*, 316–341.

therefore thoroughly steeped in the military train-
ing of the age.[1]   The first evidence of Gilbert's
great purpose was the charter by Parliament, in the
autumn of 1566, of a corporation for the discovery
of new trades.   Gilbert was a member, and in
1567 he presented an unsuccessful petition to the
queen for the use of two ships for the discovery
of a northwest passage to China and the establishment of a traffic with that country.[2]

Before long Gilbert wrote a pamphlet, entitled
"A Discourse to Prove a Passage by the Northwest
to Cathaia and the East Indies," which was shown
by Gascoigne, a friend of Gilbert, to the celebrated
mariner Martin Frobisher, and stimulated him to
his glorious voyages to the northeast coast of
North America.[3]   Before Frobisher's departure on
his first voyage Queen Elizabeth sent for him and
commended him for his enterprise, and when he
sailed, July 1, 1576, she waved her hand to him from
her palace window.[4]   He explored Frobisher's Strait
and took possession of the land called Meta Incognita
in the name of the queen.   He brought back with
him a black stone, which a gold-finder in London
pronounced rich in gold, and the vain hope of a
gold-mine inspired two other voyages (1577, 1578).
On his third voyage Frobisher entered the strait

[1] Edwards, *Life of Raleigh*, I., 77.
[2] *Cal. of State Pap., Col.*, 1513–1616, p. 8.
[3] Hakluyt, *Voyages*, III., 32–46; Edwards, *Life of Raleigh*,
I., 77; Doyle, *English in America*, I., 60.
[4] Hakluyt, *Voyages*, III., 53.

known as Hudson Strait, but the ore with which he loaded his ships proved of little value. John Davis, like Frobisher, made three voyages in three successive years (1585, 1586, 1587), and the chief result of his labors was the discovery of the great strait which bears his name.[1]

Meanwhile, the idea of building up another English nation across the seas had taken a firm hold on Gilbert, and among those who communed with him were his half-brother Sir Walter Raleigh, his brothers Adrian and John Gilbert, besides Richard Hakluyt, Sir Philip Sydney, Sir Richard Grenville, Sir George Peckham, and Secretary of State Sir Francis Walsingham. The ill success of Frobisher had no influence upon their purpose; but four years elapsed after Gilbert's petition to the crown in 1574 before he obtained his patent. How these years preyed upon the noble enthusiasm of Gilbert we may understand from a letter commonly attributed to him, which was handed to the queen in November, 1577 : " I will do it if you will allow me ; only you must resolve and not delay or dally—the wings of man's life are plumed with the feathers of death."[2]

At length, however, the formalities were completed, and on June 11, 1578, letters to Gilbert passed the seals for planting an English colony in America.[3] This detailed charter of colonization is

[1] Hakluyt, *Voyages*, III., 52–104, 132.
[2] Brown, *Genesis of the United States*, I., 9.
[3] Hakluyt, *Voyages*, III., 174–176.

most interesting, since it contains several provisions which reappear in many later charters. Gilbert was invested with all title to the soil within two hundred leagues of the place of settlement, and large governmental authority was given him. To the crown were reserved only the allegiance of the settlers and one-fifth of all the gold and silver to be found. Yet upon Gilbert's power two notable limitations were imposed: the colonists were to enjoy "all the privileges of free denizens and persons native of England"; and the protection of the nation was withheld from any license granted by Gilbert "to rob or spoil by sea or by land."

Sir Humphrey lost no time in assembling a fleet, but it was not till November 19, 1578, that he finally sailed from Plymouth with seven sail and three hundred and eighty-seven men, one of the ships being commanded by Raleigh. The subsequent history of the expedition is only vaguely known. The voyagers got into a fight with a Spanish squadron and a ship was lost.[1] Battered and dispirited as the fleet was, Gilbert had still Drake's buccaneering expedient open to him; but, loyal to the injunctions of the queen's charter, he chose to return, and the expedition broke up at Kinsale, in Ireland.[2]

In this unfortunate voyage Gilbert buried the mass of his fortune, but, undismayed, he renewed

---

[1] Hakluyt, *Voyages*, III., 186.
[2] *Cal. of State Pap., Col.*, 1574–1674, p. 17.

his enterprise. He was successful in enlisting a
large number of gentlemen in the new venture, and
two friends who invested heavily—Sir Thomas
Gerard, of Lancaster, and Sir George Peckham, of
Bucks—he rewarded by enormous grants of land and
privileges.[1] Raleigh adventured £2000 and con-
tributed a ship, the *Ark Raleigh;*[2] but probably
no man did more in stirring up interest than Richard
Hakluyt, the famous naval historian, who about
this time published his *Divers Voyages*, which fired
the heart and imagination of the nation.[3] In 1579
an exploring ship was sent out under Simon Ferdinando, and the next year another sailed under John
Walker. They reached the coast of Maine, and the
latter brought back the report of a silver-mine discovered near the Penobscot.[4]

[1] *Cal. of State Pap., Col.*, 1574–1674, pp. 8–10.
[2] Edwards, *Life of Raleigh*, I., 82, 83.
[3] Stevens, *Thomas Hariot*, 40.
[4] *Cal. of State Pap., Col.*, 1574–1660, p. 2.

CHAPTER II

GILBERT AND RALEIGH COLONIES

(1583–1602)

PREPARATIONS for Gilbert's second and fateful expedition now went forward, and public interest was much aroused by the return of Drake, in 1580, laden with the spoils of America. Gilbert invited Raleigh to accompany him as vice-admiral, but the queen would not let him accept.[1] Indeed, she seemed to have a presentiment that all would not go well, and when the arrangements for the voyage were nearing completion she caused her secretary of state, Walsingham, to let Gilbert also know that, "of her special care" for him, she wished his stay at home "as a man noted of no good hap by sea."[2] But the queen's remark only proved her desire for Gilbert's safety; and she soon after sent him word that she wished him as "great goodhap and safety to his ship as if herself were there in person," and requested his picture as a keepsake.[3]

The fleet of Sir Humphrey Gilbert, consisting of

[1] Edwards, *Life of Raleigh*, I., 81, II., 10.
[2] *Cal. of State Pap., Col.*, 1574–1674, p. 17.
[3] Edwards, *Life of Raleigh*, I., 82.

five ships bearing two hundred and sixty men,
sailed from Plymouth June 11, 1583, and the "mishaps" which the queen feared soon overtook them.
After scarcely two days of voyage the ship sent
by Raleigh, the best in the fleet, deserted. Two
more ships got separated, and the crew of one of
them, freed from Gilbert's control, turned pirates
and plundered a French ship which fell in their way.
Nevertheless, Gilbert pursued his course, and on
August 3, 1583, he reached the harbor of St. John's
in Newfoundland, where he found the two missing
ships. Gilbert showed his commission to the fishing vessels, of which there were no fewer than thirty-
six of all nations in port, and their officers readily
recognized his authority. Two days later he took
possession of the country in the name of Queen
Elizabeth, and as an indication of the national sovereignty to all men he caused the arms of England engraved on lead to be fixed on a pillar of wood
on the shore side.

Mishaps did not end with the landing in Newfoundland. The emigrants who sailed with Gilbert
were better fitted for a crusade than a colony, and,
disappointed at not at once finding mines of gold
and silver, many deserted; and soon there were not
enough sailors to man all the four ships. Accordingly, the *Swallow* was sent back to England with
the sick; and with the remainder of the fleet, well
supplied at St. John's with fish and other necessa-
ries, Gilbert (August 20) sailed south as far as forty-

four degrees north latitude. Off Sable Island a
storm assailed them, and the largest of the vessels,
called the *Delight*, carrying most of the provisions,
was driven on a rock and went to pieces.

Overwhelmed by this terrible misfortune, the
colonists returned to Newfoundland, where, yield-
ing to his crew, Gilbert discontinued his explorations, and on August 31 changed the course of the
two ships remaining, the *Squirrel* and *Golden Hind*,
directly for England. The story of the voyage
back is most pathetic. From the first the sea was
boisterous; but to entreaties that he should abandon
the *Squirrel*, a little affair of ten tons, and seek his
own safety in the *Hind*, a ship of much larger size,
Gilbert replied, "No, I will not forsake my little
company going homeward, with whom I have
passed so many storms and perils." Even then,
amid so much danger, his spirit rose supreme, and
he actually planned for the spring following two
expeditions, one to the south and one to the north;
and when some one asked him how he expected
to meet the expenses in so short a time, he replied,
"Leave that to me, and I will ask a penny of no
man."

A terrible storm arose, but Gilbert retained the
heroic courage and Christian faith which had ever
distinguished him. As often as the *Hind*, tossed
upon the waves, approached within hailing distance
of the *Squirrel*, the gallant admiral, "himself sitting
with a book in his hand " on the deck, would call out

words of cheer and consolation—"We are as near heaven by sea as by land." When night came on (September 10) only the lights in the riggings of the *Squirrel* told that the noble Gilbert still survived. At midnight the lights went out suddenly, and from the watchers on the *Hind* the cry arose, "The admiral is cast away." And only the *Golden Hind* returned to England.[1]

The mantle of Gilbert fell upon the shoulders of his half-brother Sir Walter Raleigh, whose energy and versatility made him, perhaps, the foremost Englishman of his age. When the *Hind* returned from her ill-fated voyage Raleigh was thirty-one years of age and possessed a person at once attractive and commanding. He was tall and well proportioned, had thick, curly locks, beard, and mustaches, full, red lips, bluish gray eyes, high forehead, and a face described as "long and bold."

By service in France, the Netherlands, and Ireland he had shown himself a soldier of the same fearless stamp as his half-brother Sir Humphrey Gilbert; and he was already looked upon as a seaman of splendid powers for organization. Poet and scholar, he was the patron of Edmund Spenser, the famous author of the *Faerie Queene;* of Richard Hakluyt, the naval historian; of Le Moyne and John White, the painters; and of Thomas Hariot, the great mathematician.

Expert in the art of gallantry, Raleigh won his

[1] Hakluyt, *Voyages*, III., 184–208.

way to the queen's heart by deftly placing between her feet and a muddy place his new plush coat. He dared the extremity of his political fortunes by writing on a pane of glass which the queen must see, "Fain would I climb, but fear I to fall." And she replied with an encouraging—"If thy heart fail thee, climb not at all." The queen's favor developed into magnificent gifts of riches and honor, and Raleigh received various monopolies, many forfeited estates, and appointments as lord warden of the stannaries, lieutenant of the county of Cornwall, vice-admiral of Cornwall and Devon, and captain of the queen's guard.

The manner in which Raleigh went about the work of colonization showed remarkable forethought and system. In order to enlist the active co-operation of the court and gentry, he induced Richard Hakluyt to write for him, in 1584, his *Discourse on Western Planting*, which he circulated in manuscript.[1] He not only received from the queen in 1584 a patent similar to Gilbert's,[2] but by obtaining a confirmation from Parliament in 1585 he acquired a national sanction which Gilbert's did not possess.[3]

In imitation of Gilbert he sent out first an exploring expedition commanded by Arthur Barlow and Philip Amidas; but, warned by his brother's

---

[1] Stevens, *Thomas Hariot*, 43–48.
[2] For the patent, see Hakluyt, *Voyages*, III., 297–301.
[3] Brown, *Genesis of the United States*, I., 13.

experience, he directed them to go southward. They
left the west of England April 27, 1584, and arrived
upon the coast of North Carolina July 4, where
they passed into Ocracoke Inlet south of Cape Hatteras. There, landing on an island called Wokokon
—part of the broken outer coast—Barlow and
Amidas took possession in the right of the queen
and Sir Walter Raleigh.[1]

Several weeks were spent in exploring Pamlico
Sound, which they found dotted with many small
islands, the largest of which, sixteen miles long,
called by the Indians Roanoke Island, was fifty miles
north of Wokokon. About the middle of September,
1584, they returned to England and reported as the
name of the new country "Wincondacoa," which the
Indians at Wokokon had cried when they saw the
white men, meaning "What pretty clothes you wear!"
The queen, however, was proud of the new discovery, and suggested that it should be called, in
honor of herself, "Virginia."

Pleased at the report of his captains, Sir Walter
displayed great energy in making ready a fleet of
seven ships, which sailed from Plymouth April 9,
1585. They carried nearly two hundred settlers,
and the three foremost men on board were Sir
Richard Grenville, the commander of the fleet;
Thomas Cavendish, the future circumnavigator of
the globe; and Captain Ralph Lane, the designated
governor of the new colony. The fleet went the

[1] Hakluyt, *Voyages*, III., 301.

usual way by the West Indies, and June 20 "fell in with the maine of Florida," and June 26 cast anchor at Wokokon.

After a month the fleet moved out again to sea, and passing by Cape Hatteras entered a channel now called New Inlet. August 17, the colony was landed on Roanoke Island, and eight days later Grenville weighed anchor for England. On the way back Grenville met a Spanish ship "richly loaden," and captured her, "boording her with a boate made with boards of chests, which fell asunder, and sunke at the ships side, as soone as euer he and his men were out of it." October 18, 1585, he arrived with his prize at Plymouth, in England, where he was received with great honor and rejoicing.[1]

The American loves to connect the beginnings of his country with a hero like Grenville. He was one of the English admirals who helped to defeat the Spanish Armada, and nothing in naval warfare is more memorable than his death. In an expedition led by Lord Charles Howard in 1591 against the Spanish plate-fleet, Grenville was vice-admiral, and he opposed his ship single-handed against five great Spanish galleons, supported at intervals by ten others, and he fought them during nearly fifteen hours. Then Grenville's vessel was so battered that it resembled rather a skeleton than a ship, and of the crew few were to be seen but the dead and dying. Grenville himself was captured mortally wounded,

[1] Hakluyt, *Voyages*, III., 302–310.

and died uttering these words, "Here die I, Richard Grenville, with a joyful and quiet mind, for that I have ended my life, as a true soldier ought to do, fighting for his country, queen, religion, and honor." [1]

Of the settlers at Roanoke during the winter after their landing nothing is recorded, but the prospect in the spring was gloomy. Lane made extensive explorations for gold-mines and for the South Sea, and found neither. The natives laid a plot to massacre the settlers, but Lane's soldierly precaution saved the colonists. Grenville was expected to return with supplies by Easter, but Easter passed and there was no news. In order to get subsistence, Lane divided his men into three parties, of which one remained at Roanoke Island and the other two were sent respectively to Hatteras and to Croatoan, an island just north of Wokokon.

Not long after Sir Francis Drake, returning from sacking San Domingo, Cartagena, and St. Augustine, appeared in sight with a superb fleet of twenty-three sail. He succored the imperilled colonists with supplies, and offered to take them back to England. Lane and the chief men, disheartened at the prospects, abandoned the island, and July 28, 1586, the colonists arrived at Plymouth in Drake's ships, having lost but four men during the whole year of their stay. [2]

[1] Edwards, *Life of Raleigh*, I., 144–145.
[2] Hakluyt, *Voyages*, III., 322, IV., 10.

A day or two after the departure of the colonists a ship sent by Raleigh arrived, and about fourteen or fifteen days later came three ships under Sir Richard Grenville, Raleigh's admiral. Grenville spent some time beating up and down Pamlico Sound, hunting for the colony, and finally returned to England, leaving fifteen men behind at Roanoke to retain possession.[1]   This was the second settlement.

The colonists who returned in Drake's ships brought back to Raleigh two vegetable products which he speedily popularized. One was the potato,[2] which Raleigh planted on his estate in Ireland, and the other was tobacco, called by the natives "uppowoc," which he taught the courtiers to smoke.

Most of the settlers who went with Lane were mere gold-hunters, but there were two who would have been valuable to any society—the mathematician Thomas Hariot, who surveyed the country and wrote an account of the settlement; and John White, who made more than seventy beautiful water-colors representing the dress of the Indians and their manner of living. When the engraver De Bry came to England in 1587 he made the acquaintance of Hakluyt, who introduced him to John White, and the result was that De Bry was induced to turn Hariot's account of Virginia into the

[1] Hakluyt, *Voyages*, III., 323, 340.
[2] Edwards, *Life of Raleigh*, I., 106.

first part of his celebrated *Peregrinations*, illustrating it from the surveys of Hariot and the paintings of John White.[1]

If Raleigh was disappointed with his first attempt at colonization he was encouraged by the good report of Virginia given by Lane and Hariot, and in less than another year he had a third fleet ready to sail. He meant to make this expedition more of a colony than Lane's settlement at Roanoke, and selected as governor the painter John White, who could appreciate the natural productions of the country. And among the one hundred and fifty settlers who sailed from Plymouth May 8, 1587, were some twenty-five women and children.

The instructions of Raleigh required them to proceed to Chesapeake Bay, of which the Indians had given Lane an account on his previous voyage, only stopping at Roanoke for the fifteen men that Grenville had left there; but when they reached Roanoke Simon Ferdinando, the pilot, refused to carry them any farther, and White established his colony at the old seating-place. None of Grenville's men could be found, and it was afterwards learned that they had been suddenly attacked by the Indians, who killed one man and so frightened the rest as to cause them to take to sea in a rowboat, which was never heard of again.

Through Manteo, a friendly Indian, White tried to re-establish amicable relations with the natives,

[1] Stevens, *Thomas Hariot*, 55-62.

and for his faithful services Manteo was christened and proclaimed "Lord of Roanoke and Dasamonguepeuk"; but the Indians, with the exception of the tribe of Croatoan, to which Manteo belonged, declined to make friends. August 18, five days after the christening of Manteo, Eleanor Dare, daughter to the governor and wife of Ananias Dare, one of White's council, was delivered of a daughter, and this child, Virginia, was the first Christian born in the new realm.[1]

When his granddaughter was only ten days old Governor White went to England for supplies. He reached Hampton November 8, 1587.[2] He found affairs in a turmoil. England was threatened with the great Armada, and Raleigh, Grenville, Lane, and all the other friends of Virginia were exerting their energies for the protection of their homes and firesides.[3] Indeed, the rivalry of England and Spain had reached its crisis; for at this time all the hopes of Protestant Christendom were centred in England, and within her borders the Protestant refugees from all countries found a place of safety and repose. In 1585 the Dutch, still carrying on their struggle with Spain, had offered Queen Elizabeth the sovereignty of the Netherlands, and, though she declined it, she sent an army to their assistance. The French Huguenots also looked to her for support and protection. Spain, on the

[1] Hakluyt, *Voyages*, III., 340–345.   [2] *Ibid.*, 346, 347.
[3] Brown, *Genesis of the United States*, I., 19.

other hand, as the representative of all Catholic Europe, had never appeared so formidable. By the conquest of Portugal in 1580 her king had acquired control over the East Indies, which were hardly less valuable than the colonies of Spain; and with the money derived from both the Spanish and Portuguese possessions Philip supported his armies in Italy and the Netherlands, and was the mainstay of the pope at Rome, the Guises in France, and the secret plotters in Scotland and Ireland of rebellion against the authority of Elizabeth.

This wide distribution of power was, however, an inherent weakness which created demands enough to exhaust the treasury even of Philip, and he instinctively recognized in England a danger which must be promptly removed. England must be subdued, and Philip, determining on an invasion, collected a powerful army at Bruges, in Flanders, and an immense fleet in the Tagus, in Spain. For the attack he selected a time when Amsterdam, the great mart of the Netherlands, had fallen before his general the duke of Palma; when the king of France had become a prisoner of the Guises; and when the frenzied hatred of the Catholic world was directed against Elizabeth for the execution of Mary, queen of Scots.

How to meet and repel this immense danger caused many consultations on the part of Elizabeth and her statesmen, and at first they inclined to make the defence by land only. But Raleigh, like Themistocles at Athens under similar conditions, urgently advised dependence on a well-equipped fleet, and after some hesitation his advice was followed. Then every effort was strained to bring into service every ship that could be found or constructed in time within the limits of England, so that in May, 1588, when Philip's huge Armada set sail from the Tagus, a numerous English fleet was ready to dispute its onward passage. A great battle was fought soon after in the English Channel, and there Lord Charles Howard of Effingham, and Raleigh and Drake and Hawkins joined with Grenville and Cavendish and Frobisher and Lane, and all the other glorious heroes of England, in the mighty overthrow of the Spanish enemy.[1]

Under the inspiration of this tremendous victory the Atlantic Ocean during the next three years swarmed with English cruisers, and more than eight hundred Spanish ships fell victims to their attacks. So great was the destruction that the coast of Virginia abounded in the wreckage.[2] But the way to a successful settlement in America was not entirely opened until eight years later, when the English fleet, under Howard, Raleigh, and Essex, completed the destruction of the Spanish power by another great naval victory won in the harbor of Cadiz.

Amid all this excitement and danger Raleigh did

[1] Edwards, *Life of Raleigh*, I., 111.
[2] Brown, *Genesis of the United States*, I., 20.

not forget his colony in Virginia. Twice he sent relief expeditions; but the first was stopped because in the struggle with Spain all the ships were demanded for government service; and the second was so badly damaged by the Spanish cruisers that it could not continue its voyage. Raleigh had spent £40,000 in his several efforts to colonize Virginia, and the burden became too heavy for him to carry alone. As Hakluyt said, "It required a prince's purse to have the action thoroughly followed out." He therefore consented, in 1589, to assign a right to trade in Virginia to Sir Thomas Smith, John White, Richard Hakluyt, and others, reserving a fifth of all the gold and silver extracted, and they raised means for White's last voyage to Virginia.[1]

It was not until March, 1591, that Governor White was able to put to sea again. He reached Roanoke Island August 17, and, landing, visited the point where he had placed the settlement. As he climbed the sandy bank he noticed, carved upon a tree in Roman letters, "C R O," without a cross, and White called to mind that three years before, when he left for England, it had been agreed that if the settlers ever found it necessary to remove from the island they were to leave behind them some such inscription, and to add a cross if they left in danger or distress. A little farther on stood the fort, and there White read on one of the trees an inscription in

[1] Stebbins, *Life of Raleigh*, 47.

large capital letters, "Croatoan." This left no doubt
that the colony had moved to the island of that name
south of Cape Hatteras and near Ocracoke Inlet.
He wished the ships to sail in that direction, but a
storm arose, and the captains, dreading the dangerous shoals of Pamlico Sound, put to sea and returned
to England without ever visiting Croatoan.[1] White
never came back to America, and his separation
from the colony is heightened in tragic effect by the
loss of his daughter and granddaughter.

What became of the settlers at Roanoke has been
a frequent subject of speculation. When Jamestown was established, in 1607, the search for them
was renewed, but nothing definite could be learned.
There is, indeed, a story told by Strachey that the
unfortunate colonists, finally abandoning all hope,
intermixed with the Indians at Croatoan, and after
living with them till about the time of the arrival
at Jamestown were, at the instigation of Powhatan,
cruelly massacred. Only seven of them—four men,
two boys, and a young maid—were preserved by a
friendly chief, and from these, as later legends have
declared, descended a tribe of Indians found in the
vicinity of Roanoke Island in the beginning of
the eighteenth century and known as the Hatteras
Indians.[2]

Sir Walter Raleigh will always be esteemed the
true parent of North American colonization, for

---

[1] Hakluyt, *Voyages*, III., 350–357.
[2] Strachey, *Travaile into Virginia*, 26, 85.

though the idea did not originate with him he popularized it beyond any other man. Just as he made smoking fashionable at the court of Elizabeth, so the colonization of Virginia—that is, of the region from Canada to Florida—was made fashionable through his example. His enterprise caused the advantages of America's soil and climate to be appreciated in England, and he was the first to fix upon Chesapeake Bay as the proper place of settlement.

When James I. succeeded Elizabeth on the throne Raleigh lost his influence at court, and nearly all the last years of his life were spent a prisoner in the Tower of London, where he wrote his *History of the World*. In 1616 he was temporarily released by the king on condition of his finding a gold-mine in Guiana. When he returned empty-handed he was, on the complaint of the Spanish ambassador, arrested, sentenced to death, and executed on an old verdict of the jury, now recognized to have been based on charges trumped up by political enemies.[1]

Raleigh never relinquished hope in America. In 1595 he made a voyage to Guiana, and in 1602 sent out Samuel Mace to Virginia—the third of Mace's voyages thither. In 1603, just before his confinement in the Tower, he wrote to Sir Robert Cecil regarding the rights which he had in that country, and used these memorable words, "I shall yet live to see it an English nation."[2]

[1] Edwards, *Life of Raleigh*, I., 706, 721.   [2] *Ibid.*, 91.

CHAPTER III

FOUNDING OF VIRGINIA

(1602–1608)

THOUGH a prisoner in the Tower of London who could not share in the actual work, Sir Walter Raleigh lived to see his prediction regarding Virginia realized in 1607. He had personally given substance to the English claim to North America based upon the remote discovery of John Cabot, and his friends, after he had withdrawn from the field of action, were the mainstay of English colonization in the Western continent.

Bartholomew Gosnold and Bartholomew Gilbert, son of Sir Humphrey, with Raleigh's consent and under the patronage of Henry Wriothesley, the brilliant and accomplished earl of Southampton, renewed the attempt at colonization. With a small colony of thirty-two men they set sail from Falmouth March 26, 1602, took an unusual direct course across the Atlantic, and seven weeks later saw land at Cape Elizabeth, on the coast of Maine. They then sailed southward and visited a headland which they named Cape Cod, a small island now "No Man's Land," which they called Martha's

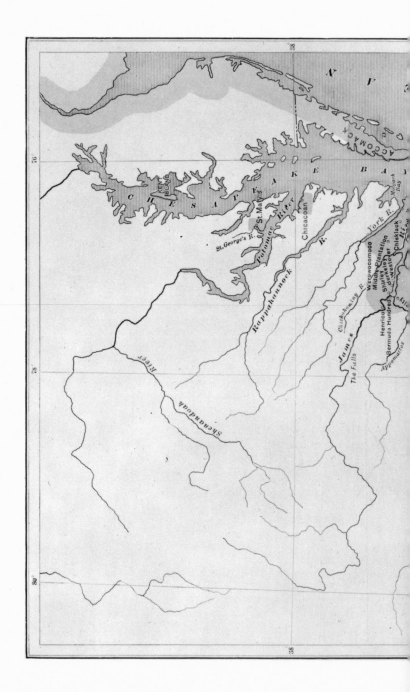

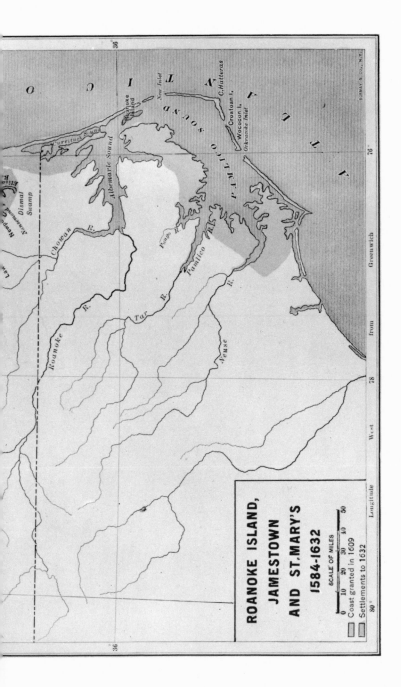

ROANOKE ISLAND,
JAMESTOWN
AND ST.MARY'S
1584-1632

SCALE OF MILES
0 10 20 30 40 50

Coast granted in 1609
Settlements to 1632

Vineyard (a name since transferred to the larger island farther north), and the group called the Elizabeth Islands. The colonists were delighted with the appearance of the country, but becoming apprehensive of the Indians returned to England after a short stay.[1]

In April, 1603, Richard Hakluyt obtained Raleigh's consent, and, aided by some merchants of Bristol, sent out Captain Martin Pring with two small vessels, the *Speedwell* and *Discovery*, on a voyage of trade and exploration to the New England coast. Pring was absent eight months, and returned with an account of the country fully confirming Gosnold's good report. Two years later, in 1605, the earl of Southampton and his brother-in-law, Lord Thomas Arundell, sent out Captain George Weymouth, who visited the Kennebec and brought back information even more encouraging.[2]

Meanwhile, Queen Elizabeth died March 24, 1603, and was succeeded by King James I. In November Raleigh was convicted of high - treason and his monopoly of American colonization was abrogated. By the peace ratified by the king of Spain June 15, 1605, about a month before Weymouth's return, the seas were made more secure for English voyages, although neither power conceded the territorial claims of the other.[3]

---

[1] Purchas, *Pilgrimes*, IV., 1647–1651; Strachey, *Travaile into Virginia*, 153–158; John Smith, *Works* (Arber's ed.), 332–340.

[2] Purchas, *Pilgrimes*, IV., 1654–1656, 1659–1667.

[3] Brown, *Genesis of the United States*, I., 27.

Owing to these changed conditions and the favorable reports of Gosnold, Pring, and Weymouth, extensive plans for colonization were considered in England.   Since the experiment of private colonization had failed, the new work was undertaken by joint-stock companies, for which the East India Company, chartered in 1600, with the eminent merchant Sir Thomas Smith at its head, afforded a model.   Not much is known of the beginnings of the movement, but it matured speedily, and the popularity of the comedy of *Eastward Ho!* written by Chapman and Marston and published in the fall of 1605, reflected upon the stage the interest felt in Virginia.   The Spanish ambassador Zuñiga became alarmed, and, going to Lord Chief-Justice Sir John Popham, protested against the preparations then making as an encroachment upon Spanish territory and a violation of the treaty of peace. Popham, with true diplomatic disregard of truth, evaded the issue, and assured Zuñiga that the only object of the scheme was to clear England of "thieves and traitors" and get them "drowned in the sea." [1]

A month later, April 10, 1606, a charter was obtained from King James for the incorporation of two companies, one consisting of "certain knights, gentlemen, merchants" in and about London, and the other of "sundry knights, gentlemen, merchants" in and about Plymouth.   The chief patron

---

[1] Brown, *Genesis of the United States*, I., 46.

of the London Company was Sir Robert Cecil,
the secretary of state; and the chief patron of the
Plymouth Company was Sir John Popham, chief-
justice of the Queen's Bench, who presided at the
trial of Raleigh in 1603.

The charter claimed for England all the North
American continent between the thirty-fourth and
forty-fifth degrees north latitude, but gave to
each company only a tract fronting one hundred
miles on the sea and extending one hundred miles
inland. The London Company was authorized to
locate a plantation called the First Colony in some
fit and convenient place between thirty-four and
forty-one degrees, and the Plymouth Company a
Second Colony somewhere between thirty-eight
and forty-five degrees, but neither was to plant
within one hundred miles of the other.

The charter contained "not one ray of popular
rights," and neither the company nor the colonists
had any share in the government. The company
must financier the enterprise, but could receive only
such rewards as those intrusted with the management by the home government could win for
them in directing trade, opening mines, and dispos-
ing of lands. As for the emigrants, while they were
declared entitled "to all liberties, franchises, and
immunities of British subjects," they were to enjoy
merely such privileges as officers not subject to
them in any way might allow them. The management of both sections of Virginia, including the

very limited grants to the companies, was conferred upon one royal council, which was to name a local council for each of the colonies in America; and both superior and subordinate councils were to govern according to "laws, ordinances, and instructions" to be given them by the king.[1]

Two days after the date of the charter these promised "laws," etc., were issued, and, though not preserved in their original form, they were probably very similar to the articles published during the following November.[2] According to these last, the superior council, resident in England, was permitted to name the colonial councils, which were to have power to pass ordinances not repugnant to the orders of the king and superior council; to elect or remove their presidents, to remove any of their members, to supply their own vacancies; and to decide all cases occurring in the colony, civil as well as criminal, not affecting life or limb. Capital offences were to be tried by a jury of twelve persons, and while to all intents and purposes the condition of the colonists did not differ from soldiers subject to martial law, it is to the honor of King James that he limited the death penalty to tumults, rebellion, conspiracy, mutiny, sedition, murder, incest, rape, and adultery, and did not include in the number of crimes either

[1] Hening, *Statutes*, I., 57–66; see also Cheyney, *European Background of American History*, chap. viii.
[2] Brown, *First Republic*, 8.

witchcraft or heresy. The articles also provided that
all property of the two companies should be held
in a "joint stock" for five years after the landing.[1]

The charter being thus secured, both companies
proceeded to procure emigrants; and they had not
much difficulty, as at this time there were many
unemployed people in England. The wool culture
had converted great tracts of arable land in England
into mere pastures for sheep,[2] and the closure of the
monasteries and religious houses removed the
support from thousands of English families. Since
1585 this surplus humanity had found employment
in the war with Spain, but the return of peace in
1605 had again thrown them upon society, and they
were eager for chances, no matter how remote, of
gold-mines and happy homes beyond the seas.[3]

Hence, in three months' time the Plymouth
Company had all things in readiness for a trial
voyage, and August 12, 1606, they sent out a ship
commanded by Henry Challons with twenty-nine
Englishmen and two Indians brought into England
by Weymouth the year before. Two months later
sailed another ship (of which Thomas Hanham
was captain and Martin Pring master), "with all
necessary supplies for the seconding of Captain
Challons and his people." Unfortunately, Captain
Challons's vessel and crew were taken by the Span-

---

[1] Hening, *Statutes*, I., 67–75.
[2] Ashley, *English Economic History*, II., 261–376.
[3] Brown, *Genesis of the United States*, I., 50.

iards in the West Indies, and, though Hanham and Pring reached the coast of America, they returned without making a settlement.[1]   Nevertheless, they brought back, as Sir Ferdinando Gorges wrote many years after, "the most exact discovery of that coast that ever came to my hands since," which wrought "such an impression" on Chief-Justice Popham and the other members of the Plymouth Company that they determined upon another and better-appointed attempt at once.[2]

May 31, 1607, this second expedition sailed from Plymouth with one hundred and twenty settlers embarked in two vessels—a fly boat called the *Gift of God* and a ship called *Mary and John*.   August 18, 1607, the company landed on a peninsula at the mouth of the Sagadahoc, or Kennebec River, in Maine.   After a sermon by their preacher, Richard Seymour, the commission of government and ordinances prepared by the authorities at home were read.   George Popham was therein designated president; and Raleigh Gilbert, James Davis, Richard Seymour, Richard Davis, and Captain Harlow composed the council.   The first work attempted was a fort, which they intrenched and fortified with twelve pieces of ordnance.   Inside they erected a church and storehouse and fifteen log-cabins.   Then a ship-builder constructed a

[1] Brown, *Genesis of the United States*, I., 127–139.
[2] Gorges, *Briefe Narration* (Mass. Hist. Soc., *Collections*, 3d series., VI. 53).

pinnace, called the *Virginia*, which afterwards was used in the southern colony. But the colonists were soon discouraged, and more than half their number went back to England in the ships when they returned in December.

The winter of 1607–1608 was terrible to the forty-five men who remained at Kennebec, where land and water were locked in icy fetters. Their storehouse took fire and was consumed, with a great part of the provisions, and about the same time President George Popham died. The other leader, Captain Raleigh Gilbert, grew discouraged when, despite an industrious exploration of the rivers and harbors, he found no mines of any kind. When Captain James Davis arrived in the spring, bringing news of the death of Chief-Justice Popham and of Sir John Gilbert, Raleigh Gilbert's brother, who had left him his estate, both leader and colonists were so disenchanted of the country that they with one accord resolved upon a return. Wherefore they all embarked, as we are told, in their newly arrived ship and newly constructed pinnace and set sail for England. "And this," says Strachey, "was the end of that northerne colony upon the river Sagadahoc." [1]

To the London Company, therefore, though slower in getting their expedition to sea, belongs the honor of the first permanent English colony in

---

[1] Strachey, *Travaile into Virginia*, 162–180; Brown, *Genesis of the United States*, I., 190–194.

America.   December 10, 1606, ten days before the departure of this colony, the council for Virginia set down in writing regulations deemed necessary for the expedition.   The command of the ships and settlers was given to Captain Christopher Newport, a famous seaman, who in 1591 had brought into the port of London the treasure-laden carrack the *Madre de Dios*, taken by Raleigh's ship the *Roe Buck*. He was to take charge of the commissions of the local council, and not to break the seals until they had been upon the coast of Virginia twenty-four hours.   Then the council were to elect their president and assume command of the settlers; while Captain Newport was to spend two months in discovery and loading his ships "with all such principal commodities and merchandise there to be had." [1]

With these orders went a paper, perhaps drawn by Hakluyt, giving valuable advice concerning the selection of the place of settlement, dealings with the natives, and explorations for mines and the South Sea. [2]   In respect to the place of settlement they were especially advised to choose a high and dry situation, divested of trees and up some river, a considerable distance from the mouth.   The emigrants numbered one hundred and twenty men— no women.   Besides Captain Newport, the admiral, in the *Sarah Constant*, of a hundred tons, the leading persons in the exploration were Bartholomew Gosnold, who commanded the *Goodspeed*, of forty

[1] Neill, *Virginia Company*, 4–8.   [2] *Ibid.*, 8–14.

tons; Captain John Ratcliffe, who commanded the *Discovery*, of twenty tons; Edward Maria Wingfield; George Percy, brother of the earl of Northumberland; John Smith; George Kendall, a cousin of Sir Edwin Sandys; Gabriel Archer; and Rev. Robert Hunt.

Among these men John Smith was distinguished for a career combining adventure and romance. Though he was only thirty years of age he had already seen much service and had many hairbreadth escapes, his most remarkable exploit having been his killing before the town of Regal, in Transylvania, three Turks, one after another, in single combat.[1] The ships sailed from London December 20, 1606, and Michael Drayton wrote some quaint verses of farewell, of which perhaps one will suffice:

> "And cheerfully at sea
> Success you still entice,
>   To get the pearl and gold,
>   And ours to hold
> Virginia,
> Earth's only paradise!"

The destination of the colony was Chesapeake Bay, a large gulf opening by a strait fifteen miles wide upon the Atlantic at thirty-seven degrees, and reaching northward parallel to the sea - coast one hundred and eighty-five miles. Into its basin a great many smooth and placid rivers discharge their contents. Perhaps no bay of the world has such

[1] Purchas, *Pilgrimes*, II., 1365.

diversified scenery. Among the rivers which enter
the bay from the west, four—the Potomac, Rappahannock, York, and James — are particularly
large and imposing. They divide what is called
tide-water Virginia into long and narrow peninsulas,
which are themselves furrowed by deep creeks
making numerous necks or minor peninsulas of
land. Up these rivers and creeks the tide ebbs and
flows for many miles. In 1607, before the English
arrived, the whole of this tide-water region, except
here and there where the Indians had a cornfield,
was covered with primeval forests, so free from
undergrowth that a coach with four horses could be
driven through the thickest groups of trees.

The numerous tribes of Indians who inhabited
this region belonged to the Algonquin race, and at
the time Captain Newport set sail from England
they were members of a confederacy, of which
Powhatan was head war chief or werowance. There
were at least thirty-four of these tribes, and to each
Powhatan appointed one of his own friends as chief.
Powhatan's capital, or "werowocomoco," was on
York River at Portan Bay (a corruption for Powhatan), about fourteen miles from Jamestown; and
Pochins, one of his sons, commanded at Point
Comfort, while Parahunt, another son, was werowance at the falls of the James River, one hundred
and twenty miles inland. West of the bay region,
beyond the falls of the rivers, were other con-
federacies of Indians, who carried on long wars with

Powhatan, of whom the most important were the
Monacans, or Manakins, and Massawomekes.[1]

Powhatan's dominions extended from the Roanoke
River, in North Carolina, to the head of Chesapeake
Bay, and in all this country his will was despotic.
He had an organized system of collecting tribute
from the werowances, and to enforce his orders kept
always about him fifty armed savages "of the
tallest in his kingdom." Each tribe had a territory
defined by natural bounds, and they lived on the
rivers and creeks in small villages, consisting of
huts called wigwams, oval in shape, and made of
bark set upon a framework of saplings. Sometimes
these houses were of great length, accommodating
many families at once; and at Uttamussick, in the
peninsula formed by the Pamunkey and Mattapony,
were three such structures sixty feet in length,
where the Indians kept the bodies of their dead
chiefs under the care of seven priests, or medicine-
men.

The religion of these Chesapeake Bay Indians,
like that of all the other Indians formerly found
on the coast, consisted in a belief in a great number
of devils, who were to be warded off by powwows
and conjurations. Captain Smith gives an account
of a conjuration to which he was subjected at
Uttamussick when a captive in December, 1607.
At daybreak they kindled a fire in one of the long

[1] On the American Indians, Farrand, *Basis of American
History*, chaps. vi.–xiv.

houses and by it seated Captain Smith. Soon the
chief priest, hideously painted, bedecked with
feathers, and hung with skins of snakes and weasels,
came skipping in, followed by six others similarly
arrayed. Rattling gourds and chanting most
dismally, they marched about Captain Smith, the
chief priest in the lead and trailing a circle of meal,
after which they marched about him again and put
down at intervals little heaps of corn of five or
six grains each. Next they took some little bunches
of sticks and put one between every two heaps of
corn. These proceedings, lasting at intervals for
three days, were punctuated with violent gesticula-
tions, grunts, groans, and a great rattling of gourds.[1]

Another custom of the Indians is linked with a
romantic incident in Virginia history. Not infre-
quently some wretched captive, already bound, to
be tortured to death, has owed his life to the interference of some member of the tribe who announced his or her desire to adopt him as a brother
or son. The motives inducing this interference
proceeded sometimes from mere business considerations and sometimes from pity, superstition,
or admiration. It was Captain Smith's fortune
during his captivity to have a personal experience
of this nature. After the conjuration at Uttamussick Smith was brought to Werowocomoco and

---

[1] For accounts of aboriginal Virginia, see Strachey, *Travaile
into Virginia;* Spelman, in Brown, *Genesis of the United States*,
I., 483–488; Smith, *Works* (Arber's ed.), 47–84.

ushered into a long wigwam, where he found
Powhatan sitting upon a bench and covered with a
great robe of raccoon skins, with the tails hanging
down like tassels. On either side of him sat an
Indian girl of sixteen or seventeen years, and along
the walls of the room two rows of grim warriors,
and back of them two rows of women with faces
and shoulders painted red, hair bedecked with the
plumage of birds, and necks strung with chains of
white beads.

At Smith's entrance those present gave a great
shout, and presently two stones were brought before
Powhatan, and on these stones Smith's head was
laid. Next several warriors with clubs took their
stand near him to beat out his brains, whereupon
Powhatan's "dearest daughter," Pocahontas, a girl
of about twelve years old, rushed forward and
entreated her father to spare the prisoner. When
Powhatan refused she threw herself upon Smith, got
his head in her arms, and laid her own upon his.
This proved too much for Powhatan. He ordered
Smith to be released, and, telling him that hence-
forth he would regard him as his son, sent him with
guides back to Jamestown.[1]

The credibility of this story has been attacked
on the ground that it does not occur in Smith's
True Relation, a contemporaneous account of the
colony, and appears first in his *Generall Historie*,
published in 1624. But the editor of the *True*

---

[1] Smith, *Works* (Arber's ed.), 400.

Relation expressly states that the published account does not include the entire manuscript as it came from Smith. Hence the omission counts for little, and there is nothing unusual in Smith's experience, which, as Dr. Fiske says, "is precisely in accord with Indian usage." About 1528 John Ortiz, of Seville, a soldier of Pamfilo de Narvaez, captured by the Indians on the coast of Florida, was saved from being roasted to death by the chief's daughter, a case very similar to that of John Smith and Pocahontas. Smith was often inaccurate and prejudiced in his statements, but that is far from saying that he deliberately mistook plain objects of sense or concocted a story having no foundation.[1]

Still another incident illustrative of Indian life is given by Smith. In their idle hours the Indians amused themselves with singing, dancing, and playing upon musical instruments made of pipes and small gourds, and at the time of another visit to Werowocomoco Smith was witness to a very charming scene in which Pocahontas was again the leading actor. While the English were sitting upon a mat near a fire they were startled by loud shouts, and a party of Indian girls came out of the woods strangely attired. Their bodies were painted, some red, some white, and some blue. Pocahontas carried a pair of antlers on her head, an otter's skin

---

[1] Cases of rescue and adoption are numerous. See the case of Conture, in Parkman, *Jesuits*, 223; Fiske, *Old Virginia and Her Neighbors*, I., 113.

at her waist and another on her arm, a quiver of arrows at her back, and a bow and arrow in her hand. Another of the band carried a sword, another a club, and another a pot-stick, and all were horned as Pocahontas. Casting themselves in a ring about the fire, they danced and sang for the space of an hour, and then with a shout departed into the woods as suddenly as they came.[1]

On the momentous voyage to Virginia Captain Newport took the old route by the Canary Islands and the West Indies, and they were four months on the voyage. In the West Indies Smith and Wingfield quarrelled, and the latter charged Smith with plotting mutiny, so that he was arrested and kept in irons till Virginia was reached. After leaving the West Indies bad weather drove them from their course; but, April 26, 1607, they saw the capes of Virginia, which were forthwith named Henry and Charles, after the two sons of King James.

Landing at Cape Henry, they set up a cross April 29, and there they had their first experience with the Indians. The Chesapeakes assaulted them and wounded two men. About that time the seals were broken, and it was found that Edward Maria Wingfield, who was afterwards elected president for one year, Bartholomew Gosnold, Christopher Newport, John Smith, John Ratcliffe, John Martin, and George Kendall were councillors.

[1] Smith, *Works* (Arber's ed.), 436.

For more than two weeks they sought a place of settlement, and they named the promontory at the entrance of Hampton Roads "Point Comfort," and the broad river which opened beyond after the king who gave them their charter. At length they decided upon a tract of land in the Paspahegh country, distant about thirty-two miles from the river's mouth; and though a peninsula they called it an island, because of the very narrow isthmus (long worn away) connecting it with the main-land. There they landed May 14, 1607 (May 24 New Style), and at the west end, where the channel of the river came close to the shore, they constructed a triangular fort with bulwarks in each corner, mounting from three to five cannon, and within it marked off the beginnings of a town, which they called Jamestown.[1]

The colonists were at first in high spirits, for the landing occurred in the most beautiful month of all the year. In reality, disaster was already impending, for their long passage at sea had much reduced the supplies, and the Paspaheghs bitterly resented their intrusion. Moreover, the peninsula of Jamestown was not such a place as their instructions contemplated. It was in a malarious situation, had no springs of fresh water, and was thickly covered with great trees and tall grass, which afforded protection to Indian enemies.

May 22 Captain Newport went up in a shallop

[1] Percy, *Discourse*, in Smith, *Works* (Arber's ed.), lvii.–lxx.

with twenty others to look for a gold-mine at the
falls of James River. He was gone only a week,
but before he returned the Indians had assaulted
the fort, and his assistance was necessary in com-
pleting the palisades. When Newport departed
for England, June 22, he left one hundred and four
settlers in a very unfortunate condition:[1] they were
besieged by Indians; a small ladle of "ill-condition-
ed" barley-meal was the daily ration per man; the
lodgings of the settlers were log-cabins and holes
in the ground, and the brackish water of the river
served them for drink.[2] The six weeks following
Newport's departure were a time of death and
despair, and by September 10 of the one hundred
and four men only forty-six remained alive.

Under such circumstances dissensions might have
been expected, but they were intensified by the
peculiar government devised by the king. In a
short time Gosnold died, and Kendall was detected
in a design to desert the colony and was shot.
Then (September 10) Ratcliffe, Smith, and Martin
deposed Wingfield from the government and elected
as president John Ratcliffe.

In such times men of strong character take the
lead. When the cape merchant Thomas Studley,
whose duty it was to care for the supplies and
dispense them, died, his important office was conferred on Smith. In this capacity Smith showed

[1] Percy, *Discourse*, in Smith, *Works* (Arber's ed.), lxx.
[2] *Breife Declaration*, in Virginia State Senate *Document*, 1874.

great abilities as a corn-getter from the Indians, whom he visited at Kecoughtan (Hampton), Warascoyack, and Chickahominy. At length, during the fall of 1607, the Indians stopped hostilities, and for a brief interval health and plenty prevailed.[1]

In December Smith went on an exploring trip up the Chickahominy, but on this occasion his good luck deserted him—two of his men were killed by the Indians and he himself was captured and carried from village to village, but he was released through the influence of Pocahontas, and returned to Jamestown (January 2, 1608) to find more dangers. In his absence Ratcliffe, the president, admitted Gabriel Archer, Smith's deadly enemy, into the council; and immediately upon his arrival these two arrested him and tried him under the Levitical law for the loss of the two men killed by the Indians. He was found guilty and condemned to be hanged the next day; but in the evening Newport arrived in the *John and Francis* with the "First Supply" of men and provisions, and Ratcliffe and Archer were prevented from carrying out their plan.[2] Newport found only thirty or forty persons surviving at Jamestown, and he brought about seventy more. Of the six members of the council living at the time of his departure in June, 1607, two, Gosnold and Kendall, were dead, Smith

---

[1] Percy, *Discourse*, in Smith, *Works* (Arber's ed.), lxxiii.

[2] Wingfield, *Discourse*, in Smith, *Works* (Arber's ed.), lxxiv. –xci.

was under condemnation, and Wingfield was a prisoner. Now Smith was restored to his seat in council, while Wingfield was released from custody.[1]

Five days after Newport's arrival at Jamestown a fire consumed nearly all the buildings in the fort.[2] The consequence was that, as the winter was very severe, many died from exposure while working to restore the town. The settlers suffered also from famine, which Captain Newport partially relieved by visiting Powhatan in February and returning in March with his "pinnace well loaden with corne, wheat, beanes, and pease," which kept the colony supplied for some weeks.[3]

Newport remained in Virginia for more than three months, but things were not improved by his stay. His instructions required him to return with a cargo, and the poor colonists underwent the severest sort of labor in cutting down trees and loading the ship with cedar, black walnut, and clapboard.[4] Captain Martin thought he discovered a gold-mine near Jamestown, and for a time the council had busied the colonists in digging worthless ore, some of which Newport carried to England.[5] These works hindered others more important to the plantation, and only four acres of land was put in corn during the spring.[6] Newport took back with him

---

[1] Wingfield, *Discourse*, in Smith, *Works* (Arber's ed.), lxxxvi.
[2] Brown, *Genesis of the United States*, I., 175.
[3] Wingfield, *Discourse*, in Smith, *Works* (Arber's ed.), lxxxvii.
[4] *Breife Declaration.*   [5] Smith, *Works* (Arber's ed.), 104.
[6] *Breife Declaration.*

the councillors Wingfield and Archer, and April 20, ten days after Newport's departure, Captain Francis Nelson arrived in the *Phœnix* with about forty additional settlers. He stayed till June, when, taking a load of cedar, he returned to England, having among his passengers Captain John Martin, another of the council.

During the summer Smith spent much time exploring the Chesapeake Bay, Potomac, and Rappahannock rivers,[1] and in his absence things went badly at Jamestown. The mariners of Newport's and Nelson's ships had been very wasteful while they stayed in Virginia, and after their departure the settlers found themselves on a short allowance again. Then the sickly season in 1608 was like that of 1607, and of ninety-five men living in June, 1608, not over fifty survived in the fall. The settlers even followed the precedent of the previous year in deposing an unpopular president, for Ratcliffe, by employing the men in the unnecessary work of a governor's house, brought about a mutiny in July, which led to the substitution of Matthew Scrivener. At length, September 10, 1608, Captain Ratcliffe's presidency definitely expired and Captain Smith was elected president.

[1] Smith, *Works* (Arber's ed.), 109–120.

CHAPTER IV

GLOOM IN VIRGINIA

(1608–1617)

WHEN Newport arrived with the "Second Supply," September 29, 1608, he brought little relief. His seventy passengers, added to the number that survived the summer, raised the population at Jamestown to about one hundred and twenty. Among the new-comers were Richard Waldo, Peter Wynne (both added to the council), Francis West, a brother of Lord Delaware; eight Poles and Germans, sent over to begin the making of pitch and soap ashes; a gentlewoman, Mrs. Forrest, and her maid, Anne Burras, who were the first of their sex to settle at Jamestown. About two months later there was a marriage in the church at Jamestown between John Laydon and Anne Burras,[1] and a year later was born Virginia Laydon, the first white child in the colony.[2]

The instructions brought by Newport expressed the dissatisfaction of the council with the paltry

---

[1] Smith, *Works* (Arber's ed.), 114, 130.
[2] Hotten, *Emigrants to America*, 245; Brown, *First Republic*, 114.

returns made to the company for their outlay, and
required President Smith to aid Newport to do three
things [1]—viz., crown Powhatan; discover a gold-
mine and a passage to the South Sea; and find
Raleigh's lost colony. Smith tells us that he was
wholly opposed to all these projects, but submitted as best he might.

The coronation of Powhatan was a formality
borrowed from Sir Walter Raleigh's peerage for
Manteo, and duly took place at Werowocomoco.
Powhatan was presented with a basin, ewer, bed,
bed-cover, and a scarlet cloak, but showed great
unwillingness to kneel to receive the crown. At
last three of the party, by bearing hard upon his
shoulders, got him to stoop a little, and while he was
in that position they clapped it upon his head.
Powhatan innocently turned the whole proceeding
into ridicule by taking his old shoes and cloak of
raccoon skin and giving them to Newport.

To seek gold-mines and the South Sea, Newport,
taking all the strong and healthy men at the fort,
visited the country of the Monacans beyond the
falls of the James. In this march they discovered
the vein of gold that runs through the present counties of Louisa, Goochland, Fluvanna, and Bucking-
ham; but as the ore was not easily extracted from
the quartz they returned to Jamestown tired and
disheartened. The search for Raleigh's lost colony
was undertaken with much less expense—several

[1] Smith, *Works* (Arber's ed.), 121.

small parties were sent southward but learned nothing important.

In December, 1608, Newport returned to England, taking with him a cargo of pitch, tar, iron ore, and other articles provided at great labor by the over-worked colonists. Smith availed himself of the op-portunity to send by Newport an account of his summer explorations, a map of Chesapeake Bay and tributary rivers, and a letter in answer to the complaints signified to him in the instructions of the home council. Smith's reply was querulous and insubordinate, and spiteful enough against Rat-cliffe, Archer, and Newport, but contained many sound truths. He ridiculed the policy of the com-pany, and told them that "it were better to give £500 a ton for pitch, tar, and the like in the settled countries of Russia, Sweden, and Denmark than send for them hither till more necessary things be provided"; "for," said he, "in overtaxing our weake and unskillful bodies, to satisfie this desire of present profit, we can scarce ever recover ourselves from one supply to another." Ratcliffe returned to England with Newport, after whose departure Smith was assisted for a short time by a council con-sisting of Matthew Scrivener, Richard Waldo, and Peter Wynne. The two former were drowned during January, 1609, and the last died not long after. Smith was left sole ruler, and, contrary to the intention of the king, he made no attempt to fill the council.[1]

[1] Smith, *Works* (Arber's ed.), 23, 125, 442, 449, 460.

The "Second Supply" had brought provisions, which lasted only two months,[1] and most of Smith's time during the winter 1608–1609 was occupied in trading for corn with the Indians on York River. In the spring much useful work was done by the colonists under Smith's directions. They dug a well for water, which till then had been obtained from the river, erected some twenty cabins, shingled the church, cleared and planted forty acres of land with Indian-corn, built a house for the Poles to make glass in, and erected two block-houses.

Smith started to build a fort "for a retreat" on Gray's Creek, opposite to Jamestown (the place is still called "Smith's Fort"), but a remarkable circumstance, not at all creditable to Smith's vigilance or circumspection, stopped the work and put the colonists at their wits' end to escape starvation. On an examination of the casks in which their corn was stored it was found that the rats had devoured most of the contents, and that the remainder was too rotten to eat.[2]

To avoid starvation, President Smith, like Lane at Roanoke Island, in May, 1609, dispersed the whole colony in three parties, sending one to live with the savages, another to Point Comfort to try for fish, and another, the largest party, twenty miles down the river to the oyster-banks, where at the end of nine weeks the oyster diet caused their skins "to

[1] *Breife Declaration.*
[2] Smith, *Works* (Arber's ed.), 133–147, 154.

peale off from head to foote as if they had been flead." [1]

While the colony was in this desperate condition there arrived from England, July 14, 1609, a small bark, commanded by Samuel Argall, with a supply of bread and wine, enough to last the colonists one month. He had been sent out by the London Company to try for sturgeon in James River and to find a shorter route to Virginia. He brought news that the old charter had been repealed, that a new one abolishing the council in Virginia had been granted, and that Lord Delaware was coming, at the head of a large supply of men and provisions, as sole and absolute governor of Virginia. [2]

The calamities in the history of the colony as thus far outlined have been attributed to the great preponderance of "gentlemen" among these early immigrants; but afterwards when the company sent over mechanics and laborers the story of misfortune was not much changed. The preceding narrative shows that other causes, purposely underestimated at the time, had far more to do with the matter. Imported diseases and a climate singularly fatal to the new-comers, the faction-breeding charter, the communism of labor, Indian attack, and the unreasonable desire of the company for immediate profit afford explanations more than

---

[1] *Breife Declaration.*
[2] Smith, *Works* (Arber's ed.), 159; Brown, *Genesis of the United States*, I., 343.

sufficient.   Despite the presence of some unworthy characters, these "gentlemen" were largely composed of the "restless, pushing material of which the pathfinders of the world have ever been made."

The ships returning from the "Second Supply" reached England in January, 1609, and the account that they brought of the dissensions at Jamestown convinced the officers of the London Company that the government in Virginia needed correction.   It was deemed expedient to admit stockholders into some share of the government, and something like a "boom" was started.   Broadsides were issued by the managers, pamphlets praising the country were published, and sermons were delivered by eminent preachers like Rev. William Simonds and Rev. Daniel Price.   Zuñiga, the Spanish minister, was greatly disturbed, and urgently advised his master, Philip III., to give orders to have "these insolent people in Virginia quickly annihilated." But King Philip was afraid of England, and contented himself with instructing Zuñiga to keep on the watch; and thus the preparations of the London Company went on without interruption.[1]

May 23, 1609, a new charter was granted to the company, constituting it a corporation entirely independent of the North Virginia or Plymouth Company.   The stockholders, seven hundred and sixty-five in number, came from every rank, profession, or trade in England, and even included the

[1] Brown, *Genesis of the United States*, I., 250–321.

merchant guilds in London.[1] The charter increased
the company's bounds to a tract fronting on the
Atlantic Ocean, "from the point of land called
Cape, or Point, Comfort all along the sea-coast to the
northward two hundred miles, and from the point
of Cape Comfort all along the sea-coast to the
southward two hundred miles," and extending "up
into the land, throughout from sea to sea, west and
northwest,"[2] a clause which subsequently caused
much dispute.

The governing power was still far from taking
a popular form, being centred in a treasurer and
council, vacancies in which the company had the
right to fill. For the colonists it meant nothing
more than change of one tyranny for another, since
the local government in Virginia was made the
rule of an absolute governor. For this office the
council selected one of the peers of the realm,
Thomas West, Lord Delaware, but as he could not
go out at once they commissioned Sir Thomas
Gates as first governor of Virginia,[3] arming him with
a code of martial law which fixed the penalty of
death for many offences.

All things being in readiness, the "Third Supply"
left Falmouth, June 8, 1609, in nine ships, carrying
about six hundred men, women, and children, and

[1] Brown, *Genesis of the United States*, I., 228.
[2] Hening, *Statutes*, I., 80–98; Brown, *Genesis of the United States*, I., 206–224.
[3] *True and Sincere Declaration*, in Brown, *Genesis of the United States*, I., 345.

in one of the ships called the *Sea Venture* sailed the governor, Sir Thomas Gates, and the two officers next in command, Sir George Somers and Captain Christopher Newport.

When within one hundred and fifty leagues of the West Indies they were caught in the tail of a hurricane, which scattered the fleet and sank one of the ships. To keep the *Sea Venture* from sinking, the men bailed for three days without intermission, standing up to their middle in water. Through this great danger they were preserved by Somers, who acted as pilot, without taking food or sleep for three days and nights, and kept the ship steady in the waves till she stranded, July 29, 1609, on one of the Bermuda Islands, where the company, one hundred and fifty in number, landed in safety. They found the island a beautiful place, full of wild hogs, which furnished them an abundance of meat, to which they added turtles, wild fowl, and various fruits. How to get away was the question, and though they had not a nail they started promptly to build two small ships, the *Patience* and *Deliverance*, out of the cedar which covered the country-side. May 10, 1610, they were ready to sail with the whole party for Jamestown, which they reached without accident May 23.[1]

At Jamestown a sad sight met their view. The

---

[1] Purchas, *Pilgrimes*, IV., 1734–1754; *Plain Description of the Barmudas* (Force, *Tracts*, III., No. iii.); Brown, *Genesis of the United States*, I., 346, 347.

place looked like "some ancient fortification" all in
ruins; the palisades were down, the gates were off
their hinges, and the church and houses were in a
state of utter neglect and desolation. Out of the
ruins tottered some sixty wretches, looking more
like ghosts than human beings, and they told a
story of suffering having hardly a parallel.[1]

The energetic Captain Argall, whose arrival at
Jamestown has been already noticed, temporarily
relieved the destitution there, first by supplies
which he brought from England and afterwards by
sturgeon which he caught in the river.[2]   August
11, 1609, four of the storm-tossed ships of Gates's
fleet entered Hampton Roads, and not long after
three others joined them. They set on land at
Jamestown about four hundred passengers, many
of them ill with the London plague; and as it was
the sickly season in Virginia, and most of their
provisions were spoiled by rain and sea-water, their
arrival simply aggravated the situation.

To these troubles, grave enough of themselves,
were added dissensions among the chief men.
Ratcliffe, Martin, and Archer returned at this time,
and President Smith showed little disposition to
make friends with them or with the new-comers,
and insisted upon his authority under the old commission until Gates could be heard from. In the

---

[1] Purchas, *Pilgrimes*, IV., 1749.
[2] *Breife Declaration;* Brown, *Genesis of the United States*, I.,
404–406

wrangles that ensued, nearly all the gentlemen opposed Smith, while the mariners on the ships took his side, and it was finally decided that Smith should continue in the presidency till September 10, when his term expired.[1]

Thus having temporarily settled their differences, the leaders divided the immigrants into three parties, retaining one under Smith at Jamestown, and sending another under John Martin to Nansemond, and a third under Francis West to the falls of the James River. The Indians so fiercely assailed the two latter companies that both Martin and West soon returned. Smith was suspected of instigating these attacks, and thus fresh quarrels broke out. About the time of the expiration of his presidency Smith was injured by an explosion of gunpowder, and in this condition, exasperated against Martin, Archer, and Ratcliffe of the former council, he would neither give up the royal commission nor lay down his office; whereupon they deposed him and elected George Percy president.[2] When the ships departed in October, 1609, Smith took passage for England, and thus the colony lost its strongest character. Whatever qualifications must be made in his prejudiced account of the colony, the positions of trust which he enjoyed after reaching home prove that his merit does not rest solely upon his own opinions.

[1] Brown, *Genesis of the United States*, I., 330–332.
[2] Smith, *Works* (Arber's ed.), 480–485; Archer's letter, in Brown, *Genesis of the United States*, I., 331–332; Ratcliffe's letter, *ibid.*, 334–335; Brown, *First Republic*, 94–97.

Under Percy the colony went from bad to worse. Sickness soon incapacitated him, and his advisers, Martin, Archer, Ratcliffe, and West, were not men of ability. Probably no one could have accomplished much good under the conditions; and though it became fashionable afterwards in England to abuse the emigrants as a "lewd company" and "gallants packed thither by their friends to escape worse destinies at home," the broadsides issued by the company show that the emigrants of the "Third Supply" were chiefly artisans of all sorts.[1] The Rev. William Croshaw perhaps stated the case fairly in a sermon which he preached in 1610,[2] when he said that "those who were sent over at the company's expense were, for aught he could see, like those that were left behind, even of all sorts, better and worse," and that the gentlemen "who went on their own account" were "as good as the scoffers at home, and, it may be, many degrees better."

The colonists at first made various efforts to obtain supplies; and at President Percy's command John Ratcliffe, in October, 1609, established a fort called Algernourne and a fishery at Point Comfort, and in the winter of 1609–1610[3] went in a pinnace to trade with Powhatan in York River; but was taken off his guard and slain by the Indians with

[1] Brown, *First Republic*, 92.
[2] Brown, *Genesis of the United States*, I., 364.
[3] Smith, *Works* (Arber's ed.), 497.

twenty-seven of his men.[1] Captain West tried to
trade also, but failing in the attempt, sailed off
to England.[2] Matters reached a crisis when the
Indians killed and carried off the hogs, drove away
the deer, and laid ambushes all around the fort
at Jamestown.[3]

Finally came a period long remembered as the
"Starving Time," when corn and even roots from
the swamps failed. The starving settlers killed and
ate the dogs and horses and then the mice and
snakes found about the fort. Some turned canni-
bals, and an Indian who had been slain was dug
out of the ground and devoured. Others crazed
with hunger dogged the footsteps of their comrades;
and one man cut his wife into pieces and ate her
up, for which barbarous act he was executed. Even
religion failed to afford any consolation, and a man
threw his Bible into the fire and cried out in the
market-place, "There is no God in heaven."

Only Daniel Tucker, afterwards governor of
Bermuda, seemed able to take any thought. He
built a boat and caught fish in the river, and "this
small relief did keep us from killing one another
to eat," says Percy. Out of more than five hundred
colonists in Virginia in the summer of 1609 there
remained about the latter part of May, 1610, not
above sixty persons—men, women, and children

[1] Brown, *Genesis of the United States*, I., 483–488.
[2] *True Declaration* (Force, *Tracts*, III., No. i.).
[3] Smith, *Works* (Arber's ed.), 498.

—and even these were so reduced by famine and disease that had help been delayed ten days longer all would have perished.[1]

The arrival of Sir Thomas Gates relieved the immediate distress, and he asserted order by the publication of the code of martial law drawn up in England.[2] Then he held a consultation with Somers, Newport, and Percy, and decided to abandon the settlement. As the provisions brought from the Bermudas were only sufficient to last the company sixteen days longer, he prepared to go to Newfoundland, where, as it was the fishing season, he hoped to get further supplies which might enable them to reach England.[3] Accordingly, he sent the pinnace *Virginia* to Fort Algernourne to take on the guard; and then embarked (June 7, 1610) the whole party at Jamestown in the two cedar vessels built in the Bermudas. Darkness fell upon them at Hog Island, and the next morning at Mulberry Island they met the *Virginia* returning up the river, bearing a letter from Lord Delaware announcing his arrival at Point Comfort, and commanding him to take his ships and company back to Jamestown; which order Gates obeyed, landing at Jamestown that very night.[4]

[1] *Breife Declaration;* Percy, *Trewe Relacyon*, quoted by Brown, *First Republic*, 94, and by Eggleston, *Beginners of a Nation*, 39; *The Tragical Relation*, in Neill, *Virginia Company*, 407–411; *True Declaration* (Force, *Tracts*, III., No. i.).

[2] *Laws Divine, Morall and Martiall* (Force, *Tracts*, III., No. ii.). [3] Brown, *Genesis of the United States*, I., 401–415.

[4] *Ibid.*, 407.

It seems that the reports which reached the council of the company in England in December, of the disappearance of Sir Thomas Gates and the ill condition of things at Jamestown, threw such a coldness over the enterprise that they had great difficulty in fitting out the new fleet. Nevertheless, March 2, 1610, Lord Delaware left Cowes with three ships and one hundred and fifty emigrants, chiefly soldiers and mechanics, with only enough "knights and gentlemen of quality" to furnish the necessary leadership.[1]

He arrived at Point Comfort June 6; and, following Gates up the river, reached Jamestown June 10. His first work was to cleanse and restore the settlement, after which he sent Robert Tindall to Cape Charles to fish, and Argall and Somers to the Bermuda Islands for a supply of hog meat. Argall missed his way and went north to the fishing banks of Newfoundland, while Somers died in the Bermudas.

Delaware next proceeded to settle matters with the Indians. The policy of the company had been to treat them justly, and after the first summer the settlers bought Jamestown Island from the Paspaheghs for some copper,[2] and during his presidency Captain Smith purchased the territory at the

---

[1] Brown, *Genesis of the United States*, I., 400–415; Purchas, *Pilgrimes*, IV., 1734–1756; *True Declaration* (Force, *Tracts*, III., No. i.).

[2] *True Declaration* (Force, *Tracts*, III., No. i.).

Falls.[1] For their late proceedings the Indians had
incurred the penalties of confiscation, but Lord
Delaware did not like harsh measures and sent to
Powhatan to propose peace. His reply was that
ere he would consider any accommodation Lord
Delaware must send him a coach and three horses
and consent to confine the English wholly to their
island territory.[2] Lord Delaware at once ordered
Gates to attack and drive Powhatan's son Pochins
and his Indians from Kecoughtan; and when this
was done he erected two forts at the mouth of
Hampton River, called Charles and Henry, about a
musket-shot distance from Fort Algernourne.

No precautions, however, could prevent the
diseases incident to the climate, and during the
summer no less than one hundred and fifty persons
perished of fever. In the fall Delaware concen-
trated the settlers, now reduced to less than two
hundred, at Jamestown and Algernourne fort.
Wishing to carry out his instructions, he sent an
expedition to the falls of James River to search
for gold-mines; but, like its predecessor, it proved a
failure, and many of the men were killed by the
Indians.[3] Delaware himself fell sick, and by the
spring was so reduced that he found it necessary to
leave the colony. When he departed, March 28,
1611, the storehouse contained only enough supplies

[1] Spelman, in Brown, *Genesis of the United States*, I., 483–488.
[2] Purchas, *Pilgrimes*, IV., 1756.
[3] Brown, *Genesis of the United States*, I., 490.

to last the people three months at short allowance; and probably another "Starving Time" was prevented only by the arrival of Sir Thomas Dale, May 10, 1611.[1]

From this time till the death of Lord Delaware in 1618 the government was administered by a succession of deputy governors, Sir Thomas Gates, Sir Thomas Dale, Captain George Yardley, and Captain Samuel Argall. For five years—1611–1616—of this period the ruling spirit was Sir Thomas Dale, who had acquired a great reputation in the army of the Netherlands as a disciplinarian. His policy in Virginia seemed to have been the advancement of the company's profit at the expense of the settlers, whom he pretended to regard as so abandoned that they needed the extreme of martial law. In 1611 he restored the settlements at forts Charles and Henry; in 1613 he founded Bermuda Hundred and Bermuda City (otherwise called Charles Hundred and Charles City, now City Point), and in 1614 he established a salt factory at Smith Island near Cape Charles.[2]

In laboring at these works the men were treated like galley - slaves and given a diet "that hogs refused to eat." As a consequence some of them ran away, and Dale set the Indians to catch them, and when they were brought back he burned

---

[1] *Breife Declaration.*
[2] Hamor, *True Discourse*, 29–31; Brown, *Genesis of the United States*, I., 501–508.

several of them at the stake. Some attempted to go to England in a barge, and for their temerity were shot to death, hanged, or broken on the wheel. Although for the most part the men in the colony at this time were old soldiers, mechanics, and workmen, accustomed to labor, we are told that among those who perished through Dale's cruelty were many young men "of Auncyent Houses and born to estates of £1000 by the year," [1] persons doubtless attracted to Virginia by the mere love of adventure, but included by Dale in the common slavery. Even the strenuous Captain John Smith testified concerning Jeffrey Abbott, a veteran of the wars in Ireland and the Netherlands, but put to death by Dale for mutiny, that "he never saw in Virginia a more sufficient soldier, (one) less turbulent, a better wit, (one) more hardy or industrious, nor any more forward to cut them off that sought to abandon the country or wrong the colony." [2]

To better purpose Dale's strong hand was felt among the Indians along the James and York rivers, whom he visited with heavy punishments. The result was that Powhatan's appetite for war speedily diminished; and when Captain Argall, in April, 1613, by a shrewd trick got possession of Pocahontas, he offered peace, which was confirmed in April, 1614, by the marriage of Poca-

---

[1] *The Tragical Relation*, in Neill, *Virginia Company*, 407-411.
[2] Smith, *Works* (Arber's ed.), 508.

hontas to a leading planter named John Rolfe. The ceremony is believed to have been performed at Jamestown by Rev. Richard Buck, who came with Gates in 1610, and it was witnessed by several of Powhatan's kindred.[1]

Dale reached out beyond the territory of the London Company, and hearing that the French had made settlements in North Virginia, he sent Captain Samuel Argall in July, 1613, to remove them. Argall reached Mount Desert Island, captured the settlement, and carried some of the French to Jamestown, where as soon as Dale saw them he spoke of "nothing but ropes" and of gallows and hanging "every one of them." To make the work complete, Argall was sent out on a second expedition, and this time he reduced the French settlements at Port Royal and St. Croix River.[2] On his return voyage to Virginia he is said to have stopped at the Hudson River, where, finding a Dutch trading-post consisting of four houses on Manhattan Island, he forced the Dutch governor likewise to submit by a "letter sent and recorded" in Virginia. Probably in one of these voyages the Delaware River was also visited, when the "atturnment of the Indian kings" was made to the king of England.[3] It appears to have received its present name from Argall in 1610.[4]

[1] Hamor, *True Discourse*, 11.

[2] Brown, *Genesis of the United States*, I., 709–725.

[3] *A Description of the Province of New Albion* (1648) (Force, *Tracts*, II., No. vii.).

[4] Brown, *Genesis of the United States*, I., 438.

Towards the end of his stay in Virginia, Dale seemed to realize that some change must be made in the colony, and he accordingly abolished the common store and made every man dependent on his own labor. But the exactions he imposed upon the settlers in return made it certain that he did not desire their benefit so much as to save expense to his masters in England. The "Farmers," as he called a small number to whom he gave three acres of land to be cultivated in their own way, had to pay two and a half barrels of corn per acre and give thirty days' public service in every year; while the "Laborers," constituting the majority of the colony, had to slave eleven months, and were allowed only one month to raise corn to keep themselves supplied for a year. The inhabitants of Bermuda Hundred counted themselves more fortunate than the rest because they were promised their freedom in three years and were given one month in the year and one day in the week, from May till harvest-time, "to get their sustenance," though of this small indulgence they were deprived of nearly half by Dale. Yet even this slender appeal to private interest was accompanied with marked improvement, and in 1614 Ralph Hamor, Jr., Dale's secretary of state, wrote, "When our people were fed out of the common store and labored jointly in the manuring of ground and planting corn, . . . the most honest of them, in a general business, would not take so much faithful

and true pains in a week as now he will do in a
day." [1]

These were really dark days for Virginia, and
Gondomar, the Spanish minister, wrote to Philip III.
that "here in London this colony Virginia is in
such bad repute that not a human being can be
found to go there in any way whatever." [2]   Some
spies of King Philip were captured in Virginia, and
Dale was much concerned lest the Spaniards would
attack the settlement, but the Spanish king and
his council thought that it would die of its own weakness, and took no hostile measure. [3]   In England
the company was so discouraged that many withdrew their subscriptions, and in 1615 a lottery
was tried as a last resort to raise money. [4]

When Dale left Virginia (May, 1616) the people
were very glad to get rid of him, and not more than
three hundred and fifty-one persons—men, women,
and children—survived altogether. [5] Within a very
short time the cabins which he erected were ready
to fall and the palisades could not keep out hogs.
A tract of land called the "company's garden"
yielded the company £300 annually, but this was
a meagre return for the enormous suffering and
sacrifice of life. [6] Dale took Pocahontas with him

---

[1] Hamor, *True Discourse*, 17; *Breife Declaration*.
[2] Brown, *Genesis of the United States*, II., 739, 740.
[3] *Ibid.*, 657.   [4] *Ibid.*, 760, 761.
[5] John Rolfe, *Relation*, in *Va. Historical Register*, I., 110.
[6] Virginia Company, *Proceedings* (Va. Hist. Soc., *Collections*,
new series, VII.), I., 65.

to England, and Lady Delaware presented her at
court, and her portrait engraved by the distinguished artist Simon de Passe was a popular curiosity.[1]
While in England she met Captain John Smith, and
when Smith saluted her as a princess Pocahontas
insisted on calling him father and having him call
her his child.[2]

It was at this juncture that in the cultivation of
tobacco, called "the weed" by King James, a new
hope for Virginia was found. Hamor says that
John Rolfe began to plant tobacco in 1612 and his
example was soon followed generally. Dale frowned
upon the new occupation, and in 1616 commanded
that no farmer should plant tobacco until he had
put down two acres of his three-acre farm in corn.[3]
After Dale's departure Captain George Yardley, who
acted as deputy governor for a year, was not so ex-
acting. At Jamestown, in the spring of 1617, the
market - place and even the narrow margin of the
streets were set with tobacco. It was hard, indeed,
to suppress a plant which brought per pound in the
London market sometimes as much as $12 in pres-
ent money. Yardley's government lasted one year,
and the colony "lived in peace and best plentye
that ever it had till that time."[4]

---

[1] Neill, *Virginia Company*, 98.
[2] Smith, *Works* (Arber's ed.), 533.
[3] Rolfe, *Relation*, in *Va. Historical Register*, I., 108.
[4] *Breije Declaration*.

CHAPTER V

TRANSITION OF VIRGINIA

(1617-1640)

DURING the period of Dale's administration the constitution of the London Company underwent a change, because the stockholders grew restless under the powers of the treasurer and council and applied for a third charter, limiting all important business to a quarterly meeting of the whole body.

As they made the inclusion of the Bermuda Islands the ostensible object, the king without difficulty signed the paper, March 12, 1612; and thus the company at last became a self-governing body.[1] On the question of governing the colony it soon divided, however, into the court party, in favor of continuing martial law, at the head of which was Sir Robert Rich, afterwards earl of Warwick; and the "country," or "patriot party," in favor of ending the system of servitude. The latter party was led by Sir Thomas Smith, who had been treasurer ever since 1607, Sir Edwin Sandys,

---

[1] Brown, *Genesis of the United States*, II., 543-554; *First Republic*, 165-167.

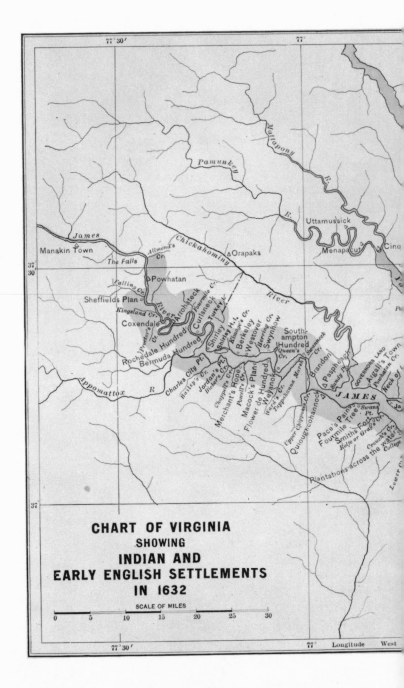

CHART OF VIRGINIA
SHOWING
INDIAN AND
EARLY ENGLISH SETTLEMENTS
IN 1632

SCALE OF MILES

0   5   10   15   20   25   30

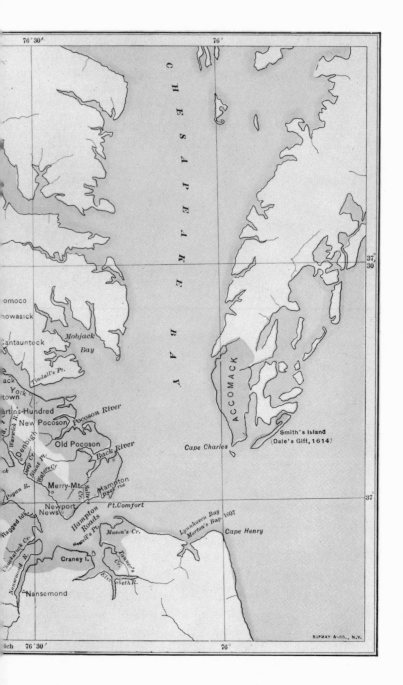

76° 30′   76′

C H E S A P E A K E   B A Y

37°
30

omoco
nowasick
Cantaunteck   Mobjack
                    Bay
                              ACCOMACK
ack   Tindall's Pt.
York
town
artins-Hundred
New Pocoson   Pocoson River
Denbigh
Old Pocoson   Buck River
                              Cape Charles   Smith's Island
                                                  (Dale's Gift, 1614)
Pagan R.   Merry-Mt.
                    Hampton
                    Buck True
Newport   Pt. Comfort   37°
News
Hampton   Lynnhaven Bay 1607
Ragged Isle.   Roads   Morton's Bay   Cape Henry
            Mason's Cr.
Craney I.
            Tanner's
            Cr.
Nansemond
            ibeth R.

ich   76° 30′   76′

the earl of Southampton, Sir John Danvers, and
John and Nicholas Ferrar.[1] Of the two, the country party was more numerous, and when the joint
stock partnership expired, November 30, 1616, they
appointed Captain Samuel Argall, a kinsman of
Treasurer Smith, to be deputy governor of Virginia,
with instructions to give every settler his own private dividend of fifty acres and to permit him to
visit in England if he chose.[2]

Argall sailed to Virginia about the first part of
April, 1617, taking with him Pocahontas's husband,
John Rolfe, as secretary of state. Pocahontas was
to go with him, but she sickened and died, and
was buried at Gravesend March 21, 1617. She left
one son named Thomas, who afterwards resided in
Virginia, where he has many descendants at this
day.[3] Argall, though in a subordinate capacity he
had been very useful to the settlers, proved wholly
unscrupulous as deputy governor. Instead of obey-
ing his instructions he continued the common
slavery under one pretence or another, and even
plundered the company of all the servants and live-
stock belonging to the "common garden." He censured Yardley for permitting the settlers to grow tobacco, yet brought a commission for himself to establish a private tobacco plantation, "Argall's Gift," and
laid off two other plantations of the same nature.

[1] Brown, *English Politics in Early Virginia History*, 24–33.
[2] Brown, *Genesis of the United States*, II., 775–779, 797–799.
[3] *Ibid.*, 967.

In April, 1618, the company, incensed at Argall's conduct, despatched the Lord Governor Delaware with orders to arrest him and send him to England, but Delaware died on the way over, and Argall continued his tyrannical government another year. He appropriated the servants on Lord Delaware's private estates, and when Captain Edward Brewster protested, tried him by martial law and sentenced him to death; but upon the petitions of the ministers resident in the colony commuted the punishment to perpetual banishment.[1]

Meanwhile, Sandys, who had a large share in draughting the second and third charters, was associated with Sir Thomas Smith in preparing a document which has been called the " Magna Charta of America."   November 13, 1618, the company granted to the residents of Virginia the "Great charter or commission of priviledges, orders, and laws"; and in January, 1619, Sir George Yardley was sent as "governor and captain-general," with full instructions to put the new government into operation.   He had also orders to arrest Argall, but, warned by Lord Rich, Argall fled from the colony before Yardley arrived. Argall left within the jurisdiction of the London Company in Virginia, as the fruit of twelve years' labor and an expenditure of money representing $2,000,000, but four hundred settlers inhabiting some broken-down settlements.

[1] Virginia Company, *Proceedings* (Va. Hist. Soc., *Collections*, new series, VII., VIII.), I., 65, II., 198.

The plantations of the private associations—Southampton Hundred, Martin Hundred, etc.—were in a flourishing condition, and the settlers upon them numbered upward of six hundred persons.[1]

Sir George Yardley arrived in Virginia April 19, 1619, and made known the intentions of the London Company that there was to be an end of martial law and communism. Every settler who had come at his own charge before the departure of Sir Thomas Dale in April, 1616, was to have one hundred acres "upon the first division," to be afterwards augmented by another hundred acres, and as much more for every share of stock (£12 6s.) actually paid by him. Every one imported by the company within the same period was, after the expiration of his service, to have one hundred acres; while settlers who came at their own expense, after April, 1616, were to receive fifty acres apiece. In order to relieve the inhabitants from taxes "as much as may be," lands were to be laid out for the support of the governor and other officers, to be tilled by servants sent over for that purpose. Four corporations were to be created, with Kecoughtan, Jamestown, Charles City, and Henrico as capital cities in each, respectively; and it was announced that thereafter the people of the colony were to share with the company in the making of laws.[2]

[1] *Discourse of the Old Company*, in *Va. Magazine*, I., 157.
[2] Instructions to Yardley, 1618, *ibid.*, II., 154–165.

Accordingly, July 30, 1619, the first legislative assembly that ever convened on the American continent met in the church at Jamestown. It consisted of the governor, six councillors, and twenty burgesses, two from each of ten plantations. The delegates from Brandon, Captain John Martin's plantation, were not seated, because of a particular clause in his patent exempting it from colonial authority. The assembly, after a prayer from Rev. Richard Buck, of Jamestown, sat six days and did a great deal of work. Petitions were addressed to the company in England for permission to change "the savage name of Kecoughtan," for workmen to erect a "university and college," and for granting the girls and boys of all the old planters a share of land each, "because that in a new plantation it is not known whether man or woman be the more necessary." Laws were made against idleness, drunkenness, gaming, and other misdemeanors, but the death penalty was prescribed only in case of such "traitors to the colony" as sold fire-arms to the Indians. To prevent extravagance in dress parish taxes were "cessed" according to apparel— "if he be unmarried, according to his own apparel; if he be married, according to his own and his wife's or either of their apparel." Statutes were also passed for encouraging agriculture and for settling church discipline according to the rules of the church of England.[1]

[1] *Assembly Journal*, 1619, in Va. State Senate *Documents*, 1874.

Another significant event during this memorable year was the introduction of negro slavery into Virginia. A Dutch ship arrived at Jamestown in August, 1619, with some negroes, of whom twenty were sold to the planters.[1]

A third event was the arrival of a ship from England with ninety "young maidens" to be sold to the settlers for wives, at the cost of their transportation—viz., one hundred and twenty pounds of tobacco (equivalent to $500 in present currency).[2] Cargoes of this interesting merchandise continued to arrive for many years.

It was fortunate that with the arrival of Yardley the supervision of Virginia affairs in England passed into hands most interested in colonial welfare. Sir Thomas Smith had been treasurer or president of the company for twelve years; but as he was also president of four other companies some thought that he did not give the proper attention to Virginia matters. For this reason, and because he was considered responsible for the selection of Argall, the leaders of his party determined to elect a new treasurer; and a private quarrel between Smith and the head of the court party, Lord Rich, helped matters to this end. To gratify a temporary spleen against Smith, Lord Rich consented to vote for Sir Edwin Sandys, and April 28, 1619, he was accord-

---

[1] Smith, *Works* (Arber's ed.), 541.
[2] Virginia Company, *Proceedings* (Va. Hist. Soc., *Collections*, new series, VII.), I., 67.

ingly elected treasurer with John Ferrar as his deputy. Smith was greatly piqued, abandoned his old friends, and soon after began to act with Rich in opposition to Sandys and his group of supporters.[1]

Sandys threw himself into his work with great ardor, and scarcely a month passed that a ship did not leave England loaded with emigrants and cattle for Virginia. At the end of the year the company would have elected him again but for the interference of King James, who regarded him as the head of the party in Parliament opposed to his prerogative. He sent word to "choose the devil if you will, but not Sir Edwin Sandys." Thereupon Sandys stepped aside and the earl of Southampton, who agreed with him in all his views, was appointed and kept in office till the company's dissolution; and for much of this time Nicholas Ferrar, brother of John, acted as deputy to the earl.[2] The king, however, was no better satisfied, and Count Gondomar, the Spanish minister, took advantage of the state of things to tell James that he had "better look to the Virginia courts which were kept at Ferrar's house, where too many of his nobility and gentry resorted to accompany the popular Lord Southampton and the dangerous Sandys. He would

---

[1] Brown, *Genesis of the United States*, II., 1014; Bradford, *Plymouth*, 47.

[2] Virginia Company, *Proceedings* (Va. Hist. Soc., *Collections*, new series, VII.), I., 78.

find in the end these meetings would prove a *seminary for a seditious parliament.*"[1] These words, it is said, made a deep impression upon the king, always jealous for his prerogatives.

For two years, however, the crown stayed its hand and the affairs of Virginia greatly improved. Swarms of emigrants went out and many new plantations sprang up in the Accomack Peninsula and on both sides of the James. The most striking feature of these settlements was the steady growth of the tobacco trade. In 1619 twenty thousand pounds were exported, and in 1622 sixty thousand pounds. This increasing importation excited the covetousness of the king, as well as the jealousy of the Spanish government, whose West India tobacco had hitherto monopolized the London market. Directly contrary to the provision of the charter which exempted tobacco from any duty except five per cent., the king in 1619 levied an exaction of one shilling a pound, equal to twenty per cent. The London Company submitted on condition that the raising of tobacco in England should be prohibited, which was granted. In 1620 a royal proclamation limited the importation of tobacco from Virginia and the Bermuda Islands to fifty-five thousand pounds, whereupon the whole of the Virginia crop for that year was transported to Flushing and sold in Holland. As this deprived the king of his revenue, the Privy Council issued an

[1] Peckard, *Ferrar,* 115.

order in 1621 compelling the company to bring
all their tobacco into England.[1]

Nevertheless, these disturbances did not interfere
with the prosperity of the settlers. Large fortunes
were accumulated in a year or two by scores of
planters;[2] and soon in the place of the old log-
cabins arose framed buildings better than many in
England. Lands were laid out for a free school at
Charles City (now City Point) and for a university
and college at Henrico (Dutch Gap). Monthly courts
were held in every settlement, and there were large
crops of corn and great numbers of cattle, swine, and
poultry. A contemporary writer states that "the
plenty of those times, unlike the old days of death
and confusion, was such that every man gave free
entertainment to friends and strangers."[3]

This prosperity is marred by a story of heart-
rending sickness and suffering. An extraordinary
mortality due to imported epidemics, and diseases
of the climate for which in these days we have found
a remedy in quinine, slew the new-comers by
hundreds. One thousand people were in Virginia
at Easter, 1619, and to this number three thousand
five hundred and seventy more were added during
the next three years,[4] yet only one thousand two
hundred and forty were resident in the colony on

---

[1] *Discourse of the Old Company*, in *Va. Magazine*, I., 161.
[2] Smith, *Works* (Arber's ed.), 562.
[3] *Breife Declaration;* Neill, *Virginia Company*, 395–406.
[4] Neill, *Virginia Company*, 334.

Good Friday, March 22, 1622, a day when the horrors of an Indian massacre reduced the number to eight hundred and ninety-four.[1]

Since 1614, when Pocahontas married John Rolfe, peace with the Indians continued uninterruptedly, except for a short time in 1617, when there was an outbreak of the Chickahominies, speedily suppressed by Deputy Governor Yardley. In April, 1618, Powhatan died,[2] and the chief power was wielded by a brother, Opechancanough, at whose instance the savages, at "the taking up of Powhatan's bones" in 1621, formed a plot for exterminating the English. Of this danger Yardley received some information, and he promptly fortified the plantations, but Opechancanough professed friendship. Under Sir Francis Wyatt for some months everything went on quietly; but about the middle of March, 1622, a noted Indian chief, called Nemmattanow, or Jack o' the Feather, slew a white man and was slain in retaliation. Wyatt was alarmed, but Opechancanough assured him that "he held the peace so firme that the sky should fall ere he dissolved it," so that the settlers again "fed the Indians at their tables and lodged them in their bedchambers."[3]

Then like lightning from a clear sky fell the

---

[1] Brown, *First Republic*, 464, 467.

[2] Smith, *Works* (Arber's ed.), 539.

[3] *William and Mary Quarterly*, IX., 203-214; Neill, *Virginia Company*, 293, 307-321; Smith, *Works* (Arber's ed.), 572-594.

massacre upon the unsuspecting settlers. The blow was terrible to the colonists: the Indians, besides killing many of the inhabitants, burned many houses and destroyed a great quantity of stock. At first the settlers were panic-stricken, but rage succeeded fear. They divided into squads, and carried fire and sword into the Indian villages along the James and the York. In a little while the success of the English was so complete that they were able to give their time wholly to their crops and to rebuilding their houses.[1]

To the company the blow was a fatal one, though it did not manifest its results immediately. So far was the massacre from affecting the confidence of the public in Southampton and his friends at the head of the company that eight hundred good settlers went to Virginia during the year 1622, and John Smith wrote, "Had I meanes I might have choice of ten thousand that would gladly go."[2] But during the summer the members of the company were entangled in a dispute, of which advantage was taken by their enemies everywhere. At the suggestion of the crafty earl of Middlesex, the lord high treasurer of England, they were induced to apply to the king for a monopoly of the sale of tobacco in England; and it was granted on two conditions—viz., that they should pay the king £20,000 (supposed to be the value of a third of the total crop of

---

[1] Neill, *Virginia Company*, 364, 366.
[2] Smith, *Works* (Arber's ed.), 263.

Virginia tobacco) and import at least forty thousand pounds weight of Spanish tobacco. Though this last was a condition demanded by the king doubtless to placate the Spanish court, with whom he was negotiating for the marriage of his son Charles to the infanta, the contract on the whole was displeasing to Count Gondomar, the Spanish minister. He fomented dissensions in the company over the details, and Middlesex, the patron of the measure, being a great favorer of the Spanish match, changed sides upon his own proposition.[1]

In April, 1623, Alderman Robert Johnson, deputy to Sir Thomas Smith during the time of his government, brought a petition to the king for the appointment of a commission in England to inquire into the condition of the colony, which he declared was in danger of destruction by reason of "dissensions among ourselves and the massacre and hostility of the natives." This petition was followed by a scandalous paper, called *The Unmasking of Virginia*, presented to the king by another tool of Count Gondomar, one Captain Nathaniel Butler.[2] The company had already offended the king, and these new developments afforded him all the excuse that he wanted for taking extreme measures. He first attempted to cow the company into a "voluntary" surrender by seizing their books and arresting their leading members. When this did not avail,

[1] *Discourse of the Old Company*, in *Va. Magazine*, I., 291–293.
[2] Neill, *Virginia Company*, 395–407.

the Privy Council, November 3, 1623, appointed a commission to proceed to Virginia and make a report upon which judicial proceedings might be had. The company fought desperately, and in April, 1624, appealed to Parliament, but King James forbade the Commons to interfere.

In June, 1624, the expected paper from Virginia came to hand, and the cause was argued the same month at Trinity term on a writ of *quo warranto* before Chief-Justice James Ley of the King's Bench. The legal status of the company was unfavorable, for it was in a hopeless tangle, and the death record in the colony was an appalling fact. When, therefore, the attorney-general, Coventry, attacked the company for mismanagement, even an impartial tribune might have quashed the charter. But the case was not permitted to be decided on its merits. The company made a mistake in pleading, which was taken advantage of by Coventry, and on this ground the patent was voided the last day of the term (June 16, 1624).[1]

Thus perished the great London Company, which in settling Virginia expended upward of £200,000 (equal to $5,000,000 in present currency) and sent more than fourteen thousand emigrants. It received back from Virginia but a small part of the money it invested, and of all the emigrants whom it sent over, and their children, only one

[1] Peckard, *Ferrar*, 145; *Discourse of the Old Company*, in *Va. Magazine*, I., 297.

thousand two hundred and twenty-seven survived the charter. The heavy cost of the settlement was not a loss, for it secured to England a fifth kingdom and planted in the New World the germs of civil liberty. In this service the company did not escape the troubles incident to the mercenary purpose of a joint-stock partnership, yet it assumed a national and patriotic character, which entitles it to be considered the greatest and noblest association ever organized by the English people.[1] However unjust the measures taken by King James to overthrow the London Company, the incident was fortunate for tne inhabitants of Virginia. The colony had reached a stage of development which needed no longer the supporting hand of a distant corporation created for profit.

In Virginia, sympathy with the company was so openly manifested that the Governor's council ordered their clerk, Edward Sharpless, to lose his ears[2] for daring to give King James's commissioners copies of certain of their papers; and in January, 1624, a protest, called *The Tragical Relation*, was addressed to the king by the General Assembly, denouncing the administration of Sir Thomas Smith and his faction and extolling that of Sandys and Southampton. The sufferings of the colony under the former were vigorously painted, and they ended

[1] Brown, *First Republic*, 615.
[2] *Cal. of State Pap., Col.*, 1574–1660, 74; Neill, *Virginia Company*, 407.

by saying, "And rather (than) to be reduced to
live under the like government we desire his ma^{tie} y^t
commissioners may be sent over wth authoritie to
hang us."

Although Wyatt cordially joined in these protests,
and was a most popular governor, the General
Assembly about the same time passed an act[1]
in the following words: "The governor shall not
lay any taxes or ympositions upon the colony,
their lands or commodities, other way than by
authority of the General Assembly to be levied and
ymployed as the said assembly shall appoynt."
By this act Virginia formally asserted the indis-
soluble connection of taxation and representation.

The next step was to frame a government which
would correspond to the new relations of the colony.
June 24, 1624, a few days after the decision of
Chief-Justice Ley, the king appointed a commission
of sixteen persons, among whom were Sir Thomas
Smith and other opponents of Sandys and Southampton, to take charge, temporarily, of Virginia
affairs; and (July 15) he enlarged this commission
by forty more members. On their advice he
issued, August 26, 1624, authority to Sir Francis
Wyatt, governor, and twelve others in Virginia, as
councillors to conduct the government of the colony,
under such instructions as they might receive from
him or them.

In these orders it is expressly stated that the

[1] Hening, *Statutes.*, I., 124.

king's intention was not to disturb the interest of either planter or adventurer; while their context makes it clear that he proposed to avoid "the popularness" of the former government and to revive the charter of 1606 with some amendments. King James died March 27, 1625, and by his death this commission for Virginia affairs expired.[1]

Charles I. had all the arbitrary notions of his father, but fortunately he was under personal obligations to Sir Edwin Sandys and Nicholas Ferrar, Jr., and for their sake was willing to be liberal in his dealing with the colonists.[2] Hence, soon after his father's death, he dismissed the former royal commissioners and intrusted affairs relating to Virginia to a committee of the Privy Council, who ignored the Smith party and called the Sandys party into consultation.[3] These last presented a paper in April, 1625, called *The Discourse of the Old Company*, in which they reviewed fully the history of the charter and petitioned to be reincorporated. Charles was not unwilling to grant the request, and in a proclamation dated May 13, 1625, he avowed that he had come to the same opinion as his father, and intended to have a "royal council in England and another in Virginia, but not to impeach the interest of any adventurer or planter in Virginia."

---

[1] *Cal. of State Pap., Col.*, 1574–1674, p. 64, 1574–1660, p. 62.
[2] Brown, *English Politics in Early Virginia History*, 89.
[3] Brown, *First Republic*, 640, 641.

Still ignorant of the death of King James, Governor Sir Francis Wyatt and his council, together with representatives from the plantations informally called, sent George Yardley to England with a petition, dated June 15, 1625, that they be permitted the right of a general assembly, that worthy emigrants be encouraged, and that none of the old faction of Sir Thomas Smith and Alderman Johnson have a part in the administration; "for rather than endure the government of these men they were resolved to seek the farthest part of the world."

Yardley reached England in October; and the king, when informed of Wyatt's desire to resign the government of Virginia on account of his private affairs, issued a commission, dated April 16, 1626, renewing the authority of the council in Virginia and appointing Yardley governor.[1] The latter returned to Virginia, but died in 1627. After his death the king sent directions to Acting Governor Francis West to summon a general assembly; and March 26, 1628, after an interval of four years, the regular law-making body again assembled at Jamestown, an event second only in importance to the original meeting in 1619.[2]

Other matters besides the form of government pressed upon the attention of the settlers. Tobacco entered more and more into the life of the colony, and the crop in the year 1628 amounted to upward

---

[1] *Cal. of State Pap., Col.*, 1574–1660, pp. 73, 74, 79.
[2] *Ibid.*, 86, 88; Neill, *Virginia Carolorum*, 55.

of five hundred thousand pounds.[1] King Charles
took the ground of Sandys and Southampton, that
the large production was only temporary, and like
his father, subjected tobacco in England to high
duties and monopoly. He urged a varied planting
and the making of pitch and tar, pipe-staves, pot-
ashes, iron, and bay-salt, and warned the planters
against "building their plantation wholly on smoke."
It was observed, however, that Charles was receiving
a large sum of money from customs on tobacco,[2]
and it was not likely that his advice would be taken
while the price was 3s. 6d. a pound. Indeed, it was
chiefly under the stimulus of the culture of tobacco
that the population of the colony rose from eight
hundred and ninety-four, after the massacre in
1622, to about three thousand in 1629.[3]

In March, 1629, Captain West went back to
England, and a new commission was issued to Sir
John Harvey as governor.[4] He did not come to
the colony till the next year, and in the interval
Dr. John Pott acted as his deputy. At the assembly
called by Pott in October, 1629, the growth of the
colony was represented by twenty-three settlements
as against eleven ten years before. As in England,
there were two branches of the law-making body, a

[1] Hening, *Statutes*, I., 134.
[2] In 1624 the crop was three hundred thousand pounds, the
total importations from Virginia, Bermuda, and Spain four
hundred and fifty thousand pounds, and the profit in customs
to the crown was £93,350.
[3] *Cal. of State Pap., Col.*, 1574–1660, p. 89.   [4] *Ibid.*, 88.

House of Burgesses, made up of the representatives of the people, and an upper house consisting of the governor and council. In the constitution of the popular branch there was no fixed number of delegates, but each settlement had as many as it chose to pay the expenses of, a custom which prevailed until 1660, when the number of burgesses was limited to two members for each county and one member for Jamestown.[1]

In March, 1630, Harvey arrived, and Pott's former dignity as governor did not save him from a mortifying experience. The council was not only an upper house of legislation, but the supreme court of the colony, and in July, 1630, Pott was arraigned before this tribunal for stealing cattle, and declared guilty. Perhaps Harvey realized that injustice was done, for he suspended the sentence, and on petition to the king the case was re-examined in England by the commissioners for Virginia, who decided that "condemning Pott of felony was very rigorous if not erroneous."[2]

The year 1630 was the beginning of a general movement of emigration northward, and in October Chiskiack, an Indian district on the south side of the York, about twenty-seven miles below the forks of the river where Opechancanough resided, was occupied in force. So rapid was the course of population that in less than two years this first

---

[1] Hening, *Statutes*, I., 147, II., 20.
[2] *Cal. of State Pap., Col.*, 1574–1660, p. 133.

settlement upon the York was divided into Chiskiack and York. One year after Chiskiack was settled, Kent Island in Chesapeake Bay was occupied by a company under William Claiborne, the secretary of state; and in 1632 Middle Plantation (afterwards Williamsburg) was laid out and defended by a line of palisades from tide - water to tide-water.[1]

Meanwhile, the old colonial parties did not cease to strive with one another in England. Harvey had been appointed by the vacillating Charles to please the former court party, but during the quarrel with his Parliament over the Petition of Right he became anxious again to conciliate the colonists and the members of the old company; and in May, 1631, he appointed[2] a new commission, consisting of the earls of Dorset and Danby, Sir John Danvers, Sir Dudley Digges, John Ferrar, Sir Francis Wyatt, and others, to advise him upon "some course for establishing the advancement of the plantation of Virginia." This commission had many consultations, and unanimously resolved to recommend to the king the renewal of the charter of 1612 with all its former privileges—except the form of government, which was to be exercised by the king through a council in London and a governor and council in Virginia, both appointed by him.

[1] Hening, *Statutes*, I., 208, 257; Mass. Hist. Soc., *Collections*, 4th series, IX., 111.
[2] *Cal. of State Pap., Col.*, 1574–1660, p. 130.

In June, 1632, Charles I. so vacillated as to grant Maryland, within the bounds of "their ancient territories," to Lord Baltimore, regardless of the protest of the Virginians; and April 28, 1634, he revoked the liberal commission of 1631, and appointed another, called "the Commission for Foreign Plantations," composed almost entirely of opponents of the popular course of government, with William Laud, archbishop of Canterbury, at the head. This commission had power to "make laws and orders for government of English colonies planted in foreign parts, to remove governors and require an account of their government, to appoint judges and magistrates, to establish courts, to amend all charters and patents, and to revoke those surreptitiously and unduly obtained." [1]

Harvey's conduct in Virginia reflected the views of the court party in England. He offended his council by acting in important matters without their consent, contrary to his instructions; and showed in many ways that he was a friend of the persons in England who were trying to make a monopoly of the tobacco trade. He attempted to lay taxes, but the assembly, in February, 1632, re-enacted the law of 1624 asserting their exclusive authority over the subject.[2] At the head of the opposition to Harvey was William Claiborne, the secretary of state, who opposed Lord Baltimore's

[1] *Cal. of State Pap., Col.*, 1574–1660, pp. 136, 177.
[2] Hening, *Statutes*, I., 171.

claim to Maryland, and, in consequence, was in the latter part of 1634 turned out of office by Harvey, to make way for Richard Kempe, one of Lord Baltimore's friends.

The people of Virginia began in resentment to draw together in little groups, and talked of asking for the removal of the governor; and matters came to a crisis in April, 1635, when Harvey suppressed a petition addressed to the king by the assembly regarding the tobacco contract, and justified an attack by Lord Baltimore's men upon a pinnace of Claiborne engaged in the fur trade from Kent Island. At York, in April, 1635, a meeting of protest was held at the house of William Warren.

Harvey was enraged at the proceeding and caused the leaders to be arrested. Then he called a council at Jamestown, and the scenes in the council chamber are interestingly described in contemporary letters. Harvey demanded the execution of martial law upon the prisoners, and when the council held back he flew into a passion and attempted to arrest George Menifie, one of the members, for high-treason. Captain John Utie and Captain Samuel Matthews retorted by making a similar charge against Harvey, and he was arrested by the council, and confined at the house of Captain William Brocas. Then the council elected Captain John West, of Chiskiack, brother of Lord Delaware, as governor, and summoned an assembly to meet at Jamestown in May following. This body promptly ratified the action of the council, and Harvey was put aboard a ship and sent off to England in charge of two members of the House of Burgesses.[1]

This deposition of a royal governor was a bold proceeding and mightily surprised King Charles. He declared it an act of "regal authority," had the two daring burgesses arrested, and on the complaint of Lord Baltimore, who befriended Harvey, caused West, Utie, Menifie, Matthews, and others of the unfriendly councillors to appear in England to answer for their crimes. Meanwhile, to rebuke the dangerous precedent set in Virginia, he thought it necessary to restore Harvey to his government.[2]

Harvey did not enjoy his second lease of power long, for the king, in the vicissitudes of English politics, found it wise to turn once more a favorable ear to the friends of the old company, and in January, 1639, Sir Francis Wyatt, who had governed Virginia so acceptably once before, was commissioned to succeed Harvey. The former councillors in Virginia were restored to power, and in the king's instructions to Wyatt the name of Captain West was inserted as "Muster-Master-General" in Charles's own handwriting.[3]

---

[1] *Va. Magazine*, I., 416, 425, VIII., 299–306; Neill, *Virginia Carolorum*, 118–120.

[2] *Cal. of State Pap., Col.*, 1574–1660, pp. 216, 217.

[3] Wyatt's commission, in *Va. Magazine*, XI., 50–54; *Cal. of State Pap., Col.*, 1574–1674, p. 83.

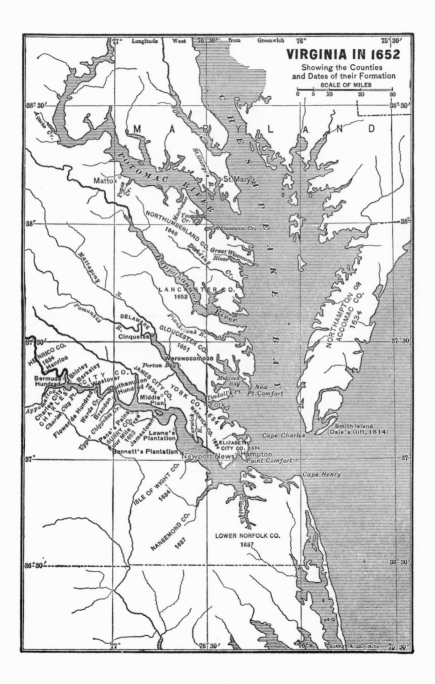

VIRGINIA IN 1652
Showing the Counties
and Dates of their Formation
SCALE OF MILES

CHAPTER VI

SOCIAL AND ECONOMIC CONDITIONS OF
VIRGINIA

(1634–1652)

DURING the vicissitudes of government in Virginia the colony continued to increase in wealth and population, and in 1634 eight counties were created;[1] while an official census in April, 1635, showed nearly five thousand people, to which number sixteen hundred were added in 1636. The new-comers during Harvey's time were principally servants who came to work the tobacco - fields.[2] Among them were some convicts and shiftless people, but the larger number were persons of respectable standing, and some had comfortable estates and influential connections in England.[3] Freed from their service in Virginia, not a few attained positions as justices of the peace and burgesses in the General Assembly.[4]

The trade of Virginia was become so extensive

[1] Hening, *Statutes*, I., 224.
[2] *Cal. of State Pap., Col.*, 1574–1660, pp. 201, 231, 268.
[3] *William and Mary Quarterly*, IV., 173–176, V., 40.
[4] *Virginia's Cure* (Force, *Tracts*, III., No. xv.).

that Dutch as well as English ships sought the colony. The principal settlements were on the north side of James River, and as the voyager in 1634 sailed from Chesapeake Bay he passed first the new fort at Point Comfort lately constructed by Captain Samuel Matthews. About five miles farther on was Newport News, chiefly remarkable for its spring, where all the ships stopped to take in water, at this time the residence of Captain Daniel Gookin, a prominent Puritan, who afterwards removed to Massachusetts. Five miles above Newport News, at Deep Creek, was Denbeigh, Captain Samuel Matthews's place, a miniature village rather than plantation, where many servants were employed, hemp and flax woven, hides tanned, leather made into shoes, cattle and swine raised for the ships outward bound, and a large dairy and numerous poultry kept.

A few hours' sail from Denbeigh was Littletown, the residence of George Menifie. He had a garden of two acres on the river-side, which was full of roses of Provence, apple, pear, and cherry trees, and the various fruits of Holland, with different kinds of sweet-smelling herbs, such as rosemary, sage, marjoram, and thyme. Growing around the house was an orchard of peach-trees, which astonished his visitors very much, for they were not to be seen anywhere else on the coast.[1]

About six miles farther was Jamestown, a village

[1] De Vries, *Voyages* (N. Y. Hist. Soc., *Collections*, 2d series, III., 34).

of three hundred inhabitants, built upon two streets at the upper end of the island.   There the governor resided with some of his council, one of whom, Captain William Pierce, had a garden of three or four acres, from which his wife a few years before obtained a hundred bushels of figs.[1] The houses there as elsewhere were of wood, with brick chimneys, but architecture was improving.

In 1637 the General Assembly offered a lot to every person who should build a house at Jamestown Island; and in pursuance of the encouragement given, "twelve new houses and stores were built in the town," one of brick by Richard Kempe, "the fairest ever known in this country for substance and uniformity."   About the same time money was raised for a brick church and a brick state-house.[2] As to the general condition of the colony in 1634, Captain Thomas Young reported that there was not only a "very great plentie of milk, cheese, and butter, but of corn, which latter almost every planter in the colony hath."[3]

Such a "plentie of corn" must be contrasted with the scarcity in 1630, for the current of prosperity did not run altogether smoothly.   The mortality still continued frightful, and "during the months of June, July, and August, the people died like cats and

[1] Smith, *Works* (Arber's ed.), 887.
[2] *Cal. of State Pap., Col.*, 1574–1660, p. 288.   In 1639 Alexander Stonar, brickmaker, patented land on Jamestown Island "next to the brick-kiln," Tyler, *Cradle of the Republic*, 46, 99.
[3] Mass. Hist. Soc., *Collections*, 4th series, IX., 108.

dogs," [1] a statement especially true of the servants, of whom hardly one in five survived the first year's hardships in the malarial tobacco-fields along the creeks and rivers.[2]   In 1630 tobacco tumbled from its high price of 3s. 6d. to 1d. per pound, and the colony was much "perplexed" for want of money to buy corn, which they had neglected to raise. To relieve the distress, Harvey, the next year, sent several ships to trade with the Indians up Chesapeake Bay and on the coast as far south as Cape Fear.[3]

Tobacco legislation for the next ten years consisted in regulations vainly intended to prevent further declines.   Tobacco fluctuated in value from one penny to sixpence, and, as it was the general currency, this uncertainty caused much trouble. Some idea of the general dependency upon tobacco may be had from a statute in 1640, which, after providing for the destruction of all the bad tobacco and half the good, estimated the remainder actually placed upon the market by a population of eight thousand at one million five hundred thousand pounds.[4]

The decline in the price of tobacco had the effect of turning the attention of the planters to other industries, especially the supply of corn to the large

---

[1] De Vries, *Voyages* (N. Y. Hist. Soc., *Collections*, 2d series, III., 37).
[2] *William and Mary Quarterly*, VII., 66, 114.
[3] *Cal. of State Pap., Col.*, 1574–1660, p. 117.
[4] Hening, *Statutes*, I., 225.

emigration from England to Massachusetts. In 1631 a ship - load of corn from Virginia was sold at Salem, in Massachusetts, for ten shillings the bushel.[1] In 1634 at least ten thousand bushels were taken to Massachusetts, besides "good quantities of beeves, goats, and hogs ";[2] and Harvey declared that Virginia had become "the granary of all his majesty's northern colonies,"[3] Yet from an imported pestilence, the year 1636 was so replete with misery that Samuel Maverick, of Massachusetts, who visited the colony, reported that eighteen hundred persons died, and corn sold at twenty shillings per bushel.[4]

Sir Francis Wyatt arrived in the colony, November, 1639, and immediately called Harvey to account for his abuse of power. The decree against Panton was repealed, and his estate, which had been seized, was returned to him, while the property of Harvey was taken to satisfy his numerous creditors.[5] The agitation for the renewal of the charter still continued, and Wyatt called a general assembly January, 1640, at which time it was determined to make another effort. George Sandys was appointed agent of the colony in England, and petitions reached England probably in the autumn of 1640. The breach between the king and Parliament was

[1] Winthrop, *New England*, I., 67.
[2] Mass. Hist. Soc., *Collections*, 4th series, IX., 110.
[3] *Cal. of State Pap., Col.*, 1574–1660, p. 184.
[4] Winthrop, *New England*, I., 228.
[5] *Va. Magazine*, V., 123–128.

then complete, and Charles had thrown himself entirely into the arms of the court party. Sandys, despairing of success from the king, appealed to Parliament in the name of the "Adventurers and Planters in Virginia," and "the Virginia patent was taken out again under the broad seal of England." [1] To what extent the new charter established the boundaries of Virginia does not appear, and the subsequent turn of affairs in Virginia made the action of Parliament at this time a nullity.

To offset these proceedings, the king commissioned [2] Sir William Berkeley, a vehement royalist, as successor to the popular Wyatt, and he arrived in Virginia in January, 1642, where he at once called an assembly to undo the work of Sandys. A petition to the king protesting against the restoration of the company was adopted, but although it was signed by the council and burgesses, as well as by Berkeley, the preamble alludes to strong differences of opinion. [3] The change of position was doubtless brought about by the issue made in England between loyalty and rebellion; and, while desirous of a recharter, the majority of the people of Virginia did not care to desert the king. The petition was presented July 5, 1642, to Charles at his headquarters at York, who returned a gracious reply that "he

[1] *Virginia and Maryland, or the Lord Baltimore's Printed Case, uncased and answered* (Force, *Tracts*, II., No. ix.).

[2] *Va. Magazine*, II., 281–288.

[3] Hening, *Statutes*, I., 230–235.

had not the least intention to consent to the introduction of any company." [1]

While loyal to the king, the people of Virginia had never been wedded to the views of the high-church party in England. Among the ministers the surplice was not usual, and there was a Puritan severity about the laws in regard to the Sabbath and attendance at church. As the strife in England became more pronounced, the people in Nansemond and lower Norfolk counties, on the south of the James, showed decided leanings towards Parliament and to the congregational form of worship.

Soon they began to think of separating from the church of England altogether, and they sent for ministers to New England in 1642. In response, the elders there despatched three of their number, who, arriving in Virginia, set zealously to work to organize the congregations on the Nansemond and Elizabeth rivers. According to their own account, these ministers met with much success till they were suddenly stopped in the work by Berkeley, who persuaded the assembly, in March, 1643, to pass severe laws against Nonconformists; and under this authority drove them out of the land in 1644. [2]

In the same year occurred an Indian attack which these preachers and John Winthrop, the governor

---

[1] *Manuscript Collection of Annals relating to Virginia* (Force, *Tracts*, II., No. vi.).

[2] Latané, *Early Relations between Maryland and Virginia* (*Johns Hopkins University Studies*, XIII., Nos. iii. and iv.).

of Massachusetts, thought to be a special visitation
of Providence. After the massacre in 1622 the war
with the Indians had continued in a desultory way
for over twelve years. Year after year squads of
soldiers were sent in various directions against the
different tribes, and by 1634 the Indians were so
punished that the whites thought it safe to make
peace. Now, after a repose of ten years, the fierce
instincts of the savages for blood were once more
excited.

April 18, 1644, was Good Friday, and Governor
Berkeley ordered it to be kept as a special fast
day to pray for King Charles; instead, it became a
day of bloodshed and mourning.[1] The chief in-
stigator of the massacre of 1622 was still alive, old
Opechancanough, who, by the death of his brother
Opitchapam, was now head chief of the Powhatan
Confederacy. Thinking the civil war in England a
favorable occasion to repeat the bloody deeds of
twenty-two years before, on the day before Good
Friday he attacked the settlers, and continued the
assault for two days, killing over three hundred
whites. The onslaught fell severest on the south
side of James River and on the heads of the other
rivers, but chiefly on the York River, where Opechancanough had his residence.[2]

The massacre of 1622 shook the colony to its
foundation, and it is surprising to see how little

---

[1] Winthrop, *New England*, II., 198, 199.
[2] *Ibid.;* Beverley, *Virginia*, 48.

that of 1644 affected the current of life in Virginia. Berkeley seemed to think so little of the attack that after making William Claiborne general of an expedition against the Pamunkey tribe he left the colony in June, 1645.[1] He was gone a whole year, and on his return found that Claiborne had driven the Indians far away from the settlements. In 1646 he received information which enabled him to close the war with dramatic effect. At the head of a body of cavalry he surprised old Opechancanough in an encampment between the falls of the Appomattox and the James, and brought him, aged and blind, to Jamestown, where, about three weeks later, one of his guards shot him to death.[2] A peace was made not long after with Necotowance, his successor, by which the Indians agreed to retire entirely from the peninsula between the York and James rivers.[3]

One of the most remarkable results of the massacre was the change it produced in Rev. Thomas Harrison, Berkeley's chaplain at Jamestown, who had used his influence with the governor to expel the Nonconformist ministers of New England. He came to the belief of John Winthrop that the massacre was a Providential visitation and turned Puritan himself. After a quarrel with Berkeley he left Jamestown and took charge of the churches on

[1] *Va. Magazine*, VIII., 71–73.
[2] *A Perfect Description of Virginia* (Force, *Tracts*, II., No. viii.); Beverley, *Virginia*, 49.
[3] Hening, *Statutes*, I., 323–326.

the Elizabeth and Nansemond rivers with their Puritan congregations. Berkeley would probably have set the law-officers upon him at once, but among his councillors was Richard Bennett, himself of Harrison's congregation, and his influence held the governor back for a time.

Three years passed, and at length Harrison and his elder, William Durand, were peremptorily directed to leave the colony. Harrison went first to New England and then to old England, while William Durand emigrated to Maryland, where, aided by Bennett, he made terms with Governor William Stone for the emigration of his flock; and in the year 1649 more than one thousand persons left Virginia and settled on the Severn and Patuxent rivers. The settlement was called Providence, and was destined to play a remarkable part in the history of Maryland.[1]

When the civil war in England was fairly on, emigration to Virginia was much improved in material, and for many years was very large. The new-comers came to make homes, not merely to make tobacco, and they no longer consisted of servants, but of the merchants and yeomanry of England. "If these troublous times hold long amongst us," wrote William Hallam, a salter of Burnham, in Essex County, England, "we must all faine come to Virginia." [2]

[1] Latané, *Early Relations* (*Johns Hopkins University Studies*, XIII.).   [2] *William and Mary Quarterly*, VIII., 239.

Hitherto the uncertainty resulting from the over-throw of the charter made it difficult to secure a good class of ministers. Those who came had been "such as wore black coats and could babble in a pulpet, and roare in a tavern, exact from their parishioners, and rather by their dissolutenesse de-stroy than feed their flocks." Now these "wolves in sheep's clothing" were by the assembly forced to depart the country and a better class of clergy-men arrived.[1] In 1649 there were twenty churches and twenty ministers who taught the doctrines of the church of England and "lived all in peace and love";[2] and at the head of them was a man of ex-emplary piety, Rev. Philip Mallory, son of Dr. Thomas Mallory, Dean of Chester.[3]

The condition of things about 1648 is thus summed up by Hammond, a contemporary writer: "Then began the gospel to flourish; civil, honorable, and men of great estates flocked in; famous build-ings went forward; orchards innumerable were planted and preserved; tradesmen set to work and, encouraged, staple commodities, as silk, flax, pot-ashes attempted on. . . . So that this country, which had a mean beginning, many back friends, two ruin-ous and bloody massacres, hath by God's grace out-grown all, and is become a place of pleasure and plenty."

---

[1] Hammond, *Leah and Rachel* (Force, *Tracts*, III., No. xiv.).
[2] *Perfect Description* (*ibid.*, II., No. viii.).
[3] Neill, *Virginia Carolorum*, 238; Tyler, *Cradle of the Republic*, 90.

Later, after the beheading of King Charles in
1649, there was a large influx of cavaliers, who, while
they raised the quality of society, much increased
the sympathy felt in Virginia for the royal cause.
Under their influence Sir William Berkeley denounced the murder of King Charles I., and the
General Assembly adopted an act making it treason
to defend the late proceedings or to doubt the right
of his son, Charles II., to succeed to the crown.[1]
Parliament was not long in accepting the challenge
which Berkeley tendered. In October, 1650, they
adopted an ordinance prohibiting trade with the re-
bellious colonies of Virginia, Barbadoes, Antigua,
and Bermuda Islands, and authorizing the Council of State to take measures to reduce them to
terms.[2]

In October, 1651, was passed the first of the
navigation acts, which limited the colonial trade to
England, and banished from Virginia the Dutch
vessels, which carried abroad most of the exports.
About the same time, having taken measures against
Barbadoes, the Council of State ordered a squadron
to be prepared against Virginia. It was placed
under the command of Captain Robert Dennis; and
Thomas Stegge, Richard Bennett, and William
Claiborne, members of Berkeley's council, were
joined with him in a commission[3] to "use their

[1] Hening, *Statutes*, I., 359–361.
[2] *Cal. of State Pap., Col.*, 1574–1660, p. 343.
[3] *Md. Archives*, III., 265–267.

best endeavors to reduce all the plantations within the Bay of Chesopiack." Bennett and Claiborne were in Virginia at the time, and probably did not know of their appointment till the ships arrived in Virginia.

The fleet left England in October, 1651, carrying six hundred men, but on the way Captain Dennis and Captain Stegge were lost in a storm and the command devolved on Captain Edmund Curtis.[1] In December they reached the West Indies, where they assisted Sir George Ayscue in the reduction of Barbadoes. In January, 1652, they reached Virginia, where Curtis showed Claiborne and Bennett his duplicate instructions. Berkeley, full of fight, called out the militia, twelve hundred strong, and engaged the assistance of a few Dutch ships then trading in James River contrary to the recent navigation act.

The commissioners acted with prudence and good sense. They did not proceed at once to Jamestown, but first issued a proclamation intended to disabuse the people of any idea that they came to make war.[2] The result was that in March, 1652, when they appeared before the little capital, the council and burgesses overruled Berkeley, and entered into an agreement with Curtis, Claiborne, and Bennett, which proves the absence of hard feelings on both sides. The Virginians recognized the authority of

[1] *Cal. of State Pap., Col.*, 1574–1660, p. 393.
[2] See report of the commissioners, *Va. Magazine*, XI., 32.

the commonwealth of England, and promised to pass no statute contrary to the laws of Parliament. On the other hand, the commissioners acknowledged the submission of Virginia, "as a voluntary act not forced nor constrained by a conquest upon the countrey"; and conceded her right "to be free from all taxes, customs, and impositions whatever, not enforced by the General Assembly." In particular it was stipulated that "Virginia should have and enjoy the antient bounds and lymitts granted by the charters of the former kings."

The articles were signed March 12, 1652, and the commissioners soon after sailed to St. Mary's and received the surrender of Maryland. They returned in time to be present at a new meeting of the assembly held at Jamestown in April, at which it was unanimously voted that until the further pleasure of Parliament was known Richard Bennett should be governor and William Claiborne secretary of state. To the burgesses, as the representatives of the people, was handed over the supreme power of thereafter electing all officers of the colony.[1] Then Virginia, the last of the British dominions to abandon the king, entered upon eight years of almost complete self-government, under the protection of the commonwealth of England.

In 1652 the settlements in Virginia were embraced in thirteen counties, of which Northampton, on the Accomack Peninsula, extended to the southern

---

[1] Hening, *Statutes*, I., 363, 371.

boundary of Maryland. On the James River were nine counties: Henrico, Charles City, James City, Surry, Warwick, Warascoyack, or Isle of Wight, Elizabeth City, Nansemond, and Lower Norfolk. On York River were York County on the south side and Gloucester on the north side.[1] On the Rappahannock was Lancaster County, extending on both sides of the river from Pianketank to Dividing Creek in the Northern Neck; and on the Potomac was the county of Northumberland, first settled about 1638 at Chicacoan and Appomattox on the Potomac, by refugees from Maryland.[2]

Towards the south the plantations, following the watercourses, had spread to the heads of the creeks and rivers, tributaries of the James, and some persons more adventurous than the rest had even made explorations in North Carolina.[3] Westward the extension was, of course, greatest along the line of the James, reaching as far as the Falls where Richmond now stands. The population was probably about twenty thousand, of whom as many as five thousand were white servants and five hundred were negroes.

The houses throughout the colony were generally of wood, a story and a half high, and were roofed with shingles. The chimneys were of brick, and the wealthier people lived in houses constructed wholly

---

[1] Virginia Land Grants, *MSS.*
[2] *Md. Archives*, IV., 268, 315.
[3] Bancroft, *United States* (22d ed.), II., 134.

of home-made brick.[1] " They had, besides, good
English furniture " and a "good store of plate."
By ordinary labor at making tobacco any person
could clear annually £20 sterling, the equivalent of
$500 to-day. The condition of the servants had
greatly improved, and their labor was not so hard
nor of such continuance as that of farmers and
mechanics in England. Thefts were seldom committed, and an old writer asserts that "he was an
eye-witness in England to more deceits and villanies
in four months than he ever saw or heard mention
of in Virginia in twenty years abode there."[2]

The plenty of everything made hospitality universal, and the health of the country was greatly
promoted by the opening of the forests. Indeed, so
contented were the people with their new homes
that the same writer declares, "Seldom (if ever) any
that hath continued in Virginia any time will or do
desire to live in England, but post back with what
expedition they can, although many are landed
men in England, and have good estates there, and
divers wayes of preferments propounded to them
to entice and perswade their continuance."

In striking contrast to New England was the absence of towns, due mainly to two reasons—first,
the wealth of watercourses, which enabled every
planter of means to ship his products from his own

---

[1] Tyler, "Colonial Brick Houses," in *Century Magazine*,
February, 1896.
[2] Hammond, *Leah and Rachel* (Force, *Tracts*, III., No. xiv.).

wharf; and, secondly, the culture of tobacco, which scattered the people in a continual search for new and richer lands. This rural life, while it hindered co-operation, promoted a spirit of independence among the whites of all classes which counteracted the aristocratic form of government. The colony was essentially a democracy, for though the chief offices in the counties and the colony at large were held by a few families, the people were protected by a popular House of Burgesses, which till 1736 was practically established on manhood suffrage. Negro slavery tended to increase this independence by making race and not wealth the great distinction; and the ultimate result was seen after 1792, when Virginia became the headquarters of the Democratic-Republican party—the party of popular ideas.[1]

Under the conditions of Virginia society, no developed educational system was possible, but it is wrong to suppose that there was none. The parish institutions introduced from England included educational beginnings; every minister had a school, and it was the duty of the vestry to see that all poor children could read and write. The county courts supervised the vestries and held a yearly "orphans' court," which looked after the material and educational welfare of all orphans.[2]

[1] Tyler, "Virginians Voting in the Colonial Period," in *William and Mary Quarterly*, VI., 9.

[2] "Education in Colonial Virginia," *William and Mary Quarterly*, V., 219–223, VI., 1–7, 71–86, 171–186, VII., 1–9, 65, 77.

The benevolent design of a free school in the colony, frustrated by the massacre of 1622, was realized in 1635, when—three years before John Harvard bequeathed his estate to the college near Boston which bears his name—Benjamin Syms left "the first legacy by a resident of the American plantations of England for the promotion of education."[1] In 1659 Thomas Eaton established[2] a free school in Elizabeth City County, adjoining that of Benjamin Syms; and a fund amounting to $10,000, representing these two ancient charities, is still used to carry on the public high-school at Hampton, Virginia. In 1655 Captain John Moon left a legacy for a free school in Isle of Wight County; and in 1659 Captain William Whittington left two thousand pounds of tobacco for a free school in Northampton County.

[1] Neill, *Virginia Carolorum*, 112.
[2] "Eaton's Deed," in *William and Mary Quarterly*, XI., 19.

CHAPTER VII

FOUNDING OF MARYLAND
(1632–1650)

THE founding of Maryland was due chiefly to the personal force of George Calvert, first Lord Baltimore, son of Leonard Calvert. He was born near Kiplin, in Yorkshire, about 1580, and graduated at Trinity College, Oxford, 1597. After making a tour of Europe he became the private secretary of Sir Robert Cecil, who rapidly advanced his fortunes. He served upon several missions to investigate the affairs of Ireland, was knighted in 1617, and in 1619 succeeded Sir Thomas Lake as principal secretary of state.

In this office he began to revolve plans of colonization in America, to which his attention was directed as a member of the Virginia Company since 1609. In 1620 he bought from Sir William Vaughan the southeastern peninsula of Newfoundland, known as Ferryland, and the next year sent some colonists thither. He supported the Spanish match; and when Charles changed his policy he obtained from the king in 1623 a charter for his province, which he called Avalon. In 1625 he resigned his secretaryship and openly avowed his adherence to the church of Rome; but the king, as a mark of favor, raised him to the Irish peerage, with the title of Baron of Baltimore, after a small town of that name in Ireland.[1]

Baltimore returned to his plans of colonization, and in 1627 went to Newfoundland with his wife and children. But the country proved too cold for him and he determined to "shift" to a warmer climate. Accordingly, in August, 1629, he wrote to the king for a "grant of a precinct of land in Virginia," with the same privileges as those which King James gave him in Newfoundland.[2] Without waiting for a reply he left Avalon, and in October, 1629, arrived in Virginia, where the governor, Dr. John Pott, and his council received him politely but coldly. Neither his religion nor his past career as a court favorite, nor the design which he made known of establishing an independent state within the confines of Virginia, commended him to the people of Jamestown.

Naturally, they wished to get rid of him, and the council tendered him the oaths of allegiance and supremacy, which, in the various instructions from the king, they were strictly enjoined to require of all new-comers. The oath of allegiance occasioned no difficulty, but the oath of supremacy, which required Baltimore to swear that he believed the king

[1] Brown, *Genesis of the United States*, II., 841.
[2] *Cal. of State Pap., Col.*, 1574–1660, pp. 83, 93, 100.

to be "the only supreme governor in his realm in all spiritual or ecclesiastical things or causes," was repugnant to him as a Catholic, and he declined to take it, but offered to subscribe to a modified form. This was refused, and after several weeks' sojourn Lord Baltimore sailed away to England to press his suit in person before the king.[1]

So far as the law of England stood at that time, the effect of the dissolution of the London Company was to extinguish the debts of the corporation and vest all its property undisposed of in the crown. On the other hand, there were the repeated official pledges of Charles and his father not to disturb the interest of either planter or adventurer in any part of the territory formerly conveyed by the charter of 1609.[2]   Nevertheless, the king preferred law to equity, and October 30, 1629, granted to Sir Robert Heath the province of Carolana in the southern part of Virginia, between thirty-one and thirty-six degrees.[3]   But there was a clause in this charter excepting any land "actually granted or in possession of any of his majesty's subjects."

About the same time Cottington, the secretary of state, was directed to answer Lord Baltimore's letter written from Newfoundland and promise him "any part of Virginia not already granted." Lord Baltimore arrived in London soon after this letter

---

[1] *Cal. of State Pap., Col.*, 1574–1660, p. 104; *Md. Archives*, III., 17.   [2] *Md. Archives*, III., 19.
[3] Heath's grant, in *Cal. of State Pap., Col.*, 1574–1674, p. 70.

was written, and in December, 1629, petitioned to be permitted to "choose for his part" a tract south of James River and north of Carolana. A charter was made out for him in February, 1631, and would have passed the seals but for the intervention of William Claiborne, one of those Virginia councillors who had offered the oath to Baltimore.[1]

William Claiborne, the second son of Sir Edward Claiborne, of Westmoreland County, England, went over to Virginia with Governor Wyatt in 1621 as surveyor-general of the colony. Shortly afterwards he was made a councillor, and in 1625 secretary of state of the colony. In the Indian war, which began with the massacre in 1622, he was appointed general, and in 1629 received lands in the Pamunkey Neck for valuable military service. Active and fearless, he engaged with great success in the trade for furs in the bay, and was recognized as the foremost man in Virginia. Sent in May, 1630, by the Virginia council to watch the movements of Lord Baltimore, he co-operated in England with ex-Governor Francis West, of Virginia, Sir John Wolstenholme, and other gentlemen who wished the restoration of the London Company.

Aided by these friends, Claiborne defeated the proposed grant, but Baltimore persevered, and, · in April, 1632, received from the crown a patent for a portion of the Virginia territory lying north of Point Comfort, and having for bounds the ocean, the

[1] Neill, *Founders of Maryland*, 46, 47.

fortieth parallel of north latitude, the meridian of
the western fountain of the Potomac, the southern
bank of the Potomac River, and a line drawn east
from Watkins Point.   In the grant the land was
described as "hitherto unsettled and occupied only
by barbarians ignorant of God."   The king first
proposed to call it Mariana, in honor of his wife,
Henrietta Maria, but on Baltimore objecting that
it was the name of a Spanish historian who had
written against the doctrine of passive obedience,
Charles modified the appellation, and said, "Let it
be called Terra Mariæ—Maryland." [1]

April 15, 1632, George Calvert died, and the
charter was made out in the name of his eldest son,
Cecilius, and was signed by the king, June 20, 1632.
Cecilius Calvert, named after Sir Robert Cecil, was
born in 1605, and in 1621 entered Trinity College,
Oxford University.   He married Anne Arundel,
daughter of Lord Thomas Arundel, of Wardour.
As Cecilius, unlike his father, never held public
positions in England, his character is best revealed
by his conduct of his province in America, which
shows him to have been a man of consummate
prudence and tact.

Baltimore's grant called forth a strong remonstrance from members of the Virginia Company and
all the leading planters in Virginia, including Claiborne.   The matter was referred by the king to
the Commissioners for Foreign Plantations, who

---

[1] Neill, *Terra Mariæ*, 53; Ogilby, *America*, 183.

heard the complaint, and July 3, 1633, decided to
"leave Lord Baltimore to his patent" and "the
other partie to the course of the law."[1] This certainly meant a decision against the wholesale claim
of Virginia to the ancient limits, and was deemed by
Lord Baltimore as authorizing him to go on with
his settlement; and his patent authorized a form of
government entirely different from anything yet
tried in America.

The English colonies of Virginia and Massachusetts were founded by joint-stock companies really
or ostensibly for profit. After the suppression of
the London Company in 1624, the powers of government in Virginia devolved upon the king, and the
government was called a crown government. Had
Charles been a Spanish or French king he would have
appointed an absolute governor who would have
tyrannized over the people. But Charles, as an
English king, admitted the colonists into a share of
the government by permitting them to elect one of
the branches of the law-making body. This concession effectually secured the liberties of the people,
for the House of Burgesses, possessing the sole right
to originate laws, became in a short time the most
influential factor of the government.

Baltimore's government for Maryland, on the
other hand, was to be a palatinate similar to the
bishopric of Durham, in England, which took its
origin when border warfare with Scotland prevailed,

[1] *Md. Archives*, III., 21.

and the king found it necessary to invest the bishop, as ruler of the county, with exceptionally high powers for the protection of the kingdom. Durham was the solitary surviving instance in England of the county palatinate, so called because the rulers had in their counties *jura regalia* as fully as the king had in his palace. In Durham the bishop had the sole power of pardoning offences, appointing judges and other officers, coining money, and granting titles of honor and creating courts. In the other counties of England all writs ran in the king's name, but in Durham they ran in the bishop's. The county had no representation in the House of Commons, and were it not that the bishop was a member of the House of Lords, an officer of the church, paid taxes into the national treasury, and had to submit to appeals to the court of exchequer in London, in cases to which he was a party, he was, to all intents and purposes, a king, and his county an independent nation.

Baltimore by his charter was made even more independent of the king of England than the bishop, for neither he nor his province had any taxes to pay into the British treasury, and he held his territory in free and common socage by the delivery of two Indian arrows yearly at the palace of Windsor and a promise of the fifth part of all gold and silver mined. In legislation the bishop had decidedly the advantage, for his power to make law was practically uncontrolled, while the proprietor of Maryland could only legislate "with the advice, assent, and approbation of the freemen or the greater part of them or their representatives."[1]

One cardinal feature of Lord Baltimore's colony found no expression either in the government of Durham or in his own charter. On their liberality in the question of religion the fame of both George and Cecilius Calvert most securely rests. While neither realized the sacredness of the principle of religious freedom, there is no doubt that both father and son possessed a liberality of feeling which placed them ahead of their age. Had policy been solely their motive, they would never have identified themselves with a persecuted and powerless sect in England. In the charter of Maryland, Baltimore was given "the patronage and advowsons of all churches which, with the increasing worship and religion of Christ within the said region, hereafter shall happen to be built, together with the license and faculty of erecting and founding churches, chapels, and places of worship in convenient and suitable places within the premises, and of causing the same to be dedicated and consecrated according to the ecclesiastical laws of England." This clause was far from establishing religious freedom; but while it permitted Baltimore to found Anglican churches, it did not compel him to do so or prohibit him from per-

[1] Fiske, *Old Virginia and Her Neighbors;* Bassett, *Constitutional Beginnings of North Carolina;* Lapsley, *County Palatinate of Durham.*

mitting the foundation of churches of a different stamp.

About the middle of October, 1633, Baltimore's two ships got under way for America—the *Ark*, of three hundred tons, and the *Dove*, of sixty tons. The emigrants consisted of twenty gentlemen and about three hundred laborers; and, while most of the latter were Protestants, the governor, Leonard Calvert, brother of Lord Baltimore, was a Catholic, as were Thomas Cornwallis and Gabriel Harvey, the two councillors associated with him in the government, and the other persons of influence on board. Among the latter were two Jesuit priests, to one of whom, Father Andrew White, we owe a charming account of the voyage. Baltimore, in his written instructions to his brother, manifested his policy of toleration, by directing him to allow no offence to be given to any Protestant on board, and to cause Roman Catholics to be silent "upon all occasions of discourse concerning matters of religion."[1]

The expedition did not get away from England without trouble. The attempt to divide the territory of Virginia was not popular, and Catholics were looked upon as dangerous persons. The effort of the emigrants to sail without subscribing the necessary oaths caused the ships to be brought back by Admiral Pennington.[2] It was not until November

[1] *Calvert Papers* (Md. Hist. Soc., *Fund Publications*, No. 28), p. 132.   [2] *Md. Archives*, III., 23.

22, 1633, that they got off, and the ships took the old route to Virginia—by way of the West Indies.

February 27, 1634, they reached Point Comfort, where the king's letter addressed to Sir John Harvey insured them a kind reception. Here they learned that the Indians of the Potomac were excited over a rumor that they were Spaniards coming to subdue the country. After a stay of eight or nine days for fresh provisions the emigrants set sail up Chesapeake Bay and soon entered the Potomac River, " in comparison with which the Thames seemed a rivulet." At its mouth they saw natives on shore in arms, and at night their watch-fires blazed throughout the country.

March 25 the settlers landed on St. Clement's Island and erected a cross. Then leaving the *Ark* with most of the passengers, Governor Calvert, with the *Dove*, and a pinnace bought at Point Comfort, explored the river and made friends with the Indians. He found that they all acknowledged the sovereignty of the "emperor of Piscataqua," who, relieved of his apprehensions, gave them permission to settle in the country. The final choice of a seating-place was due to Captain Henry Fleet, a well-known member of the Virginia colony, who guided them up St. George's River, about nine miles from its juncture with the Potomac; and there, on its north bank, March 27, 1634, Leonard Calvert laid out the city of St. Mary's.[1]

[1] White, *Relation* (Force, *Tracts*, IV., No. xii.); letter of Leonard Calvert, *Calvert Papers* (Md. Hist. Soc., *Fund Publications*, No. 35), pp. 32-35; Baltimore, *Relation* (London, 1635).

Though we have little record of the early social and economic conditions of the settlers, the colony appears to have been remarkably free from the sufferings and calamities that befell the Virginians. This exemption was probably due to the following causes: there was no common stock, but the property was held in severalty; there was a proper proportion of gentlemen and laborers, few of one class and many of the other; Virginia was near at hand and provisions and cattle could be easily secured; and they had immediate use of Indian-cleared fields, because when they arrived at St. Mary's, the Yaocomocos, harassed by the Susquehannas, were on the point of removing across the Potomac to Virginia, and were glad to sell what they had ceased to value.   It seems, too, that Maryland was healthier than Virginia.

Hence, the very first year they had an excellent crop of corn, and sent a ship-load to New England to exchange for salt fish and other provisions.[1] Imitating the example of the Virginians, they began immediately to plant tobacco, which, as in Virginia, became the currency and leading product.   Its cultivation caused the importation of a great number of servants, "divers of very good rank and quality," [2] who, after a service of four or five years, became freemen.   In the assembly of 1638 several of the servants in the first emigration took their

---

[1] Winthrop, *New England*, I., 166.
[2] Neill, *Founders of Maryland*, 80.

seats as burgesses. As the demand for houses and casks for tobacco was great, a good many carpenters and coopers came out at their own expense and received shares of land by way of encouragement.

A state of society developed similar in many respects to that in Virginia. Baltimore, accustomed to the type of life in England, expected the settlements in Maryland to grow into towns and cities; and, under this impression, in January, 1638, he erected the population on the south side of St. George's River into a "hundred," and afterwards created other hundreds in other parts of the colony. But the wealth of watercourses and the cultivation of tobacco caused the population to scatter, and made society from the first distinctly agricultural and rural. St. Mary's and St. George's Hundred, in Maryland, shared the fate of Jamestown and Bermuda Hundred, in Virginia, and no stimulus of legislation could make them grow.

The application of the powers of the palatinate intensified these conditions by creating an agricultural and landed aristocracy. There was a council like that in Durham, whose members, appointed by the lord proprietor, held all the great offices of state.

Outside of the council the most important officer was the sheriff, who, like the sheriff of Durham, executed the commands of the governor and the courts, of which there were (in addition to the council) the county court and the manorial courts, answering respectively to the court of quarter-sessions and the

courts baron and leet in Durham. As for the manorial courts, feudal relicts transplanted to America,
they sprang from Lord Baltimore's attempt to build
up an aristocracy like that which attended upon the
bishop in his palace in Durham. In his "Conditions
for Plantations," August 8, 1636, after providing
liberally for all who brought emigrants to the colony, he directed that every one thousand acres or
greater quantity so given to any adventurer "should
be erected into a manor with a court-baron and
court-leet to be from time to time held within
every such manor respectively."

There were many grants of one thousand acres or
more, and Maryland "lords of the manor" became
quite common. These "lords" were the official
heads of numerous tenants and leaseholders who
were settled on their large estates. Yet the manor,
as a free-governing community, was a stronghold of
liberty. At the courts baron and leet the tenants
elected the minor officers, tried offences, and made
by-laws for their own government. Later, when
negroes substituted white laborers, these feudal
manors changed to plantations worked by slaves
instead of free tenants.[1]

Even great office-holders and a landed aristocracy
were insufficient to sustain the regal dignity to which
Lord Baltimore aspired. Apparently, his right of
initiating legislation and dictating the make-up of

[1] Johnson, *Old Maryland Manors* (*Johns Hopkins University
Studies*, I., No. iii.).

the assembly ought to have been sufficient.   But political and social equality sprang from the very conditions of life in the New World; and despite the veneering of royalty, Maryland came soon to be a government of the people.   The struggle began in the assembly which met in February, 1635, but not much is known of the proceedings of this assembly beyond the fact that it assumed the initiative and drew up a code to which Lord Baltimore refused his assent.

Of subsequent assemblies the record is copious enough.   Lord Baltimore had the right under his charter to summon " all the freemen, or the greater part of them, or their representatives," and thus for a long time there was a curious jumble of anomalies, which rendered the assembly peculiarly sensitive to governmental influence.   The second assembly met at St. Mary's, January 25, 1638, and consisted of the governor and council, freemen specially summoned, freemen present of their own volition, and proxies.[1] Governor Calvert submitted a code of laws sent from Lord Baltimore, and it was rejected by a vote of thirty-seven to fourteen; but twelve of the minority votes were in two hands, the governor and Secretary Lewger, an illustration of the danger of the proxy system.

Not long after, in a letter August 21, 1638, the proprietor yielded by authorizing Leonard in the future to consent to laws enacted by the freemen, which assent should temporarily make them valid

[1] *Md. Archives*, I., 1–24.

until his own confirmation or rejection should be received. To the next assembly, held February 25, 1639, Leonard Calvert, instead of summoning all the freemen, issued writs to different hundreds for the election of representatives.

Among the laws which they enacted was one limiting seats in the assembly to councillors, persons specially summoned by the proprietor's writ, and burgesses elected by the people of the different hundreds. This law controlled the make-up of the next four assemblies (October, 1640, August, 1641, March and July, 1642). Nevertheless, in September, 1642, Baltimore reverted to the old practice.

In 1649 Baltimore made another and last attempt for his initiative. He sent over a learned and complicated code of sixteen laws which he asked the assembly to adopt; but they rejected his work and sent him a code of their own, begging him in their letter not to send them any more such "bodies of laws, which served to little end than to fill our heads with jealousies and suspicions of that which we verily understand not." The next year, 1650, a constitutional system was perfected not very different from the plan adopted in the mother-country and Virginia. The assembly was divided into two chambers, the lower consisting exclusively of burgesses representing the different hundreds, and the upper of the councillors and those specially summoned by the governor.[1]

[1] *Md. Archives*, I., 32, 74, 243, 272.

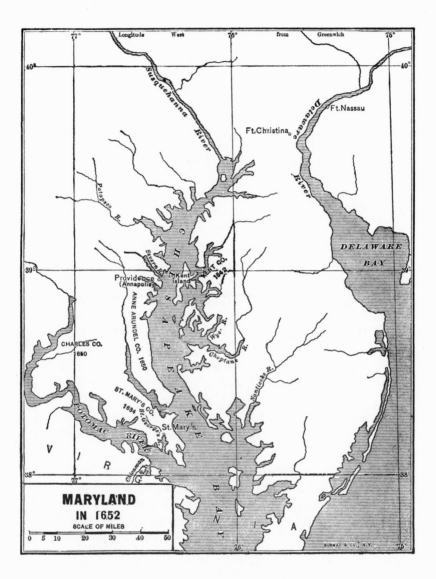

MARYLAND
IN 1652
SCALE OF MILES
0 5 10   20   30   40   50

CHAPTER VIII

CONTENTIONS IN MARYLAND

(1633–1652)

THE delay in the constitutional adjustment of Maryland, while mainly attributable to the proprietors, was partially due to the prolonged struggle with Virginia, which for years absorbed nearly all the energies of the infant community. The decision of the Commissioners for Foreign Plantations in July, 1633, disallowing the Virginia claim to unoccupied lands, was construed by the Virginians to mean that the king at any rate intended to respect actual possession. Now, prior to the Maryland charter, colonization in Virginia was stretching northward. In 1630, Chiskiack, on the York River, was settled; and in August, 1631, Claiborne planted a hundred men on Kent Island, one hundred and fifty miles from Jamestown.[1]

Though established under a license from the king for trade, Kent Island had all the appearance of a permanent settlement. Its inhabitants were never at any time as badly off as the settlers in the early days at Jamestown and Plymouth, and the

---

[1] *Md. Archives*, III., 32.

island itself was stocked with cattle and had orchards and gardens, fields of tobacco, windmills for grinding corn, and women resident upon it. Had it, however, been only a trading-post, the extension over it of the laws of Virginia made the settlement a legal occupation. And we are told of Kent that warrants from Jamestown were directed there. "One man was brought down and tried in Virginia for felony, and many were arrested for debt and returned to appear at James City."[1] In February, 1632, Kent Island and Chiskiack were represented at Jamestown by a common delegate, Captain Nicholas Martian.[2] The political existence of the whole Virginia colony, and its right to take up and settle lands, the king expressly recognized.

Accordingly, when Leonard Calvert, on his arrival at Point Comfort in February, 1634, called upon Claiborne to recognize Baltimore's paramount sovereignty over Kent Island, because of its lying within the limits of his charter, the council of Virginia, at the request of Claiborne, considered the claim, and declared that the colony had as much right to Kent Island as to "any other part of the country given by his majesty's patent" in 1609.[3] After this, acquiescence in Baltimore's wishes would have been treason, and Claiborne declined to acknowledge Lord Baltimore's authority in Kent

[1] *Md. Archives*, V., 158.   [2] Hening, *Statutes*, I., 154.
[3] *Md. Archives*, III., 33.

Island, and continued to trade in the bay as freely as formerly.

Calvert's instructions[1] had been, in case of such a refusal, not to molest Claiborne for at least a year. But Captain Fleet, Claiborne's rival in the fur trade, started a story that Claiborne was the originator of the rumor which so greatly alarmed the Indians at the time of the arrival of the emigrants at St. Mary's. Though Claiborne promptly repelled the calumny, Baltimore, in September, 1634, sent an order to his brother Leonard to seize Kent Island, arrest Claiborne, and hold him prisoner.[2] As this mandate was contrary to the order in July, 1633, of the lords commissioners, which enjoined the parties to preserve "good correspondence one with another," Claiborne's partners petitioned the king against it.

Thereupon the king, by an order[3] dated October 8, 1634, peremptorily warned Lord Baltimore, or his agents, "not to interrupt the people of Kent Island in their fur trade or plantation." Nevertheless, April 5, 1635, Thomas Cornwallis, one of the Maryland councillors, confiscated a pinnace of Claiborne's for illegal trading, and this act brought on a miniature war in which several persons on both sides were killed.[4] Great excitement prevailed in both colonies, and in Virginia the people arrested

[1] Browne, *George and Cecilius Calvert*, 49.
[2] *Md. Archives*, V., 164–168.   [3] *Ibid.*, III., 29.
[4] Neill, *Founders of Maryland*, 51.

Harvey, their governor, who upheld Cornwallis's conduct, and shipped him off to England; while two of the councillors were sent to Maryland to protest against the violent proceedings affecting Claiborne.[1]

These measures induced a truce, and for nearly three years there were no further hostilities in the bay. Claiborne brought his case before the king, who referred it to the Lords Commissioners for Plantations; then, as his partners feared to take further risk, he carried on the trade in the bay almost solely with his own servants and resources. In December, 1636, these partners, becoming dissatisfied at their loss of profit, made the capital mistake of sending, as their agent to Kent Island, George Evelin, who pretended at first to be an ardent supporter of Claiborne, but presently, under a power of attorney, claimed control over all the partnership stock.

Claiborne, naturally indignant and not suspecting any danger, sailed for England in May, 1637, to settle accounts with his partners, having just previously established another settlement on Palmer's Island at the mouth of the Susquehanna River, believed by him to be north of the Maryland patent. After he was gone, Evelin tried to persuade the inhabitants to disown Claiborne and submit to Lord Baltimore; and when they declined he urged Governor Calvert to attempt the reduction of the island by force. After some hesitation the latter con-

[1] *Md. Archives* III., 37.

sented, and while the assembly was sitting at St. Mary's, in February, 1638, Calvert made a landing at night with thirty men, and, taking the inhabitants by surprise, succeeded in reducing the island to submission.[1]

Calvert's after-conduct reflects little credit upon his reputation for leniency. In March, 1638, he caused Claiborne to be attainted by the assembly as a rebel and his property confiscated, and Thomas Smith, who commanded one of Claiborne's pinnaces in the battles three years before, was tried and hanged for murder and piracy.[2] In England, in the mean time, Claiborne and Baltimore were contending zealously for the favor of the king. Both had powerful interests behind them, but Baltimore's were the stronger. At last the Commissioners for Foreign Plantations rendered a report (April 4, 1638), giving Kent Island and the right of trade in the bay wholly to Lord Baltimore, leaving all personal wrongs to be redressed by the courts.

The question of title at least seemed settled, and in October, 1638, Sir John Harvey, now restored as governor of Virginia, issued a proclamation recognizing the validity of the decision. Claiborne submitted, and, being left to "the course of the law," empowered George Scovell to recover, if possible, some of the confiscated property in Maryland; but Scovell was told that the law-courts of Maryland

---

[1] Browne, *George and Cecilius Calvert*, 69.
[2] *Md. Archives*, V., 187.

were closed against such a rebel as Claiborne.[1] The justice of the English decision depends on the impartiality of the board which made it, and of any board with Bishop Laud at the head only partisanship could be expected.

While these turbulent proceedings were going on, the Jesuit priests introduced into the colony by Lord Baltimore were performing a work of peace and love. They visited the Indian tribes and made many Christian converts. Tayac, chief of the Piscataquas, received baptism, and his example was followed by the chiefs and inhabitants of Port Tobacco. The main trouble came from the Nanticokes on the eastern shore, and the fierce Susquehannas to the north of the settlements, and at different times armed expeditions were sent out against them; but there was nothing like a war.

For sixteen years the only clergy in the colony were priests, who were so zealous in their propaganda that nearly all the Protestants who came in 1638 were converted to Catholicism and many later conversions were made.[2] Nevertheless, the Catholic governor and council acted up to the spirit of the instructions given by Baltimore to his brother on the sailing of the first emigrants from the port of London, and would permit no language tending to insult or breach of peace. Not long after the arrival at St. Mary's a proclamation to this end was issued,

[1] *Md. Archives*, III., 42–93.
[2] White, *Relation* (Force, *Tracts*, IV., No. xii.).

of which only two violations appear in the records; in both cases the offenders were Roman Catholics, and they were arrested and promptly punished.[1]

Baltimore would not even exempt the Jesuit priests in Maryland from the ordinary laws as to lands and taxes, and by the "Conditions of Plantations," published in 1648, he prohibited any society, temporal or spiritual, from taking up land.[2] In 1643 his liberality carried him so far as to induce him to extend, through Major Edward Gibbons, an invitation to the Puritans of Massachusetts to emigrate to Maryland, with a full assurance of "free liberty of religion"; but Winthrop grimly writes, "None of our people had temptation that way."[3]

In the year of this invitation the possibility of a new shuffle of the political cards occurred through the breaking out of the war so long brewing in England between the king and Parliament. The struggle of party made itself strongly felt in Maryland, where, among the Protestants, sympathy with Parliament was supplemented by hatred of Catholics. In 1643, Governor Leonard Calvert repaired to England, where he received letters of marque from the king at Oxford commissioning him to seize ships belonging to Parliament. Accordingly, when, three months later, in January, 1644, Captain

---

[1] *Md. Archives*, I., 119, IV., 38.
[2] *Calvert Papers* (Md. Hist. Soc., *Fund Publications*, No. 35), 166, 216, 217; *Md. Archives*, III., 227.
[3] Winthrop, *New England*, II., 179.

Richard Ingle arrived in his ship at St. Mary's and uttered some blatant words against the king, he was arrested by Acting Governor Brent, for treason. The charges were dismissed by the grand jury as unfounded, but Brent treated Ingle harshly, and fined and exiled Thomas Cornwallis for assisting the captain in escaping.[1]

In September, 1644, when Calvert returned to Maryland, there were strong symptoms of revolt, which came to a head when Ingle came back to St. Mary's with a commission from Parliament in February, 1645. Chaotic times ensued, during which Catholics were made victims of the cruel prejudices of the Protestants. The two Jesuit priests, Father Andrew White and Father Philip Fisher, were arrested, loaded with irons,[2] and sent prisoners into England, while Leonard Calvert himself was driven from Maryland into Virginia.[3]

During these tumults so many persons went over from Virginia to Maryland that the Virginia assembly sent Captain Edward Hill and Captain Thomas Willoughby to compel the return of the absentees,[4] with curious result. As the province was without a governor, some of the council of Maryland issued, in the name of the refugee Calvert, a commission to Hill to act as governor of Maryland. The revolutionists flattered themselves that a stable govern-

---

[1] *Md. Archives*, IV., 246–249.
[2] Neill, *Founders of Maryland*, 75; *Md. Archives*, III., 165, 177.   [3] Bozman, *Maryland*, II., 293.
[4] Hening, *Statutes*, I., 321.

ment under a Protestant governor was now at hand. But the unexpected came to pass, when, in December, 1646, Governor Calvert suddenly appeared with a strong body of soldiers furnished by Sir William Berkeley and re-established his authority by capturing both Hill and the Protestant assembly then sitting at St. Mary's.

These two years of civil war in Maryland are called the "plundering time." Claiborne again appears, though there is no evidence that he had any part in Ingle's spoliations.[1] He did visit Kent Island about Christmas, 1645, and put Captain Brent, to whom Governor Calvert had assigned his house and property, in a terrible fright. One year later he visited the island a second time, when he offered to aid the Kent Islanders in marching upon St. Mary's with a view of reinstating Hill. When the men of Kent declined to take the risk, Claiborne returned to Virginia, and Kent Island fell once more under the government of Lord Baltimore.[2] On this visit Claiborne, instead of posing as a friend of the Parliament, showed a commission and letter from the king, by whom he appears to have stood till the king's death in 1649. Charles I., in his turn, who deposed Lord Baltimore as a "notorious parliamentarian," appointed Claiborne, in 1642, treasurer of Virginia;[3] and Charles II. included

---

[1] Bozman, *Maryland*, II., 296.
[2] *Md. Archives*, IV., 281, 435, 458, 459.
[3] Hazard, *State Papers*, I., 493.

his name among the list of councillors in the commission issued by Sir William Berkeley in 1650.[1]

While Maryland was thus convulsed with civil war an ordinance settling the Maryland government in Protestant hands passed the House of Lords. Before the Commons could concur, Lord Baltimore appeared and asked for time to inquire into the charges. This was after the battle of Marston Moor, and perhaps marks the moment when Lord Baltimore, conceiving the king's cause desperate, began to trim his sails to the parliamentary side. His request was granted, and Parliament, diverted from immediate action, left Baltimore's authority unaffected for several years.[2]

In this interval Baltimore busied himself in reorganizing his government on a Protestant basis. Leonard Calvert died in June, 1647, not long after his *coup d'état* at St. Mary's, and upon his deathbed he appointed Thomas Greene, a Catholic and royalist, as his successor. Lord Baltimore removed him and appointed in his stead a Protestant, Captain William Stone, of Northampton County, Virginia, giving him a Protestant secretary and a Protestant majority of councillors. Yet Baltimore took care not to surrender the cardinal principle of his government. Before Stone and his chief officers were allowed to take office they were required to swear not to "molest any person in the colony pro-

---

[1] *Cal. of State Pap., Col.,* 1574–1660, p. 340.
[2] *Md. Archives,* III., 164, 180, 187.

fessing to believe in Jesus Christ for or in respect of his or her religion, and in particular no Roman Catholic." [1]

The famous Toleration Act of 1649 was passed at the first assembly succeeding Stone's appointment. It was very probably in great part a copy of a bill in the code of sixteen laws which Baltimore sent over at this time, and it very nearly repeated the provisions of the oath required of Governor Stone. While the terms of the act did not place the right on that broad plane of universal principle stated later in the Virginia Declaration of Rights, it proclaimed toleration, even if it was a toleration of a very limited nature. [2]

Stone had recommended himself to Calvert by promising to lead five hundred persons of British or Irish descent [3] into Maryland; and this engagement he was soon able to perform through the Puritans, whose story of persecution in Virginia has been already related. The new emigrants called the country where they settled "Providence," from feelings akin to those which led Roger Williams to give that comforting name to his settlement on Narragansett Bay. They were to prove a thorn in Baltimore's flesh, but for the moment they seemed tolerably submissive. In January, 1650, soon after their arrival, Governor Stone called an assembly to meet at St. Mary's in April, and to this assembly

[1] *Md. Archives*, III., 211, 214.
[2] *Ibid.*, I., 244-247.   [3] *Ibid.*, III., 201.

the colony at "Providence" sent two representatives, one of whom was made speaker.

Apprehension of William Claiborne was still felt, and the assembly, though dominated by the newcomers, declared their readiness to resist any attempts of his to seize Kent Island.[1] Only in one particular at this time did they oppose Lord Baltimore's policy. The oath of fidelity required them to acknowledge Lord Baltimore as "absolute lord" and his jurisdiction as "royal jurisdiction."[2] The Puritans, having scruples about these words, struck them out and inserted a proviso that the oath "be not in any wise understood to infringe or prejudice liberty of conscience."[3] About this time Charles II., although a powerless exile, issued an order deposing Baltimore from his government and appointing Sir William Davenant as his successor, for the reason that Baltimore "did visibly adhere to the rebels in England and admit all kinds of schismatics and sectaries and ill-affected persons into the plantation."[4]

Thus when Parliament soon after took up his case again, Lord Baltimore came full-handed with proofs of loyalty to the commonwealth. His enemies produced evidence that Charles II., in 1649, was proclaimed in Maryland, but Baltimore showed that it was done without his authority by Thomas Greene, who acted as governor a second time during a brief

[1] *Md. Archives*, I., 261, 287.   [2] *Ibid.*, III., 196.
[3] *Ibid.*, I., 305.   [4] Neill, *Terra Mariæ*, 88.

absence of Captain Stone from Maryland. When they accused him of being an enemy of Protestants he produced the proclamation of Charles II., deposing him from the government on account of his adherence to them. Finally, he exhibited a declaration in his behalf signed by many of the Puritan emigrants from Virginia, among whom were William Durand, their elder, and James Cox and Samuel Puddington, the two burgesses from Providence in the assembly of 1650.[1]

Nevertheless, Baltimore played a losing game. At heart the Puritans in England were unfriendly to him because of his religion; and, when persistent rumors reached Maryland that Baltimore's patent was doomed, some of the men of Providence appeared in England and urged that it be revoked.[2] At length, October 3, 1650, Parliament passed an ordinance authorizing the Council of State to reduce to obedience Barbadoes, Antigua, Bermudas, and "Virginia," the last being a term which in England was often used to include Maryland. Baltimore struggled hard to have Maryland left out of the instructions drawn up afterwards by the Council of State; but though he was apparently successful, a descriptive phrase including his province was inserted, for the commissioners, Curtis, Claiborne, and Bennett, with an armed fleet, were instructed "to use their best endeavors to reduce *all the plantations*

---

[1] Bozman, *Maryland*, II., 672.
[2] *Md. Archives*, III., 259.

within the Bay of Chesopiack to their due obedience to the Parliament of England."[1]

After the commissioners had reduced Virginia, they found even less resistance in Maryland. The commissioners landed at St. Mary's, and, professing their intention to respect the "just rights" of Lord Baltimore, demanded that Stone should change the form of the writs from the name of Lord Baltimore to that of Parliament. Stone at first declined to comply, and the commissioners, March 29, 1652, put the government into the hands of a council of leading Protestants. Stone then reconsidered his action, and Claiborne and Bennett, returning to St. Mary's, restored him to the government, June 28, 1652, in conjunction with the councillors already appointed. The ascendency of Claiborne seemed complete, but beyond renewing his property claim to Kent and Palmer islands, he did not then further interfere.[2]

Maryland consisted at this time of four counties: St. Mary's, erected in 1634, Kent, 1642, and Charles and Anne Arundel in 1650, and contained a population perhaps of eight thousand. The settlements reached on both sides of the bay, from the Potomac to the Susquehanna. Society was distinctly democratic, for while there were favored families there was no privileged class, and the existence of African slavery and the temporary servitude of convicts and redemptioners tended to place all freemen on an equality. As there was no state church, educational

[1] *Md. Archives*, III., 265.   [2] *Ibid.*, 271–277.

opportunities in the province were small, but it was a land of plenty and hospitality, and charity in religion made the execution of the criminal law singularly mild. In spite of turmoils and dissensions, Maryland prospered and flourished. A home feeling existed, and there were many even among the recent exiles from Virginia who looked with hope to its future and spoke of it as "a country in which I desire to spend the remnant of my days, in which I covet to make my grave." [1]

[1] Hammond, *Leah and Rachel* (Force, *Tracts*, III., No. xiv.).

CHAPTER IX

FOUNDING OF PLYMOUTH

(1608–1630)

AFTER the disastrous failure of the Popham colony in 1608 the Plymouth Company for several years was inactive. Its members were lacking in enthusiastic co-operation, and therefore did not attract, like the London Company, the money and energy of the nation. After Sir John Popham's death, in 1607, his son Francis Popham was chiefly instrumental in sending out several vessels, which, though despatched for trade, served to keep up interest in the northern shores of America.

That coast threatened to be lost to Englishmen, for the French, in 1603, began to make settlements in Nova Scotia and in Mount Desert Island, near the mouth of the Penobscot, while their ships sailed southward along the New England shores. The Dutch, too, explored the Hudson (1609) and prepared the way for a colony there. It was, therefore, a great service to England when Captain Argall, under the authority of Sir Thomas Dale, in 1613, dislodged the French at Mount Desert, Port Royal, and St. Croix.

Shortly after Argall's visit John Smith sailed, in 1614, for the northern coast, with two ships fitted out by some private adventurers. While the ships were taking a freight of fish, Smith, with a view to colonization, ranged the neighboring coast, collecting furs from the natives, taking notes of the shores and the islands, and making soundings of the water. Smith drew a map of the country, and was the first to call it "New England" instead of North Virginia, Norumbega, or Canada. This map he submitted to Prince Charles, who gave names to some thirty points on the coast. Only Plymouth, Charles River, and Cape Ann have permanently kept the names thus fastened upon them. Boston, Hull, Cambridge, and some others were subsequently adopted, but applied to localities different from those to which Prince Charles affixed them.

While he was absent one day Thomas Hunt, master of one of his vessels, kidnapped twenty-four savages, and, setting sail, carried them to Spain, where he sold most of them. The outrage soured the Indians in New England, but of the captives, one, named Squanto or Tisquantum, was carried to England, and his later friendliness worked to the benefit of subsequent English colonization.[1]

In 1615 Captain Smith entered into the service of the Plymouth Company and was complimented with the title of "Admiral of New England." With

[1] Smith, *Works* (Arber's ed.), 699; Bradford, *Plimoth Plantation*, 117.

great difficulty they provided two ships and despatched them to effect a settlement, but the result
was the old story of misfortune. The ship in which
Smith sailed was captured by the French, and Smith
himself was detained in captivity for some time.
Captain Dormer, with the other vessel, proceeded
on his voyage to New England, but did not attempt
anything beyond securing a cargo of furs.

Smith tried to stir up interest in another expedition, and travelled about England in 1616, dis-
tributing his maps and other writings, but he says
"all availed no more than to hew rocks with oyster-
shells." Smith's connection with the American
coast then ceased altogether; but his plans of
colonization were not without fruit, since his liter-
ary works, making known the advantages of New
England, kept the attention of the public fastened
upon that region.[1]

At this time the most prominent member of the
Plymouth Company was Sir Ferdinando Gorges, son
of Edward Gorges, of Worcestershire, born about
1566. He served at Sluys in 1587, was knighted by
Essex before Rouen, in October, 1591, and in 1593
was made governor of the port of Plymouth in England, which office he still held. Despite the ill-
fortune attending past efforts, he continued to send
out vessels under color of fishing and trade, which
ranged the coast of New England and brought news
of a calamity to the natives unexpectedly favorable

[1] Smith, *Works* (Arber's ed.), 699–701, 731–742, 745.

to future colonization.   In 1616–1617 the country
from Penobscot River to Narragansett Bay was almost left "void of inhabitants" by a pestilence
which swept away entire villages of Indians.   This
information, together with the better knowledge
due to Gorges of the value of the fisheries, caused a
revival of interest regarding New England among
the members of the Plymouth Company,[1]

Under the name of "the Council for New England," they obtained from the king in 1620 a new
charter,[2] granting to them all the territory in
North America extending "in breadth from forty
degrees of northerly latitude, from the equinoctial
line, to forty-eight degrees of the said northerly latitude, and in length by all the breadth aforesaid
throughout the main-land from sea to sea."   In the
new grant the number of grantees was limited to
forty, and all other persons enjoying rights in the
company's lands stood in the position of their tenants.   Thus, like the Plymouth Company, the new
company proved defective in co-operative power, and
the first actual settlement of New England was due
to an influence little fancied by any of its members.

Religious opinions during the sixteenth and sev-
enteenth centuries were great political forces.   The
Christian church of Europe, before the days of
Luther, held the view that the pope of Rome was

[1] Gorges, *Description of New England* (Mass. Hist. Soc.,
Collections, 3d series, VI.), 57.
[2] Poore, *Charters and Constitutions*, I., 921.

the only infallible interpreter of the Holy Scriptures, and against this doctrine Luther led a revolt denominated Protestantism, which insisted upon the right of private judgment.   Nevertheless, when the reformed churches came to adopt articles and canons of their own they generally discarded this fundamental difference, and, affirming infallibility in themselves, enlisted the civil power in support of their doctrines.

Hence, in 1559, Queen Elizabeth caused her Parliament to pass two famous statutes, the Act of Supremacy, which required all clergymen and officeholders to renounce the spiritual as well as temporal jurisdiction of all foreign princes and prelates; and the Act of Uniformity, which forbade any minister from using any other liturgy or service than that established by Parliament.[1]

These acts, though directed originally against the Roman Catholics, were resented by many zealous English clergymen who, during the reign of Queen Mary, had taken refuge in Switzerland and Germany, and learned while there the spiritual and political doctrines of John Calvin.   These English refugees were the first Puritans, and in the beginning the large majority had no desire of separating from the church of which the sovereign was the head, but thought to reform it from within, according to their own views of ecclesiastical policy.   They wanted, among other things, to discard the surplice and Book

[1] Cf. Cheyney, *European Background of Am. Hist.*, chap. xi.

of Common Prayer and to abolish the order of bish-
ops. Queen Elizabeth looked upon their opinions
as dangerous, and harassed them before the Court
of High Commission, created in 1583 for enforcing
the acts of supremacy and uniformity. But her
persecution increased rather than diminished the
opposition, and finally there arose a sect called
Independents, who flatly denied the ecclesiastical
supremacy of the queen and claimed the right to set
up separate churches of their own. The Scotch
Calvinists worked out an elaborate form of Presbyterian government, by synods and assemblies, which
later played a great part in England.

For a long time the "Separatists," as they were
called, were as unpopular with the great body of
Puritans as with the churchmen. Popular aver-
sion was expressed by the derisive name of "Brownists," given them from Robert Browne, the first to
set forth their doctrines in a formal pamphlet, entitled *The Life and Manners of True Christians.*
Their meetings were broken up by mobs, and worshippers were subjected to insults.[1]

Holland at that time was the only country en-
lightened enough to open its doors to all religions
professing Jesus Christ; and as early as 1593 a Separatist congregation, which had come into existence
at London, took refuge at Amsterdam, and they
were followed by many other persons persecuted

---

[1] Neal, *Puritans*, I., 149–151, 202; cf. Cheyney, *European
Background of Am. Hist.*, chap. xii.

under the laws of Queen Elizabeth. When she died, in 1603, there were hopes at first of a milder policy from King James, but they were speedily dispelled, and at a conference of Puritans and High Churchmen at Hampton Court in 1604 the king warned dissenters, "I will make them conform or I will harry them out of this land, or else worse"; and he was as good as his word.[1]

Several congregations of Separatists were located in the northeastern part of England, in some towns and villages in Nottinghamshire, Lincolnshire, and Yorkshire. One held meetings, under Rev. John Smith, a Cambridge graduate, at Gainsborough, and another, under Richard Clifton as pastor and John Robinson as teacher, at the small village of Scrooby. Persecuted by the king's officers, these congregations began to consider the advisability of joining their brethren in Holland. That of Gainsborough was the first to emigrate, and, following the example of the London church, it settled at Amsterdam.

In the second, or Scrooby, congregation, destined to furnish the "Pilgrim Fathers" of New England,[2] three men were conspicuous as leaders. The first was John Robinson, a man, according to the testimony of an opponent, of "excellent parts, and the most learned, polished, and modest spirit" that ever separated from the church of England. The second was the elder, William Brewster, like Robinson,

---

[1] Neal, *Puritans*, I., 232; Hart, *Source-Book*, No. 15.
[2] Bradford, *Plimoth Plantation*, 13.

educated at Cambridge, who had served as one of the under-secretaries of state for many years. After the downfall of his patron, Secretary Davison, he accepted the position of postmaster and went to live at Scrooby in an old manor house of Sir Samuel Sandys, the elder brother of Sir Edwin Sandys, where, in the great hall, the Separatists held their meetings.[1] The third character was William Bradford, born at Austerfield, a village neighboring to Scrooby, and at the time of the flight from England seventeen years of age, afterwards noted for his ability and loftiness of character.

In 1607 the Scrooby congregation made their first attempt to escape into Holland. A large party of them hired a ship at Boston, in Lincolnshire, but the captain betrayed them to the officers of the law, who rifled them of their money and goods and confined them for about a month in jail. The next year another party made an attempt to leave. The captain, who was a Dutchman, started to take the men aboard, but after the first boat-load he saw a party of soldiers approaching, and, "swearing his countries oath Sacramente, and having the wind faire, weighed anchor, hoysted sayles & away." The little band was thus miserably separated, and men and women suffered many misfortunes; but in the end, by one means or another, all made good their escape from England and met together in the city of Amsterdam.

[1] Hunter, *Founders of New Plymouth.*

They found there both the church of the London Separatists and that of the Gainsborough people stirred up over theological questions, which bid fair to tear them to pieces. Hence, Robinson determined to remove his flock, and in May, 1609, they made the city of Leyden, twenty miles distant, their permanent abode. Their pastor, Richard Clifton, remained in Amsterdam, and the care of the congregation in their new home was confided to John Robinson and William Brewster.[1]

In Leyden the Pilgrims were compelled to adapt themselves, as they had in Amsterdam, to conditions of life very different from those to which they had been trained in their own country. As far as they can be traced, a majority seem to have found employment in the manufacture of woollen goods, for which the city was famous. Their uprightness, diligence, and sobriety gave them a good name and pecuniary credit with their Dutch neighbors, who testified twelve years later that in all their stay in Holland "we never had any suit or accusation against any of them."[2]

To Robinson, Brewster, and Bradford the change was a decided gain. As the site of a great university, Leyden furnished them intercourse with learned men and access to valuable libraries. Robinson was admitted a member of the university, and before long appeared as a disputant on the Calvinist side in the public discussions. Brewster taught the

---

[1] Bradford, *Plimoth Plantation*, 15–29.   [2] *Ibid.*, 27.

English language to the Dutch, and, opening a publishing house, printed many theological books. Bradford devoted himself to the study of the ancient languages, "to see with his own eyes the ancient oracles of God in all their native beauty." [1]

Their stay at Leyden covered the period of the famous twelve years' truce between Spain and Holland, and their number increased from one hundred to three hundred. Among the new-comers from England were John Carver, Robert Cushman, Miles Standish, and Edward Winslow. Towards the end of the period the exiles began to think of a second emigration, and this time it was not persecution that suggested the thought. In expectation of the renewal of hostilities with Spain, the streets of Leyden sounded with the beating of drums and preparations of war. Although Holland afforded them religious freedom, they won their subsistence at the price of unremitting toil, which might be made even harder by renewal of hostilities. A more sentimental reason was found in the desire to perpetuate their existence as a religious body of Englishmen.

By the summer of 1617 the majority of the Scrooby congregation had fully decided to emigrate, and it only remained to determine the new place of residence. Some talked of Guiana, others of New York, but the majority inclined to Virginia; and the conclusion was to emigrate as a distinct body to a

---

[1] Bradford, *Plimoth Plantation*, 28, 488–493; Mather, *Magnalia*, I., 113.

place under the London Company, but not so near Jamestown as to be troubled by the Episcopalian planters there.

With this design they sent two of their number, John Carver and Robert Cushman, to London, and Sir Edwin Sandys tried to obtain for them a patent recognizing their religious rights. To aid him, Robinson and Brewster drew up a confession of faith which, as it contains an admission of the right of the state to control religion, seems strangely at variance with the doctrines of the Separatists. But the king was not easily persuaded, and he promised only that "he would connive at them and not molest them, provided they carried themselves peaceably."[1]

Sandys passed through the London Company two "particular patents" in their behalf, one taken out in the name of John Wincop and the other in that of John Pierce, two of their associates in England; under the latter, granted in February, 1620, the Pilgrims prepared to leave Holland.[2] Capital to the amount of £7000 was furnished by seventy merchant adventurers in London, and it was agreed with them that for several years everything was to be held in joint stock, the shares of which were to be valued at £10 each and to be paid for in money or by personal service.[3]

[1] Bradford, *Plimoth Plantation*, 29–38.
[2] Brown, *First Republic*, 424.
[3] Smith, *Works* (Arber's ed.), 783; Bradford, *Plimoth Plantation*, 56–58.

As they had not resources for all to go, the major part of the congregation, with Robinson, stayed behind, promising to follow later. The emigrants under Carver, Bradford, and Brewster started out from Delft-Haven in July, 1620, in the leaky ship the *Speedwell*. At Southampton, in England, they met the *Mayflower* with friends from London, and soon after both ships made an attempt to start to sea. They had not sailed any distance before the *Speedwell* let in so much water that it was necessary to put in at Dartmouth for repairs. Again they set sail, and this time they had left old England one hundred leagues behind when the captain reported the *Speedwell* in danger of foundering. There was nothing to do but to bear up again and return to England, where they put in at Plymouth. Upon examination the *Speedwell* was pronounced unseaworthy and sent to London with about twenty of the company. With the rest, one hundred and two in number, the *Mayflower* cleared the port, September 6, for America.

Her destination was some point south of the Hudson River, within the Virginia patent; but foul weather prevented any accurate calculation, and November 9, 1620, the emigrants found themselves in the neighborhood of Cape Cod. They tacked and sailed southward, but ran into "dangerous shoals and roaring breakers," which compelled them to turn back and seek shelter in the harbor now called Provincetown. The anxiety of the sailors to be rid of the emigrants prevented any further attempt southward, and forced them to make their permanent habitation near this accidental lodgment.

As the patent under which they sailed had no force in the territory of the Plymouth Company, they united themselves by the so-called " Mayflower compact," November 11, 1620, into a "civill body politic," and promised "submission and obedience to all such ordinances as the general good of the colony might require from time to time." Under the patent John Carver had been chosen governor, and he was now confirmed in that office under the new authority, which followed pretty nearly the terms of the old.[1]

For five weeks they stayed in the ship, while Captain Miles Standish with a small company explored the country. In the third expedition, after an attack from the Indians and much suffering from snow and sleet, Standish's men reached a landing nearly opposite to the point of Cape Cod, which they sounded and "found fit for shipping." There "divers cornfields" and an excellent stream of fresh water encouraged settlement, and they landed, December 11 (Old Style), 1620, near a large bowlder, since known as Plymouth Rock.

By the end of the week the *Mayflower* had brought over her company of emigrants — seventy - three males and twenty-nine females—and December 25,

[1] Bradford, *Plimoth Plantation*, 90–110; Eggleston, *Beginners of a Nation*, 184, note 4.

1620, they began to erect the first house "for the common use to receive them and their goods." The Indian name of the place was Patuxet, but the emigrants called it New Plymouth "after Plymouth, in old England, the last town they left in their native country ";[1] and it was a curious coincidence that the spot had already received from John Smith the name of Plymouth.   Later the town was called simply Plymouth, while the colony took the name of New Plymouth.

[1] Morton, *New England's Memorial*, 56.

CHAPTER X

DEVELOPMENT OF NEW PLYMOUTH

(1621–1643)

DURING the winter of 1620–1621 the emigrants suffered greatly from scurvy and exposure. More than half the company perished, and the seamen on the *Mayflower* suffered as much.[1] With the appearance of spring the mortality ceased, and a friendly intercourse with the natives began. These Indians were the Pokanokets, whose number had been very much thinned by the pestilence. After the first hostilities directed against the exploring parties they avoided the whites, and held a meeting in a dark and dismal swamp, where the medicine-men for three days together tried vainly to subject the new-comers to the spell of their conjurations.

At last, in March, 1621, an Indian came boldly into camp, and, in broken English, bade the strangers "welcome." It was found that his name was Samoset, and that he came from Monhegan, an island distant about a day's sail towards the east, where he had picked up a few English words from

[1] Bradford, *Plimoth Plantation*, 112.

163

the fishermen who frequented that region. In a short time he returned, bringing Squanto, or Tisquantum, stolen by Hunt seven years before, and restored to his country in 1620 by Sir Ferdinando Gorges. Squanto, who could speak English, stated that Massasoit was near at hand, and on invitation that chief appeared, and soon a treaty of peace and friendship was concluded; after which Massasoit returned to his town of Sowams, forty miles distant, while Squanto continued with the colonists and made himself useful in many ways.[1]

In the beginning of April, 1621, the *Mayflower* went back to England, and the colonists planted corn in the fields once tilled by Indians whom the pestilence had destroyed. While engaged in this work the governor, John Carver, died, and his place was supplied by William Bradford, with Isaac Allerton as assistant or councilman. During the summer the settlers were very busy. They fitted up their cabins, amassed a good supply of beaver, and harvested a fair crop of corn. In the fall a ship arrived, bringing thirty - five new settlers poorly provided. It also brought a patent, dated June 1, 1621, from the Council for New England, made out to John Pierce, by whom the original patent from the London Company had been obtained. The patent did not define the territorial limits, but allowed one hundred acres for every emigrant and fifteen hundred acres for

[1] Bradford, *Plimoth Plantation*, 114-117.

public buildings, in the same proportion of one
hundred acres to every workman.[1]

The ship tarried only fourteen days, and returned
with a large cargo of clapboard and beaver skins
of the value of £500, which was, however, captured
on the way to England by a French cruiser. After
the departure the governor distributed the new-
comers among the different families, and because
of the necessity of sharing with them, put every-
body on half allowance. The prospect for the winter was not hopeful, for to the danger from starvation was added danger from the Indians.

West of the Pokanokets were the Narragansetts, a
tribe of two thousand warriors, whose chief, Canonicus, sent to Plymouth in January, 1622, a bundle
of arrows tied with a snake's skin, signifying a challenge of war. Bradford knew that it was fatal to
hesitate or show fear, and he promptly stuffed the
snake's skin with bullets and returned it to the
sender with some threatening words. This answer
alarmed Canonicus, who thought that the snake's skin
must be conjured, and he did not pursue the matter
further. But the colonists took warning, and the
whole settlement was enclosed with a paling, and strict
military watch was maintained. Thus the winter
passed and the spring came, but without the hoped-for
assistance from the merchant partners in England.[2]

[1] Mass. Hist. Soc., *Collections*, 4th series, II., 158–163.
[2] Bradford, *Plimoth Plantation*, 130–133; Winslow, "Relation,"
in Young, *Chronicles of the Pilgrims*, 280–284.

On the contrary, the arrival in May, 1622, "without a bite of bread," of sixty-seven other persons, sent out on his own account under a grant from the Council for New England, by Thomas Weston, one of the partners, plunged them into dire distress, from which they were happily saved by a ship-captain, John Huddleston, from the colony on James River, who shared his supplies with them, and thus enabled them to "make shift till corn was ripe again." Weston's emigrants were a loose set, and before they left in August they stole most of the green corn, and thus Plymouth was threatened with another famine.   Fortunately, about this time another ship from Virginia, bearing the secretary of state, John Pory, arrived, and sold the colonists a supply of truck for trading; by which they bought from the Indians not only corn, but beaver, which proved afterwards a source of much profit.

Weston's people removed to Wessagusset (modern Weymouth), on Massachusetts Bay, where they conducted themselves in so reckless a manner that they ran the double risk of starvation and destruction from savages.   To save them, Bradford, in March, 1623, despatched a company under Captain Miles Standish, who brought them corn and killed several of the Indians. Then Standish helped Weston's "rude fellows " aboard ship and saw them safely off to sea.   Shortly after Weston came over to look after his emigrants, fell into the hands of the Indians, escaped to Plymouth, where the colonists helped him away, and returned in October, 1623, to create more disturbance.

Weston was not the only one of the partners that gave the colonists trouble. John Pierce took advantage of the prominence given him by the patent issued in his name for the benefit of all, to get a new one which made him sole actual owner of the territory. His partners resented this injustice, and the Council for New England, in March, 1623, was induced to revoke the grant to Pierce.[1]

About this time Bradford made a great change in the industrial system of the colony. At Plymouth, as at Jamestown, communism was found to breed "confusion and discontent," and he tried the experiment of assigning to every family, in proportion to its size, a tract of land. In July, 1623, arrived sixty other settlers, and the old planters feared another period of starvation. Nevertheless, when harvest-time arrived, the wisdom of Bradford's appeal to private interest was demonstrated, for instead of misery and scarcity there was joyfulness, and "plentie of corn." Later experience was equally convincing, for, as Bradford wrote many years after, "any general wante or famine hath not been known amongst them since to this day."

While the Pilgrim fathers were overcoming their difficulties in Massachusetts, the Council for New England were struggling with the London Company

[1] Bradford, *Plimoth Plantation*, 149–168; *Cal. of State Pap., Col.*, 1574–1660, p. 40.

to maintain the monopoly of fishing and fur trading on the North Atlantic coast granted to them by their charter. The London Company complained to the king in 1620 and to Parliament in 1621, but the king refused any relief, and prevented Parliament from interfering by dissolving it.[1] Thereupon, the Council for New England, appreciating the danger, made a grand effort to accomplish something in America. As a preliminary step they induced the king to publish a proclamation, November 6, 1622, against all unlicensed trading and other infringements upon the rights granted them,[2] and shortly afterwards sent out Francis West as admiral to reduce the fishermen on the coast to obedience. West came to America, but found them "stuberne fellows,"[3] and he returned in about a year to England without effecting anything.

During his absence the Council for New England set to work to send out a colony under Robert Gorges, son of Sir Ferdinando; and, June 29, 1623, a division was made among twenty patentees, of the North Atlantic coast from the Bay of Fundy to Narragansett Bay.[4] In September, 1623, Gorges arrived at Plymouth attended by an Episcopal minister, William Morell, and a company of settlers, whom he planted at Wessagusset. He remained in

---

[1] Gorges, *Description of New England* (Mass. Hist. Soc., *Collections*, 3d series, VI., 80).

[2] *Cal. of State Pap., Col.*, 1574–1660, p. 33.

[3] Bradford, *Plimoth Plantation*, 170.

[4] Maine Hist. Soc., *Collections*, 2d series, VII., 73–76.

New England throughout the winter, and in the effort to exert his authority had a long wrangle with Weston. In the spring of 1624 he received news from his father that discouraged his further stay. It seems that in March, 1624, a committee of Parliament, at the head of which was Sir Edward Coke, had reported the charter of the Council for New England as a national grievance, which so discouraged the patentees that most of them abandoned the enterprise, and it became, in the language of the elder Gorges, "a carcass in a manner breathless." [1] After Robert Gorges' departure most of his party dispersed, some going to England and some to Virginia, but a few remained at Wessagusset, which was never entirely abandoned.

The relations between the colony and the London merchant adventurers, never very pleasant, became more unsatisfactory as time went on. The colonists naturally wanted to bring over their friends at Leyden, but the partners regarded Robinson as the great leader of the Independents, and London was already rife with rumors of the heretical character of the rulers at Plymouth. It seemed to the partners evidently for their interest to introduce settlers of a different religious opinion from Bradford and Brewster, and to this was largely due the fact that the emigrants who came over after the *Mayflower's* return in 1621 had little in common with the original band of Pilgrims.

---

[1] Adams, *Three Episodes of Mass. Hist.*, I., 152.

In January, 1624, arrived another miscellaneous cargo, including a minister named John Lyford. Upon his arrival he professed intense sympathy with the settlers, and when they received him as a member of their church he renounced, pursuant to the extreme tenets of Separatism, "all universall, nationall, and diocessan churches."[1] Nevertheless, he joined with John Oldham, who came the year before, in a conspiracy to overturn the government; but was detected and finally banished from the colony.   In March, 1625, Lyford and Oldham went to Wessagusset, from which they moved with Roger Conant and other friends to Nantasket, where, in the mean time, a new settlement had sprung up.

In the division of 1623, the region around Cape Ann fell to Lord Sheffield, and the same year he conveyed the country to Robert Cushman and Edward Winslow in behalf of the colonists at Plymouth.[2] The next year the new owners sent a party to establish a fishing stage at Cape Ann, but they found other persons on the spot, for in 1623 some merchants of Dorchester, England, who regularly sent vessels to catch fish in the waters of New England, had conceived the idea of planting a colony on the coast, and in the summer of that year landed fourteen men at Cape Ann, soon increased to thirty-four.

For some months the two parties got along amicably together and fished side by side.   An element

---

[1] Bradford, *Plimoth Plantation,* 238.
[2] Palfrey, *New England,* I., 222, 285.

of discord was introduced in 1625 when the Dorchester men invited Roger Conant and Rev. Mr. Lyford from Nantasket, and made the former manager and the latter minister of their settlement; while John Oldham was asked to become their agent to trade with the Indians. A short time after, the crew of a vessel belonging to the Dorchester adventurers, instigated, it is said, by Lyford, took from the Plymouth men their fishing stage; whereupon Miles Standish came with soldiers from Plymouth, and the rival parties would have come to blows had not Conant interfered and settled the matter.[1]   The Plymouth settlers built a new stage, but, as the war with Spain affected the sale of fish, they soon abandoned the enterprise altogether. The Dorchester men had no better fortune, and the discouraged merchants at home, in 1626, broke up their colony and sold their shipping and most of their other property.[2]   Lyford went to Virginia, where he soon died, and all the other settlers, except Conant and three others, returned to England.

The colony at Plymouth, in the mean time, was signally prospering, and soon felt strong enough to dissolve the troublesome relations with the merchant partners, who had fallen into dissensions

---

[1] Hubbard, *New England* (Mass. Hist. Soc., *Collections*, 2d series, VI., 110).

[2] Bradford, *Plimoth Plantation*, 237; *Planters' Plea* (Force, *Tracts*, II., No. iii.).

among themselves. For this purpose the colonists made, in 1627, an agreement by which for £1800, to be paid in nine annual instalments of £200 each, the colonists were relieved from all vassalage under their original contract.[1]

Custodians of their own fortunes, they now established trading-posts at several places on the coast — at Manomet, on Buzzard's Bay (1627), at Kennebec (1628), and at Penobscot and Machias Bay (1629). In addition they made arrangements for reunion with their friends in Holland, one party of whom arrived in 1629 and another in 1630, though Robinson, the Moses of the Pilgrims, was never permitted to join them, having died March 1, 1626,[2] in Leyden.

They tried also to obtain a charter from the king, but they never could get anything better than a fresh patent from the Council for New England. This patent,[3] dated January 13, 1630, empowered Bradford and his associates "to incorporate by some usual and fit name and title him and themselves, or the people there inhabiting under him or them, with liberty to them and their successors from time to time to frame and make orders, ordinances, and constitutions" not contrary to the laws of England or to any government established by the council.

The patent had the merit of defining the extent of

---

[1] Bradford, *Plimoth Plantation*, 237–258.
[2] *Ibid.*, 248.   [3] Hazard, *State Papers*, I., 298.

territory belonging to the Plymouth settlers, and
granted "all that part of New England in America
aforesaid and Tracte and Tractes of Land that lye
within or betweene a certaine Reuolett or Runlett
there commonly called Coahassett alias Conahassett
towards the North and the Riuer commonly called
Narragansett Riuer towards the South and the
great Westerne Ocean towards the East, and betweene, and within a Streight Line directly Extending up Jnto the Maine Land towards the west from
the mouth of the said Riuer called Narragansett
Riuer to the utmost bounds of a Country or place
in New England Commonly called Pokenacutt als
Sowamsett, westward, and another like Streight line
Extending it Self Directly from the mouth of the
said Riuer called Coahassett als Conahassett towards
the West so farr up into the Main Land Westwards
as the Vtmost Limitts of the said place or Country
Commonly called Pokenacutt als Sowamsett Do
Extend togeather with one half of the sᵈ Riuer
called Narragansett and the sᵈ Reuolett or Runlett
called Coahassett als Conahassett and all Lands
Riuers waters hauens Ports Crecks ffihings fowl-
ings and all hereditaments Proffitts Commodityes
and Jmoluments Whatsoeuer Scituate Lyeing and
being or ariseing within or betweene the said
Limitts or bounds or any of them." For trading
purposes the patent also gave them a tract extending fifteen miles in breadth on each bank of the
Kennebec.

Among the "scattered beginnings" in the neighborhood of Plymouth, the most interesting, because the most contrasted with the Puritan colony at Plymouth, was Captain Wollaston's settlement, established in 1625 a little north of Wessagusset. His men were, for the most part, servants, and Wollaston finding, soon after his arrival, that they could be used to better advantage in Virginia, transported some of them to that colony.

During his absence one Thomas Morton, a lawyer of Clifford's Inn, asserted his authority, freed the rest of the settlers, and engaged in a successful traffic with the Indians for beaver and other skins. This circumstance was itself calculated to excite the jealousy of the Plymouth settlers, but the ceremonies and customs at "Merry Mount," which name Morton gave to the settlement in lieu of "Mount Wollaston," caused them to regard him with even greater disgust. He instituted the Episcopal service and planted a May-pole eighty feet high, around which, for many days together, the settlers "frisked" hand-in-hand with the Indian girls.

As Morton was outside of the Plymouth jurisdiction, the colonists there had no right to interfere except in self-defence. But the Plymouth people asserted that Morton sold arms to the Indians and received runaway servants. This made him dangerous, and all the other "straggling settlements," though, like Morton's, of the church of England, united with the people at Plymouth in suppressing

Morton's settlement. In June, 1628, a joint force under Captain Miles Standish was sent against Merry Mount, and Morton was captured and shipped to England in charge of John Oldham, who had made his peace with Plymouth, and now took with him letters to the Council for New England and to Sir Ferdinando Gorges, in which Morton's offences were duly set forth.[1]

The settlements besides Plymouth which took part in the expedition were Piscataqua (Portsmouth); Nantasket (now Hull), then the seat of John Oldham; Naumkeag (now Salem); Winnisimmet (now Chelsea), where Mr. Jeffrey and Mr. Burslem lived; Cocheco, on the Piscataqua, where Edward Hilton lived; Thompson's Island, where the widow of David Thompson lived; and Shawmut (now Boston), where Rev. William Blackstone lived. Besides the settlements, there were in the neighborhood of Plymouth plantations of some solitary settlers whose names do not appear in this transaction. Thomas Walford lived at Mishawum (now Charlestown), and Samuel Maverick on Noddle's Island; Wessagusset also had probably a few inhabitants.

In 1627 De Rasières, the secretary of state of the Dutch colony at New Netherland, opened a correspondence with Governor Bradford and assured him of his desire to cultivate friendly relations. Brad-

[1] Bradford, *Letter-Book* (Mass. Hist. Soc., *Collections*, 1st series, III., 63); *Plimoth Plantation*, 284–292.

ford gave a kind reply, but questioned the right of the Dutch on the coast, and invited Rasières to a conference. He accepted the invitation, and in 1628 visited the Puritan settlement. A profitable exchange of merchandise succeeded, and the Dutch taught the Plymouth men the value of wampum in trading for furs, and sold them £50 worth of it. It was found useful both as a currency and commodity, and afterwards the settlers learned to make it from the shells on the sea-shore.[1] It was not till five years later that this peaceful correspondence with the Dutch was disturbed.

Unfriendliness characterized, from the first, the relations with the French. They claimed that Acadia extended as far south as Pemaquid, and one day in 1631, when the manager of the Penobscot factory was away, a French privateer appeared in port and landed its crew. In the story, as told by Bradford, the levity of the French and the solemn seriousness of the Puritans afford a delightful contrast. The Frenchmen were profuse in "compliments" and "congees," but taking the English at a disadvantage forced them to an unconditional surrender. They stripped the factory of its goods, and as they sailed away bade their victims tell the manager when he came back "that the Isle of Rhé gentlemen had been there."[2] In 1633, after Ra-

---

[1] Bradford, *Letter-Book* (Mass. Hist. Soc., *Collections*, 1st series, III., 53).

[2] Bradford, *Plimoth Plantation*, 350.

zilly's appointment as governor-general, De la Tour, one of his lieutenants, attacked and drove away the Plymouth men at Machias Bay,[1] and in 1635 D'Aulnay, another lieutenant, dispossessed the English at Penobscot.

The Plymouth people, greatly incensed, sent two armed ships to punish the French, but the expedition proved a failure. Then they appealed to Massachusetts for help, but the great men of that colony, hoping, as Bradford intimates, to arrange a trade with the French on their own account, declined to be at any expense in the matter,[2] and so the Penobscot remained in unfriendly hands for many years.

This appeal to Massachusetts showed that another power had stepped to the front in New England. After John Winthrop set up his government in 1630 on Massachusetts Bay the history of the Plymouth colony ceased to be of first importance, and therefore the remaining events in her annals need not take much space. In 1633 the people of Plymouth established a fort on Connecticut River above the Dutch post, so as to intercept the Indian trade, and in 1639 they renewed the ancient league with Massasoit.[3] In 1640 they had a dispute with Massachusetts over the boundary-line, which was arranged by a compromise, and in 1641 William

---

[1] Winthrop, *New England*, I., 139.
[2] Bradford, *Plimoth Plantation*, 395–401.
[3] *Plymouth Col. Records*, I., 133.

Bradford deeded to the freemen of the corporation of New Plymouth the patent of 1630, granted by the Council for New England to him as trustee for the colony.[1]   Finally, in 1643, Plymouth became a member of the New England confederation.

A survey of these twenty-three years (1620–1643) shows that during the first eleven years the increase in population was very slow.   In 1624 there were one hundred and eighty settlers and in 1630 but three hundred.   The emigration to Massachusetts, beginning in 1629, brought about a great change. It overflowed into Plymouth, and in twelve years more the population had increased to three thousand.[2]   The new settlers were a miscellaneous set, composed for the most part of "unruly servants" and dissipated young men, whose ill conduct caused the old rulers like Bradford to question "whether after twenty years' time the greater part be not grown worser."[3]   Nevertheless, the people increased their "outward estate," and as they scattered in search of fertile land, Plymouth, "in which they lived compactly till now, was left very thin and in a short time almost desolate."   In 1632 a separate church and town of the name of Duxbury was formed north of Plymouth; and eleven years later the towns of the Plymouth colony were ten in

---

[1] Bradford, *Plimoth Plantation*, 437–444.
[2] Palfrey, *New England*, I., 223, II., 6; Hazard, *State Papers*, I., 300.   [3] Bradford, *Plimoth Plantation*, 459.

number: Plymouth, Duxbury, Scituate, Taunton, Sandwich, Yarmouth, Barnstable, Marshfield, See-conck, or Rehoboth, and Nausett.[1]

At the first arrival the executive and judicial powers were exercised by John Carver, without any authorized adviser. After his death, in 1621, the same powers were vested in William Bradford as governor and Isaac Allerton as assistant.[2] In 1624 the number of assistants was increased to five and in 1633 to seven, and the governor was given a double voice.[3] The elective and legislative powers were vested in a primary assembly of all the free-men, called the "General Court," held at short in-tervals.   One of these meetings was called the court of elections, and at this were chosen the governor and other officers of the colony for the ensuing year.

As the number of settlements increased, it be-came inconvenient for freemen to attend the general courts in person, and in 1638 the representative system was definitely introduced. Plymouth was allowed four delegates, and each of the other towns two, and they, with the governor and his council of assistants, constituted the law-making body of the colony.   To be entitled to hold office or vote at the court of elections, the person had to be "a free-man"; and to acquire this character, he had to be specially chosen one of the company at one of the

---

[1] Bradford, *Plimoth Plantation*, 444. [2] *Ibid.*, 122.
[3] *Ibid.*, 187.

general courts. Thus suffrage was regarded as a privilege and not a right.[1]

Although the first of the colonies to establish a Separatist church, the Puritans of Plymouth did not make church-membership a condition of citizenship; still, there can be no doubt that this restriction practically prevailed at Plymouth, since up to 1643 only about two hundred and thirty persons acquired the suffrage. In the general laws of Plymouth, published in 1671, it was provided as a condition of receiving the franchise that "the candidate should be of sober and peaceable conversation, orthodox in the fundamentals of religion," which was probably only a recognition of the custom of earlier times.[2] The earliest New England code of statutes was that of Plymouth, adopted in 1636. It was digested under fifty titles and recognized seven capital offences, witchcraft being one.[3]

In the Plymouth colony, as in other colonies of New England, the unit of government was the town, and this town system was borrowed from Massachusetts, where, as we shall see, the inhabitants of Dorchester set the example, in 1633, of coming together for governmental purposes. Entitled to take part in the town-meetings under the Plymouth laws were all freemen and persons "admitted inhabitants" of a town. They elected the deputies of the general

[1] Palfrey, *New England*, II., 8.

[2] *Ibid.* In August, 1643, the number of males of military age was 627.

[3] Brigham, *Plymouth Charter and Laws*, 43, 244.

court and the numerous officers of the town, and
had the authority to pass local ordinances of nearly
every description.[1]

During the early days, except for the short time
of Lyford's service, Elder William Brewster was the
spiritual guide for the people.   For a long time they
kept the place of minister waiting for Robinson, but
when he died they secured, in 1628, the services of
Mr. Rogers, who proved to "be crazed in his brain "
and had to be sent back the following year.   Then,
in 1629, Mr. Ralph Smith was minister, and Roger
Williams assisted him.   Smith was a man of small
abilities, and after enduring him for eight years they
persuaded him to resign.   After Smith's resignation
the office of minister at Plymouth was filled by
Rev. John Rayner.[2]

The educational advantages of the Plymouth
colony were meagre, and the little learning that
existed was picked up in the old English way by
home instruction.   This deficiency was due to the
stern conditions of a farmer's life on Cape Cod
Bay, where the soil was poor and the climate severe, necessitating the constant labor of the whole
family.

Nevertheless, the Plymouth colony was always an
example to its neighbors for thrift, economy, and integrity, and it influenced to industry by proving

---

[1] Palfrey, *New England*, II., 7; Howard, *Local Constitutional
History*, 50–99.
[2] Bradford, *Plimoth Plantation*, 314, 418, 419.

what might be done on a barren soil.   Its chief claim
to historical importance rests, of course, on the fact
that, as the first successful colony on the New England coast, it was the cause and beginning of the
establishment of the other colonies of New England,
and the second step in founding the great republic
of the United States.

CHAPTER XI

GENESIS OF MASSACHUSETTS

(1628–1630)

THE abandonment, in 1626, of their colony at Cape Ann by the Dorchester adventurers, did not cause connection to be entirely severed either in America or in England. In America, Conant and three of the more industrious settlers remained, but as the fishery was abandoned, they withdrew with the cattle from the exposed promontory at Cape Ann to Naumkeag, afterwards Salem.[1] In England a few of the adventurers, loath to give up entirely, sent over more cattle, and the enterprise, suddenly attracting other support, rose to a greater promise than had ever been anticipated.[2]

Among those in England who did not lose hope was the Rev. John White, of Dorchester, a merchant as well as a preacher, and his large figure stands on the threshold of the great commonwealth of Massachusetts. Thomas Fuller says that he had absolute command of two things not easily controlled—"his

[1] Hubbard, *New England* (Mass. Hist. Soc., *Collections*, 2d series, V.), 107, 108.
[2] *Planters' Plea* (Force, *Tracts*, II., No. iii.).

183

own passions and the purses of his parishioners."
White wrote Conant and his associates to stick by
the work, and promised to obtain for them a patent
and fully provide them with means to carry on the
fur trade.   The matter was discussed in Lincolnshire and London, and soon a powerful association
came into being and lent its help.

Other men, some of whom are historic personages,
began to take a leading part, and there was at first
no common religious purpose among the new associates.   The contemporary literature is curiously
free from any special appeal to Puritanic principles,
and the arguments put forward are much the same
as those urged for the settlement of Virginia.   The
work of planting a new colony was taken up en-
thusiastically, and a patent, dated March 19, 1628,
was obtained from the Council for New England,
conceding to six grantees, Sir Henry Rosewell, Sir
John Young, Thomas Southcot, John Humphrey,
John Endicott, and Simon Whitcombe, "all that
Parte of New England in America aforesaid, which
lyes and extendes betweene a greate River there
comonlie called Monomack alias Merriemack, and a
certen other River there, called Charles River, being in the Bottome of a certayne Bay there, comonlie
called Massachusetts alias Mattachusetts, . . . and
. . . lyeing within the Space of three English Myles
on the South Parte of the said Charles River, . . .
and also . . . within the space of three English Myles
to the Northward of the said River called Monomack,

. . . throughout the Mayne Landes there, from the Atlantick and Westerne Sea and Ocean on the East Parte, to the South Sea on the West Parte."

The patent also gave to the company "all Jurisdiccons, Rights, Royalties, Liberties, Freedoms, Ymmunities, Priviledges, Franchises, Preheminences, and Commodities, whatsoever, which they, the said Council established at Plymouth, . . . then had, . . . within the saide Landes and Premisses."[1] On account of the reckless manner in which the Council for New England granted away its territory, the patent conflicted with several others of an earlier date. In March, 1622, they had granted to John Mason a patent for all the land between Naumkeag and the Merrimac River. Then, in December, 1622, a part of this territory having a front of ten miles "upon the northeast side of Boston Bay," and extending thirty miles into the interior, was granted to Captain Robert Gorges.[2] Next, at the division in June, 1623, the part of New England about Boston Bay fell to Lord Sheffield, the earl of Warwick, and Lord Edward Gorges, a cousin of Sir Ferdinando. The rights under the first and last of these grants were surrendered in 1629,[3] but, according to Ferdinando Gorges, he, as one of the

[1] The patent is not preserved, but there is a recital of its main feature in the Massachusetts charter. Poore, *Charters and Constitutions*, I., 932.

[2] *Cal. of State Pap., Col.*, 1574–1660, pp. 25, 35; Gorges, *Description of New England* (Mass. Hist. Soc., *Collections*, 3d series, VI., 75).   [3] *Cal. of State Pap., Col.*, 1661–1668, p. 347.

council, only sanctioned the patent to Rosewell and his partners on the understanding that the grant to his son should not be interfered with; and the maintenance of this claim was the occasion of dispute for some years.[1]

June 20, 1628, the new company sent out a party of emigrants under John Endicott, who arrived, September 6, at Naumkeag, where, with the number already on Boston Bay at their coming, they made about fifty or sixty persons. He found the remains of Conant's company disposed to question the claims of the new-comers, but the dispute was amicably arranged, and in commemoration Naumkeag was given the name of Salem, the Hebrew word for "Peaceful."[2]

For nearly a year little is known of the settlers except that in the winter some died of the scurvy and others of an "infectious fever."[3] Endicott wrote to Plymouth for medical assistance, and Bradford sent Dr. Samuel Fuller, whose services were thankfully acknowledged. One transaction which has come down to us shows that Endicott's government early marked out the lines on which the Massachusetts colony travelled for many years afterwards. Endicott made it evident that he would make no compromise with any of the "ungodly" in Massachusetts. Morton's settlement fell within

---

[1] Gorges, *Description of New England*, 80.
[2] Hubbard, *New England* (Mass. Hist. Soc., *Collections*, 2d series, V., 109).   [3] Bradford, *Plimoth Plantation*, 314.

Endicott's jurisdiction, and he resolved to finish the work which the Plymouth people began. So, about three months after the first visit, Endicott, with a small party, crossed the bay, hewed down the abominable May-pole, and, solemnly dubbing the place Mount Dago, in memory of the Philistine idol which fell down before the ark of the Lord, "admonished Morton's men to look ther should be better walking."

In the mean time, important events were happening in England. John Oldham, having Thomas Morton in custody, landed at Plymouth, England, not long after Endicott left for America. Morton posed as a martyr to religious persecution, and Oldham, who remembered his own troubles with the Plymouth settlers, soon fraternized with him. They acted in connection with Ferdinando Gorges and his son John Gorges, who, instead of punishing Morton for illicit trading, made use of him and Oldham to dispute the title of the grant to Endicott and his associates. Robert Gorges was then dead, and his brother John was heir to his patent for the northeast side of Massachusetts Bay.

Accordingly, John Gorges, in January, 1629, executed two deeds—one to John Oldham and the other to Sir William Brereton—for two tracts of land out of the original grant to Robert Gorges. Oldham planted himself on his new rights, and tried to make his patent the means to obtain from the Massachusetts Company in England the exclusive management of the colony's fur trade, or the recognition of his rights as an independent trader. But the company had already set aside the profits of the fur trade as a fund for the defence of the colony and the support of the public worship, and they would make no concession.[1] Instead, they took the best means to strengthen their title and suppress such disturbers as Oldham.

A royal charter was solicited, and March 4, 1629, one of liberal powers passed the seals, chiefly through the influence of the earl of Warwick.[2] It created a corporation by the name of the "Governor and Company of Massachusetts Bay in New England," and confirmed to them all the territory given by the patent from the Council for New England. The administration of its affairs was intrusted to a governor, deputy, and eighteen assistants, who were annually, on the last Wednesday of Easter term, to be elected by the freemen or members of the corporation, and to meet once a month or oftener "for despatching such business as concerned the company or plantation." Four times a year the governor, assistants, and all the freemen were to be summoned to "a greate generall, and solemne assemblie," and these "greate and generall courts" were invested with full power to choose and admit into the company so many as they should think fit, to elect and

---

[1] Young, *Chronicles of Massachusetts*, 148; Adams, *Three Episodes of Mass. Hist.*, I., 216.
[2] See charter in Poore, *Charters and Constitutions*, I., 932.

constitute all requisite subordinate officers, and to make laws and ordinances for the welfare of the company and for the government of the plantation.

The company was given the power to transport to its American territory all persons who should go willingly, but the corporate body alone was to decide what liberties, if any, the emigrants should enjoy. In fact, the only restrictions in the charter upon the company and its court of assistants were that they should license no man " to rob or spoil," hinder no one from fishing upon the coast of New England, and pass "no law contrary or repugnant to the lawes and statutes of England." Matthew Cradock was named in the charter the governor of the company.

One of the first steps taken by the company under the new charter was to organize a temporary local government for the colonists in Massachusetts. This was to consist of a governor, a deputy governor, and thirteen councillors, of whom seven were to be named by the company, three were to be chosen by these seven and the governor, and three more were to be appointed by the "old planters" found in Massachusetts at the arrival of Endicott. Land was allotted on a plan like that adopted by the London Company: each shareholder was to have two hundred acres for every £50 that he invested, and if he settled in that country, fifty more for himself and fifty more for each member of his family.[1]

---

[1] Young, *Chronicles of Massachusetts*, 192–200.

A letter of instructions was draughted, April 17, to Governor Endicott, in which mention was made of the negotiations with Oldham, and orders given to effect an occupation of the territory covered by his grant from John Gorges. This letter was sent off by a special ship which reached Salem June 20, 1629, and Endicott promptly despatched three brothers of the name of Sprague, and a few others, who planted themselves at Mishawum, within the disputed territory, where they found but "one English palisadoed and thatched house wherein lived Thomas Walford, a smith." Other emigrants followed, and there, in July, was laid out by Endicott a town which was named Charlestown. This practically ended the difficulty with Oldham, who was kept in the dark till the ship sailed from England, and was then told by the company that they were determined, on advice of counsel, to treat his grant as void. As for Brereton, he was made a member of the company and did not give any real trouble.[1]

May 11, 1629, sailed from London five ships carrying about four hundred settlers, most of whom were servants, and one hundred and forty head of cattle and forty goats. They arrived at Salem, June 27, and about four weeks later the ecclesiastical organization of the colony was effected by John Endicott, who had already written to Bradford that the worship at Plymouth was "no other than is

[1] Hutchinson, *Massachusetts Bay*, I., 17; Adams, *Three Episodes of Mass. Hist.*, I., 216–220.

warranted by the evidence of the truth." He set apart July 20 for the work, and, after a portion of the morning spent in prayer, Samuel Skelton and Francis Higginson, two of the four ministers who accompanied the last arrivals, avowed their belief in the doctrines of the Independents, and were elected respectively pastor and teacher. A confession of faith and a church covenant were drawn up, and August 6 thirty persons associated themselves in a church.[1]

Two of the gentlemen emigrants, John and Samuel Browne, presumed to hold a separate service with a small company, using the Prayer Book. Thereupon the hot-headed Endicott arrested them, put them on shipboard, and sent them back to England. This conduct of Endicott's was a flagrant aggression on vested rights, since the Brownes appear in the charter as original promoters of the colony, and were sent to Massachusetts by the company in the high capacity of assistants or councillors to Endicott himself. The two brothers complained in England, and in October, 1629, the company sent Endicott a warning against "undigested counsels . . . which may have any ill construction with the state here and make us obnoxious to an adversary."[2]

In another particular Endicott showed the summary character which distinguished him. When Morton arrived in London a prisoner, in 1628, Isaac

---

[1] Bradford, *Plimoth Plantation*, 315, 316.
[2] Young, *Chronicles of Massachusetts*, 89, 290.

Allerton was trying to secure from the Council for New England a new patent for Plymouth colony. In Morton he appears to have recognized a convenient medium for reaching Sir Ferdinando Gorges; at any rate, when Allerton returned to New England in the summer of 1629, he brought Thomas Morton back with him, to the scandal of the Plymouth community.[1] After a few weeks at Plymouth, Morton repaired to Merry Mount and resumed the business of a fur-trader, but, as might have been expected, he was soon brought into conflict with his neighbors.

Endicott, it appears, not long after Morton's return, in pursuance of instructions from England, summoned all the settlers in Massachusetts to a general court at Salem. At this meeting, according to Morton, Endicott tendered to all present for signature articles binding them "to follow the rule of God's word in all causes as well ecclesiasticall as politicall." The alternative was banishment, but Morton says that he declined to subscribe without the words in the Massachusetts charter, "so as nothing be done contrary or repugnant to the Lawes of the Kingdome of England." Endicott took fire at the independent claims of Morton and sent a party to arrest him. They found Morton gone, whereupon they broke into his house and appropriated his corn and other property.[2]

[1] Bradford, *Plimoth Plantation*, 302.
[2] Morton, *New English Canaan* (Force, *Tracts*, II., No. v.), 106, 107.

Meanwhile, in England, an important determination had been reached by the leaders of the Massachusetts Company. At a general court, July 28, 1629, Cradock, the governor, read "certain propositions conceived by himself" for transferring the headquarters of the company to America.[1]   The matter was held in abeyance, and the members present were instructed to consider the question "privately and secretely."   August 26 twelve of the most influential members, among whom were John Winthrop, Isaac Johnson, Thomas Dudley, and Richard Saltonstall, bound themselves by a written agreement at Cambridge to emigrate with their families to New England if a transfer of the government could be effected.[2]

Three days later the company held another meeting, when the removal was formally proposed and carried.   Accordingly, such of the old officers as did not wish to take part in the emigration resigned their places, and for governor the choice fell upon John Winthrop, a wealthy gentleman of Groton, in Suffolk, and for deputy governor upon Thomas Dudley, who had been steward of the earl of Lincoln. The ultimate effect of this brilliant stroke was to convert the company into a colony.[3]

This change of policy was taken when affairs looked particularly dark in England, for it was about

[1] *Mass. Col. Records*, I., 49.
[2] Young, *Chronicles of Massachusetts*, 282–284.
[3] *Mass. Col. Records*, I., 51.

this time that King Charles, provoked at the opposition of Parliament, entered upon his policy of ruling without one.   March 10, 1629, Parliament was
dissolved, and no other was called for a space of
eleven years.   Several of the most eminent members were languishing in the Tower of London, and
the king's proclamation of March 27 announced that
he would "account it as a presumption for any to
prescribe any time unto us for Parliaments, the calling, continuing, and dissolving of which is always in
our power." [1]

The result was a general stir throughout England,
and in a few months a thousand persons prepared to
leave.   They went in several parties in seventeen
ships, and there was probably a greater proportion of
men of wealth and solid respectability than ever had
left England for America in any one year before.   The
colonists, though Puritans, were church of England
men, and the idea of any separation from their old
religious connections was expressly disclaimed in a
pamphlet published in 1630, entitled the "Planters'
Plea," [2] which has been, with good reason, assigned
to Rev. John White.   In this paper the writer appeals to the address of the colonists at their departure, wherein they termed the church of England
"our dear mother." [3]   Apparently anxious to repel the imputation of nonconformity against "our
New England colony," he adds the confident asser-

[1] Rymer, *Fœdera*, XIX., 63.   [2] Force, *Tracts*, II., No. iii.
[3] Palfrey, *New England*, I., 312.

tion that John Winthrop, the chosen governor, has been "in every way regular and conformable in the whole course of his practice"; and that "three parts of four of the men planted in New England are able to justify themselves to have lived in a constant conformity unto our church government and orders."

The party with which Winthrop sailed arrived at Salem June 12, 1630, after a nine weeks' voyage, in which they were exposed to stormy and boisterous weather. They found the colony of Endicott in "a sad and unexpected condition." More than a fourth part had died during the previous winter, and many of the survivors were weak and sick. There was a general scarcity of bread and corn, and the arrival of Winthrop and his emigrants did not improve matters, for many of the new-comers were suffering from scurvy, and a quantity of supplies which had been bought in England had by some mistake been left behind.[1]

[1] Thomas Dudley, letter to the countess of Lincoln (Force, *Tracts*, II., No. iv.).

CHAPTER XII

FOUNDING OF MASSACHUSETTS

(1630–1642)

WINTHROP'S government superseded Endi-cott's; but Winthrop, not liking the appear-ance of the country around Salem, repaired to Charlestown with most of the new-comers. Here, as elsewhere, there was much sickness and death. Owing to the dearth of provisions it was found necessary to free all the servants sent over within the last two years at a cost of £16 or £20 each. The discouragement was reflected in the return to England within a few months of more than a hundred persons in the ships that brought them over.

The gloom of his surroundings caused Winthrop to set apart July 30 as a day of prayer, and on that day Rev. John Wilson, after the manner of proceed-ing the year before at Salem, entered into a church covenant with Winthrop, Dudley, and Isaac John-son, one of the assistants. Two days later they as-sociated with themselves five others; and more being presently added, this third congregational church established in New England, elected, August 27,

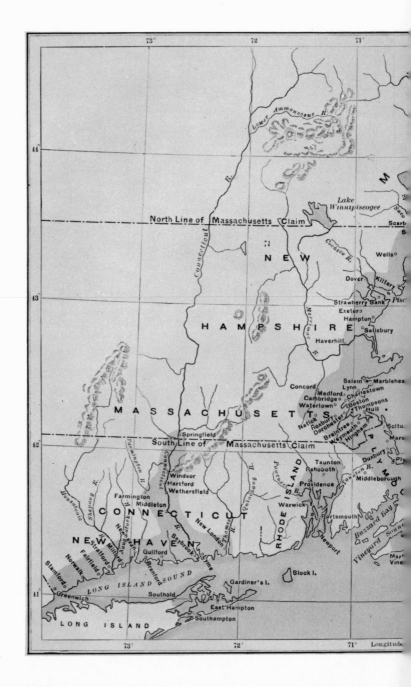

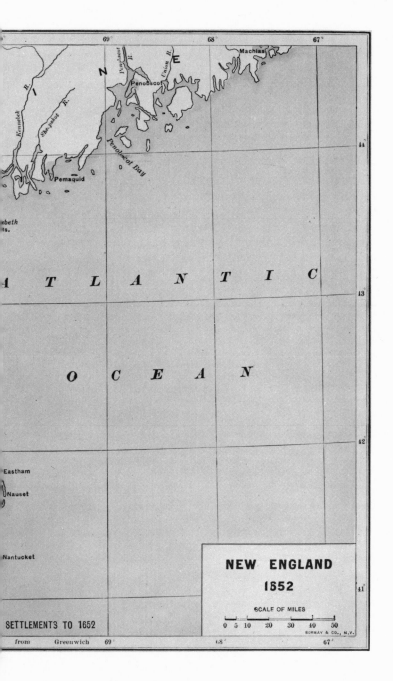

SETTLEMENTS TO 1652

NEW ENGLAND
1852

SCALE OF MILES

0 5 10   20   30   40   50

BORMAY & CO., N.Y.

from   Greenwich   69°   68°   67°

John Wilson to be their teacher and Increase Nowell to be ruling elder.[1]

Still the guise of loyalty to the church of England was for some time maintained. In a letter to the countess of Lincoln, March 28, 1631, the deputy governor, Thomas Dudley, one of the warmest of the Puritans, repelled "the false and scandalous report," which those who returned "the last year" had spread in England that "we are Brownists in religion and ill affected to our state at home"; "and for our further cleareinge," he said, " I truely affirme that I know noe one person who came over with us the last yeare to be altered in his judgment and affection eyther in ecclesiasticall or civill respects since our comeinge hither."[2]

Winthrop and his assistants held their first formal session at Charlestown, August 23, 1630, and took vigorous measures to demonstrate their authority. Morton challenged attention on account not only of his religious views and his friendship for Gorges, but of his defiant attitude to the colony, and an order was issued that "Morton, of Mount Wolliston, should presently be sent for by process." Two weeks later his trial was had, and he was ordered "to be set into the bilboes," and afterwards sent prisoner to England. To defray the charges of his transportation, his goods were seized, and "for the many wrongs he had done the Indians" his house was

---

[1] Bradford, *Plimoth Plantation*, 332; Winthrop, *New England*, I., 36.   [2] Force, *Tracts*, II., No. iv., 15.

burned to the ground,[1] a sentence which, according to Morton, caused the Indians to say that "God would not love them that burned this good man's house." [2]

Death was still playing havoc with the immigrants at Charlestown. Several hundred men, women, and children were crowded together in a narrow space, and had no better protection than tents, wigwams, booths, and log-cabins. By December two hundred of the late arrivals had perished, and among the dead were Francis Higginson, who had taken a leading part in establishing the church at Salem, the first in Massachusetts.[3] The severity of the diseases was ascribed to the lack of good water at Charlestown, and, accordingly, the settlers there broke up into small parties and sought out different places of settlement.

On the other side of the Charles River was a peninsula occupied by William Blackstone, one of the companions of Robert Gorges at Wessagusset in 1626. It was blessed with a sweet and pleasant spring, and was one of the places now selected as a settlement. September 7, 1630, the court of assistants gave this place the name of Boston; and at the same court Dorchester and Watertown began their career under legislative sanction.[4] Before

---

[1] *Mass. Col. Records*, I., 75.

[2] Morton, *New English Canaan* (Force, *Tracts*, II., No. v.), 109.   [3] Dudley's letter (*ibid.*, No. iv.).

[4] *Mass. Col. Records*, I., 75, 77.

winter the towns scattered through Massachusetts were eight in number—Salem, Charlestown, Dorchester, Boston, Watertown, Roxbury, Mystic, and Lynn.[1]

October 19, 1630, a general court, the first in New England, was held in Boston. The membership consisted of the governor, deputy, eight assistants, and one or two others, for these were all at that time in Massachusetts possessing the franchise of the company.[2] The former officers were reelected, and a resolution was adopted that "the freemen should have the power to choose assistants when they are to be chosen, and the assistants to choose from among themselves the governor and his deputy." The rule implied a strong reluctance to leave out of the board any person once elected magistrate.

From the last week in December to the middle of February, 1631, the suffering in the colony was very great, especially among the poorer classes, and many died. Were it not for the abundance of clams, mussels, and fish gathered from the bay there might have been a "starving time," like that of Jamestown in 1609. Winthrop appointed a fast to be kept February 22, 1631; but February 5 the *Lyon* arrived with supplies, and a public thanksgiving was substituted for a public fasting.[3]

---

[1] Palfrey, *New England*, I., 323, 324   [2] *Ibid.*, 323.
[3] Hubbard, *New England* (Mass. Hist. Soc., *Collections*, 2d series, V.), 138, 139; Winthrop, *New England*, I., 52.

From this time the colony may be said to have secured a permanent footing. The court of assistants, who had suspended their sessions during the winter, now began to meet again, and made many orders with reference to the economic and social affairs of the colonists. There were few natives in the neighborhood of the settlement, and Chickatabot, their sachem, anxious to secure the protection of the English against the Taratines, of Maine, visited Boston in April and established friendly communications.[1] At the courts of elections of 1631, 1632, and 1633 Winthrop was re-elected governor. His conduct was not deemed harsh enough by some people, and in 1634 Thomas Dudley succeeded him. In 1635 John Haynes became governor, and in 1636 Henry Vane, known in English history as Sir Harry Vane, after which time the governorship was restored to Winthrop.

Puritanism entered the warp and woof of the Massachusetts colony, and a combination of circumstances tended to build up a theocracy which dominated affairs. The ministers who came over were among the most learned men of the age, and the influence which their talents and character gave them was greatly increased by the sufferings and the isolation of the church members, who were thus brought to confide all the more in those who, under such conditions, dispensed religious consolation. Moreover, the few who had at first the direction of civil matters

[1] Winthrop, *New England*, I., 64.

were strongly religious men, and inclined to promote the unity of the church by all the means at
hand.

We have noticed the turn of affairs given by
Endicott at Salem, and how Winthrop followed his
example on his arrival at Charlestown. After the
court of assistants resumed their meetings in March,
1631, the upbuilding of the theocracy was rapidly
pushed. Various people deemed inimical to the
accepted state of affairs were punished with banishment from the colony, and in some cases the penalties
of whipping, cropping of ears, and confiscation of
estate were added. In some cases, as that of Sir
Christopher Gardiner, a secret agent of Sir Ferdinando Gorges, there was reason for parting with these
people; but in other cases the principle of punishment was persecution and not justice. There is a
record of an order for reshipping to England six
persons of whose offence nothing more is recorded
than "that they were persons unmeet to inhabit
here." [1]

The most decided enlargement of the power of
the theocracy was made in the general court which
met at Boston in May, 1631, when it was resolved
that the assistants need not be chosen afresh every
year, but might keep their seats until removed by a
special vote of the freemen. [2] The company was enlarged by the addition of one hundred and eighteen
"freemen"; but "to the end that the body of the

[1] *Mass. Col. Records*, I., 82.   [2] *Ibid.*, 87.

commons may be preserved of honest and good men," it was ordered that "for the time to come no man should be admitted to the freedom of this body politic but such as are members of some of the churches within the limits of the same."

These proceedings practically vested all the judicial and legislative powers in the court of assistants, whose tenure was permanent, and left to the freemen in the general court little else than the power of admitting freemen. Not only was citizenship based on church-membership, but the Bible was the only law-book recognized by the court of assistants. Of this book the ministers were naturally thought the best interpreters, and it thus became the custom for the magistrates to consult them on all questions of importance. Offenders were not merely law-breakers, but sinners, and their offences ranged from such as wore long hair to such as dealt in witchcraft and sorcery.

Fortunately, this system did not long continue without some modification. In February, 1632, the court of assistants assessed a tax upon the towns for the erection of a fortification at Newtown, subsequently Cambridge. The inhabitants of Watertown grumbled about paying their proportion of this tax, and at the third general court, May 9, 1632, it was ordered that hereafter the governor and assistants in laying taxes should be guided by the advice of a board composed of two delegates from every town; and that the governor and other magistrates should be elected by the whole body of the freemen assembled as the charter required.

Two years later a general court consisting of the governor, assistants, and two " committees," or dele-gates, elected by the freemen resident in each town, assembled and assumed the powers of legislation.[1] This change, which brought about a popular repre-sentative body—second in point of time only to Virginia—was a natural extension of the proceed-ings of 1632. In 1644 the assistants and delegates quarrelled over an appeal in a lawsuit, and as a result the division of the court into two co-ordinate branches occurred.[2]

Nevertheless, the authority of the court of as-sistants, for several reasons, continued to be very great. In the first place, unlike the Council of Virginia, which could only amend or reject the action of the lower house, the assistants had the right of originating laws. Then the custom at the annual elections of first putting the names of the incum-bents to the vote made the tenure of its members a pretty constant affair. Next, as a court, it exercised for years a vast amount of discretionary power. Not till 1641 was the first code, called the *Body of Liberties*, adopted, and this code itself permitted the assistants to supply any defect in the law by the "word of God," a phrase which to the followers

[1] Winthrop, *New England*, I., 84, 90, 152.
[2] *Mass. Col. Records*, II., 58, 59; Winthrop, *New England*, II., 115–118, 193.

of Calvin had especial reference to the fierce legislation of the Old Testament.

The course of the colonial authorities speedily
jeopardized the charter which they obtained so readily from the king.   Upon the arrival in England, in
1631, of Morton, Gardiner, and other victims of the
court of assistants, they communicated with Gorges
(now powerfully assisted by John Mason); and he
gladly seized upon their complaints to accuse the
ministers and people of Massachusetts of railing
against the state and church of England, and of an
evident purpose of casting off their allegiance at the
first favorable opportunity.   The complaint was
referred, in December, 1632, to a committee of the
council,[1] before whom the friends of the company
in London—Cradock, Saltonstall, and Humphrey—
filed a written answer.   Affairs bore a bad appearance for the colonists, but the unexpected happened.   Powerful influences at court were brought
to bear upon the members of the committee, and to
the astonishment of every one they reported, January 19, 1633, against any interference until "further
inquiry" could be made.[2]   King Charles not only
approved this report, but volunteered the remark
that "he would have them severely punished who
did abuse his governor and the plantation."[3]

Though the danger for the present was avoided,

---

[1] *Cal. of State Pap., Col.* 1574–1660, p. 158.
[2] Bradford, *Plimoth Plantation*, 356.
[3] Winthrop, *New England*, I., 122, 123.

it was not wholly removed.   In August, 1633, Laud
was made archbishop of Canterbury, and his accession to authority was distinguished by a more
rigorous enforcement of the laws against Nonconformists.   The effect was to cause the lagging emigration to New England to assume immense volume.
There was no longer concealment of the purposes of
the emigrants, for the Puritan preachers began everywhere to speak openly of the corruptions of the
English church.[1]   In September, 1633, the theocracy of Massachusetts were reinforced by three eminent ministers, John Cotton, Thomas Hooker, and
Thomas Shepard; and so many other persons accompanied and followed them that by the end of
1634 the population was not far short of four thousand.   The clergy, now thirteen or fourteen in number, were nearly all graduates of Oxford or Cambridge.

This exodus of so many of the best, "both ministers and Christians,"[2] aroused the king and
Archbishop Laud to the danger threatened by the
Massachusetts colony.   Gorges, Mason, and the rest
renewed the attack, and in February, 1634, an order
was obtained from the Privy Council for the deten-
tion of ten vessels bound for Massachusetts.   At the
same time Cradock, the ex-governor of the company, was commanded by the Privy Council to hand
in the Massachusetts charter.[3]   Soon after, the

---

[1] *Cal. of State Pap., Col.*, 1574–1660, p. 174.
[2] Winthrop, *New England*, I., 161.
[3] Hazard, *State Papers*, I., 341.

king announced his intention of "giving order for a
general governor" for New England; and in April,
1634, he appointed a new commission for the government of the colonies, called "The Commission
for Foreign Plantations," with William Laud, archbishop of Canterbury, at the head. Mr. Cradock
transmitted a copy of the order of council, requiring
a production of the charter, to Boston, where it was
received by Governor Dudley in July, 1634.

This was a momentous crisis in the history of the
colony. The governor and assistants made answer
to Mr. Cradock that the charter could not be returned
except by command of the general court, not then
in session. At the same time orders were given for
fortifying Castle Island, Dorchester, and Charlestown. In this moment of excitement the figure of
Endicott again dramatically crosses the stage of history. Conceiving an intense dislike to the cross in
the English flag, he denounced it as antichrist, and
cut it out with his own hands from the ensign borne
by the company at Salem. Endicott was censured
by the general court for the act, but soon the cross
was left out of all the flags except that of the fort
at Castle Island, in Boston Harbor.[1]

Massachusetts, while taking these bold measures
at home, did not neglect the protection of her interests in England. The government of Plymouth, in
July, 1634, sent Edward Winslow to England, and
Governor Dudley and his council engaged him to

---

[1] Winthrop, *New England*, I., 161, 163, 166, 186, 188, 224.

present an humble petition in their behalf.[1] Winslow was a shrewd diplomat, but was so far from succeeding with his suit that upon his appearance before the lords commissioners in 1635 he was, through Laud's "vehement importunity," committed to Fleet Prison, where he lay seventeen weeks.[2]

Gorges and Mason lost no time in improving their victory. February 3, 1635, they secured a redivision of the coast of New England by the Council for New England, into twelve parts, which were assigned to as many persons. Sir William Alexander received the country from the river St. Croix to Pemaquid; Sir Ferdinando Gorges, the province of Maine from Penobscot to Piscataqua; Captain John Mason, New Hampshire and part of Massachusetts as far as Cape Ann, while the coast from Cape Ann to Narragansett Bay fell to Lord Edward Gorges, and the portion from Narragansett Bay to the Connecticut River to the marquis of Hamilton.[3]

April 25, 1635, the Council for New England issued a formal declaration of their reasons for resigning the great charter to the king, chief among which was their inability to rectify the complaints of their servants in America against the Massachusetts Company, who had "surreptitiously" obtained a charter for lands "justly passed to Captain Robert

[1] Winthrop, *New England*, I., 163.
[2] Bradford, *Plimoth Plantation*, 393.
[3] Maine Hist. Soc., *Collections*, 2d series, VII., 183–188.

Gorges long before." [1]   June 7 the charter was surrendered to the king, who appointed Sir Ferdinando
Gorges "general governor."   The expiring company
further appointed Thomas Morton as their lawyer
to ask for a *quo warranto* against the charter of the
Massachusetts Company.

In September, 1635, judgment was given in Westminster Hall that "the franchises of the Massachusetts Company be taken and seized into the king's
hands." [2]   But, as Winthrop said, the Lord "frustrated their designs."   King Charles was trying to
rule without a Parliament, and had no money to
spend against New England.   Therefore, the cost
of carrying out the orders of the government devolved upon Mason and Gorges, who set to work to
build a ship to convey the latter to America, but it
fell and broke in the launching, [3] and about November, 1635, Captain John Mason died.

After this, though the king in council, in July,
1637, named Gorges again as "general governor," [4]
and the Lords Commissioners for Plantations, in
April, 1638, demanded the charter anew, [5] the
Massachusetts general court would not recognize
either order.   Gorges could not raise the necessary
funds to compel obedience, and the attention of the
king and his archbishop was occupied with forcing

[1] *Cal. of State Pap., Col.*, 1574–1660, pp. 200, 204.
[2] Hazard, *State Papers*, I., 423–425.
[3] Winthrop, *New England*, II., 12.
[4] *Cal. of State Pap., Col.*, 1574–1660, p. 256.
[5] Hazard, *State Papers*, I., 432.

episcopacy upon Scotland. In 1642 war began in England between Parliament and king, and Massachusetts was left free to shape her own destinies. It was now her turn to become aggressive. Construing her charter to mean that her territory extended to a due east line three miles north of the most northerly branch of Merrimac River, she possessed herself, in 1641, of New Hampshire, the territory of the heirs of John Mason; and in 1653–1658, of Maine, the province of Gorges.

When the Long Parliament met, in 1641, the Puritans in England found enough occupation at home, and emigration greatly diminished. In 1643 Massachusetts became a member of the New England confederation, and her population was then about fifteen thousand; but nearly as many more had come over and were distributed among three new colonies —Rhode Island, Connecticut, and New Haven.

CHAPTER XIII

RELIGION AND GOVERNMENT IN MASSA-CHUSETTS

(1631–1638)

THE history of the beginnings of the Massachusetts colony shows that there was no real unity in church matters among the first emigrants. The majority were strongly tinctured with Puritanism, but nonconformity took on many shades of opinion. When it came to adopting a form of religion for Massachusetts, the question was decided by the ministers and the handful who then enjoyed the controlling power in the colony, and not by the majority of inhabitants. It was in this way that the Congregational church, and not the Presbyterian church, or a simplified form of the Anglican church, obtained its first hold upon the colony.

The adoption of the law of 1631 making membership in the Congregational church the condition of citizenship, and the arrival at a later day of so many talented ministers embittered by persecution against the Anglican church, strengthened the connection and made it permanent. "God's word" was the law of the state, and the interpretation of it was the natural function of the clergy. Thus, through church influence, the limitations on thought and religious practice became more stringent than in the mother-country, where the suffrage took in all freeholders, whether they were adherents of the established church or not.

In Massachusetts even Puritans who declined to acknowledge the form of church government pre-scribed by the self - established ecclesiastical au-thority were practically aliens, compelled to bear the burdens of church and state, and without a chance of making themselves felt in the govern-ment. And yet, from their own point of view, the position of the Puritan rulers was totally illogical. While suffering from persecution in England, they had appealed to liberty of conscience; and when dominant in America the denouncers of persecu-tion turned persecutors.

A spirit of resistance on the part of many was the natural consequence of a position so full of contra-diction. Instances of contumacy happened with such frequency and determination as should have given warning to those in control. In November, 1631, Richard Brown, an elder in the Watertown church, was reported to hold that "the Romish church was a Christian church." Forthwith the court of assistants notified the Watertown congregation that such views could not be allowed, and Winthrop, who went in person with the deputy governor, Dudley, used such summary arguments that Richard Brown, though "a man of violent spirit," thought it prudent to hold his tongue thereafter. In November, 1634, John Eliot, known afterwards so well for his noble work among the Indians, in a sermon censured the court for proceeding too arbitrarily towards the Pequots. He, too, thought better of his words when a solemn embassy of ministers presented the matter in a more orthodox light.

In March, 1635, Captain Israel Stoughton, one of the deputies from Dorchester to the general court, incurred the resentment of the authorities. This "troubler of Israel," as Governor Winthrop termed him, wrote a pamphlet denying the right of the governor and assistants to call themselves "Scriptural Magistrates." Being questioned by the court, the captain made haste, according to the record, to desire that "the said book might be burned as being weak and oppressive." Still unsatisfied, the court ordered that for his said offence he should for three years be disabled from bearing any office in the colony.[1]

The first great check which this religious despotism received proceeded from Roger Williams, who arrived in February, 1631, in the *Lyon*, which brought supplies to the famishing colonists of Massachusetts. He was the son of a merchant in London and a graduate of Pembroke College, Cambridge, where he

[1] Winthrop, *New England*, I., 70, 81, 113, 179, 185; *Cal. of State Pap., Col.*, 1574–1660, p. 180.

took the degree of master of arts in 1627. In his mere religious creed Williams was harsher than even the orthodox ministers of Massachusetts. Soon after his arrival he was invited to become one of the ministers of the Boston church, but refused because that church declined to make a public declaration of their repentance for holding communion in the churches of England while they lived in the home country.

He was then invited to Salem, where he made himself very popular by his talents and eloquence. Nevertheless, within two months he advanced other "scrupulosities," denying the validity of land-titles proceeding from the Massachusetts government, and the right of the magistrates to impose penalties as to Sabbath-breaking or breaches of the laws of the first table. Winthrop and his assistants complained to the Salem church, and this interference prevented his intended ordination at Salem.[1]

Williams presently removed to Plymouth, where his peculiar views were indulged, and where he improved his time in learning the Indian language and cultivating the acquaintance of the chief sachems of the neighboring Indian tribes. When, two years later, in 1633, Williams returned to live at Salem for the purpose of assisting the minister, Mr. Skelton, who was sick, the rulers of the church at Plymouth granted him a dismissal, but accompanied it

[1] Winthrop, *New England*, I., 49, 63.

with some words of warning about his "unsettled judgment and inconsistency."[1]

Williams was soon in trouble in Massachusetts. While at Plymouth his interest in the Indians led him to prepare for the private reading of Bradford a pamphlet which argued that the king of England had no right to give away the lands of the Indians in America. The pamphlet had never been published, but reports of its contents reached Boston, and the court of assistants, following, as usual, the advice of the ministers, pounced upon the author and summoned him to answer for what it was claimed was a denial of their charter rights.

When Williams appeared for this purpose, in January, 1634, the objections of the court shifted to some vague phrases in the document which they construed to reflect upon the king. These expressions were readily explained by Williams, and he was promptly forgiven by the court on his professing loyalty and taking the usual oath of allegiance to his majesty.[2] Perhaps this singular behavior on the part of the court is explained by the apprehension generally felt that Ferdinando Gorges, in England, would succeed in his attempt to vacate the charter of Massachusetts. If the charter had been successfully called in, Williams's ground of the suffi-

---

[1] Bradford, *Plimoth Plantation*, 370; Hubbard, *New England* (Mass. Hist. Soc., *Collections*, 2d series, V.), 203.
[2] Winthrop, *New England*, I., 145, 147.

ciency of the Indian title to lands might have proved useful as a last resort.[1]

Nevertheless, in November, 1634, the authorities were on his track again. The pretext now was that Williams "taught publicly against the king's patent," and that "he termed the churches of England antichristian." This revamping of an old charge which had been explained and dropped was probably due to a change of attitude towards the English government. In May, 1634, the general court elected the intolerant deputy governor, Thomas Dudley, governor in the place of Winthrop; and when in July the news of the demand of the Lords Commissioners for Foreign Plantations for the surrender of the colony charter was received at Boston, the new governor took steps, as we have seen, to commit the colony to a fight rather than yield compliance.[2]

Nothing, however, resulted from the charges against Williams, and it was not until March, 1635, that he again excited the wrath of the government. Then his scruples took the shape of objections to the recent legislation requiring every resident to swear to defend the provincial charter. Williams declared that the state had no right to demand an oath of an "unregenerate man," for that "we thereby had communion with a wicked man in the worship of God and caused him to take the name of God in vain."

---

[1] Eggleston, *Beginners of a Nation*, 282.
[2] Winthrop, *New England*, I., 163, 166, 180.

Williams was, accordingly, summoned to Boston in April, and subjected to confutation by the ministers, but positive action was deferred. While the matter remained thus undetermined, the church at Salem elected him teacher, and this action was construed as a contempt on the part of both Williams and the Salem church. Accordingly, when the general court met in July, 1635, Haynes now being governor, it entered an order giving them till next court to make satisfaction for their conduct. At the same court a petition of the Salem church for some land in Marblehead Neck was rejected "because they had chosen Mr. Williams their teacher."

Affairs had now drawn to a crisis. The Salem church wrote a letter to all the other churches protesting against their treatment, and Williams notified his own church that he would not commune with them unless they declined to commune with the other churches of the colony.

When the general court met in September, Salem was punished with the loss of representation, and thereupon gave way and submitted. Not so Williams. In October, 1635, he was again "convented," and on his refusing, in the presence of all the ministers of the colony, to renounce his opinions, he was banished from Massachusetts. The time given him to depart was only six weeks, and though some of the laymen in the church opposed the decree, every clerical member save one approved it.

Liberty to remain till spring was afterwards granted Williams, but he was admonished not to go about
to draw others to his opinions. As Williams was
one of those contentious people who must talk, this
inhibition was futile. It is true that he no longer
preached in his church, as the congregation had
submitted to the will of those in power. But he
conversed in private with some of his friends, and
arranged a plan of establishing a new settlement on
the shores of Narragansett Bay.

When information of this design reached Boston
in January, 1636, the authorities, on the plea that
an heretical settlement in the neighborhood might
affect the peace of the colony, determined to get rid
of Williams altogether by shipping him to England.
An order was sent to him to come to Boston, which
he declined to obey on account of ill-health. Captain Underhill was then sent to take him by force,
but before the doughty captain could arrive, Williams, getting intelligence of his purpose, sick as he
was, left his wife and two infant children and hur-
ried away, and no one at Salem would give Underhill any information.[1]

Thirty-five years later Williams wrote, "I was
sorely tossed for one fourteen weeks, in a bitter
winter season, not knowing what bed or bread did
mean." In this extremity he experienced the
benefits of the friendly relations which he had cultivated with the Indians at Plymouth, for the Po-

[1] Winthrop, *New England*, I., 188, 193, 198, 204, 209, 210.

kanokets received him kindly and gave him some land on the Seekonk River.

The long arm of the Massachusetts authorities reached out for him even here. He was soon advised by his friend, Governor Winslow, of Plymouth, that as his plantation was within the limits of the Plymouth colony he had better remove to the other side of the river, as his government was "loath to displease the Bay." So Williams, with five of his friends, who now joined him, embarked in his canoe and established his settlement in June, 1636, at Providence, where he was joined by many members of the church of Salem.[1] This was the beginning of Rhode Island, or, rather, of one of the beginnings of their complex colony.

The religion of the ruling class in Massachusetts, though bitterly hostile to the ritual of the English church, was a matter of strict regulation — there were rules regarding fast days, Sabbath attendance, prayer-meetings, apparel, and speech. The wrath of God and eternal punishment formed the substance of every sermon. In the church at Boston this rigid system found a standard exponent in the pastor, John Wilson; but the "teacher," John Cotton, a man of far greater ability, sometimes preached sermons in which he dwelt upon the divine mercy and love. The result was that the people crowded to hear him, and more persons were converted and added to the church in Boston in the earlier months

[1] Mass. Hist. Soc., *Collections*, 1st series, I., 276.

of Cotton's residence than in all the other churches in the colony.[1]

Among the members of Cotton's church was Mrs. Anne Hutchinson, who knew Cotton in England and had crossed the sea to hear his teachings. After her arrival, in June, 1636, she made herself very popular by her ministrations "in time of child-birth and other occasions of bodily infirmities." Soon she ventured to hold open meetings for women, at which the sermons of the ministers furnished the subject of comment. From a mere critic of the opinions of others Mrs. Hutchinson gradually presumed to act the part of teacher herself, and her views on the questions of "a covenant of works" and "a covenant of grace" attracted much attention.[2] The former of these terms had been used by Protestants to designate the condition of the Catholic church, which imposed as the condition of salvation penances, confessions, pilgrimages, legacies to the church, etc.; while the latter expression described the condition of all true Protestant Christians who found peace in the consciousness of holiness of spirit and faith in Jesus Christ.

Mrs. Hutchinson gave an emotional rendering to the "covenant of grace," and held that the divine spirit dwelt in every true believer and no demeanor in life could evidence its existence. To the Massachusetts ministers this doctrine seemed like a claim

[1] Wintnrop, *New England*, I., 144.
[2] Adams, *Three Episodes of Mass. Hist.*, I., 339.

to inspiration, and struck at the whole discipline of the church.   But what disturbed them more than anything else was the report that she had singled out two of the whole order, John Cotton and her brother-in-law John Wheelwright, to praise as walking in "the covenant of grace." [1]

The quarrel began first in the bosom of the Boston church.   Wilson, the pastor, resented Mrs. Hutchinson's preference of Mr. Cotton, the teacher, and began to denounce Mrs. Hutchinson's opinions. The congregation divided into two factions; on the one side was the pastor, supported by John Winthrop and a few others, and on the other were Mrs. Hutchinson, young Harry Vane, then governor, and the large majority of the members.   Mr. Cotton was not identified with either side, but sympathized with the latter.   Matters verged to a crisis when the Hutchinsonians announced their intention of electing Mr. Wheelwright, who had not long since arrived, as a second teacher in the church.

The election was to take place on Sunday, October 30, 1636; but October 25 the general court met and the ministers from other parts of the colony came to Boston and held a conference at which Cotton, Wheelwright, and Wilson were present, and there was a general discussion of all points in controversy. They agreed that "sanctification" (*i.e.*, a holy deportment) did help to evidence "justification"

---

[1] Winthrop, *New England*, I., 239; Hutchinson, *Massachusetts Bay*, I., 435.

(salvation); but there was more or less difference on the question of the "indwelling of the Holy Ghost." Mr. Wheelwright argued in its favor, but held that the indwelling referred to did not amount to "a personal union with God," as Mrs. Hutchinson and Governor Vane contended.

The conference instead of quieting aggravated the difficulty. Five days later, when Mr. Wheelwright's name was voted upon, Winthrop rose and hotly objected to him on the ground that he held unorthodox opinions respecting the indwelling of the Holy Ghost and was apt to raise "doubtful disputations." As a consequence the church would not elect Wheelwright in the face of an objection from so prominent a member as Winthrop. Next day Winthrop continued his attack, insisting that Wheelwright must necessarily believe in a "personal union."

At this juncture Governor Harry Vane unfortunately gave to the existing difficulties a political aspect. Vane was the son of one of the secretaries of state of England. Having taken a religious turn, he forsook all the honors and preferments of the court and obtained the consent of his parents to visit Massachusetts. Almost immediately after his arrival, he was elected, in May, 1636, when only twenty-four years of age, governor of the colony, with John Winthrop as deputy governor. After the quarrel in regard to the election of Wheelwright, Vane, who had become tired of the distractions in

the colony, convened the general court, December
10, 1636, to tender his resignation upon the half-
reason that his private affairs required his presence
in England.

Next day one of the assistants very feelingly re-
gretted the coming loss, especially in view of threatened attacks from the French and Indians. The
remarks took Vane off his guard. Carried away by
his feelings, he burst into tears and protested that,
though his outward estate was really in peril, yet he
would not have thought of deserting them at this
crisis had he not felt the inevitable danger of God's
judgments upon them for their dissensions. Thereupon the court, of which a majority were his opponents, declined to allow his departure on the grounds
assigned. Vane saw his mistake and reverted to his
private estate. The court then consented to his
departure, and a court of elections was called for
December 15 to supply the vacancy caused by his
resignation.

Before this time arrived the religious drama took
a new turn. The friends of Mrs. Hutchinson knew
the value of having the head of the government with
them, and would not dismiss Vane from the church,
whereupon he withdrew his resignation altogether.
Till the next election in May the colony was more
divided than ever. Mr. Wheelwright was appointed
to take charge of a church at Mount Wollaston, but
his forced withdrawal from Boston was a source of
irritation to his numerous friends. Mrs. Hutchin-

son remained and was the storm-centre, while Vane,
who now sought a re-election, was freely accused of
subterfuge and deception.

A day or two after December 15 the ministers
and the court held a meeting at which very hot words
passed between Governor Vane and Rev. Hugh Peter.
Wilson, the pastor of Boston, also indulged in caustic
criticisms directed at Governor Vane and the other
friends of Mrs. Hutchinson. By this speech Wilson
gave great offence to his congregation, who would
have laid a formal church censure upon him had not
Cotton interfered and in lieu of it gave his fellow-
preacher a good scolding, under the guise of what
Winthrop calls "a grave exhortation."

The clergy were very anxious to win over Mr.
Cotton, and about a week later held a meeting at
Boston and solemnly catechised Cotton on many abstruse points. The storm of theological rancor was
at its height. Harsh words were hurled about, and
by some orthodox ministers Mrs. Hutchinson and her
friends were denounced as Familists, Antinomians,
etc., after certain early sects who cherished the doctrines of private inspiration and had committed
many strange offences. On the other hand, some
of Mrs. Hutchinson's friends scornfully referred to
the orthodox party as legalists and antichrists,
"who walked in a covenant of works."

Harsh words are only one step removed from
harsh measures. The legalists were in a majority
in the general court, and they resolved to retaliate

for the treatment Mr. Wilson had received at the hands of his congregation.[1] At the general court which convened March 9, 1637, Wilson's sermon was approved and Wheelwright was summoned to answer for alleged "seditious and treasonable words" that were used by him in a sermon preached in Boston on a recent fast day. This action brought forth a petition from the church of Boston in Wheelwright's behalf, which the court declared "presumptious" and rejected. Wheelwright himself was pronounced guilty, and thereupon a protest was offered by Vane, and a second petition came from Boston, which, like the first, went unheeded, and only served at a later day to involve those who signed it.

Amid great excitement the legalists carried a resolution to hold the May election at Newtown (Cambridge) instead of Boston, a partisan move, for Newtown was more subject to their influence than Boston. At this court in May the turbulence was so great that the parties came near to blows. Threats resounded on all sides, and Wilson was so carried away with excitement that he climbed a tree to harangue the multitude. The Vane forces struggled hard, but were badly defeated, and Winthrop was restored to his former office as governor, while the stern Thomas Dudley was made deputy governor. Vane and his assistants, Coddington and

[1] Winthrop, *New England*, I., 240-255; *Mass. Col. Records*, I., 185.

Dummer, were defeated and "quite left out," even from the magistracy.[1]

Secure in the possession of power, the legalists now proceeded to suppress the opposing party altogether. An order was passed commanding that no one should harbor any new arrival for more than three weeks without leave of the magistrates. This was to prevent any dangerous irruption of sympathizers with Mrs. Hutchinson from England, and it was applied against a brother of Mrs. Hutchinson and some others of her friends who arrived not long after.

August 3, 1637, Vane sailed for England, and thenceforward the Hutchinson faction, abandoned by their great leader, made little resistance. In the latter part of the same month (August 30) a great synod of the ministers was held at Newtown, which was the first thing of the sort attempted in America, and included all the teaching elders of the colony and some new-comers from England. This body set to work to lay hold of the heresies which infected the atmosphere of the colony, and formulated about "eighty opinions," some "blasphemous," but others merely "erroneous and unsafe." How many of them were really entertained by Mrs. Hutchinson's followers and how many were merely inferences drawn from their teachings by their opponents it is hard to say.

When these heresies were all enumerated and

[1] Winthrop, *New England*, I., 256–263.

compared with the opinions of Cotton and Wheelwright, only five points of possible heterodoxy on
their part appeared. Over these there was a solemn
wrangle for days, till Cotton, shrinking from his
position, contrived, through abundant use of doubt-
full expressions, to effect his reconciliation with the
dominant party. After a session of twenty-four
days the synod adjourned, and Wheelwright, alone
of the ministers, was left as the scapegoat of the
Antinomians, and with him the majority determined
to make short work.[1]

At the general court which met November 2,
1637, the transgressions of Wheelwright through his
fast-day sermon were made the basis of operations.
For this offence Wheelwright had been judged guilty
more than nine months before, but sentence had
been deferred; he was now sentenced to disfranchise-
ment and banishment. Many of his friends at
Boston, including William Aspinwall and John Coggeshall, delegates to the general court, experienced
similar treatment for signing the petition presented
to the court in March, 1637, after the verdict against
Wheelwright.[2]

An order was passed for disarming Mrs. Hutchinson's followers, and finally the arch-heretic herself
was sent for and her examination lasted two days.
In the dialogue with Winthrop which began the proceedings, Mrs. Hutchinson had decidedly the best
of the controversy; and Winthrop himself confesses

[1] Winthrop, *New England*, I., 261–288.   [2] *Ibid.*, 291–296.

that "she knew when to speak and when to hold her tongue." The evidence failed wretchedly upon the main charge, which was that Mrs. Hutchinson alleged that all the ministers in Massachusetts except Mr. Cotton preached "a covenant of works." On the contrary, by her own evidence and that of Mr. Cotton and Mr. Leverett, it appeared that Mrs. Hutchinson had said that "they did not preach a covenant of grace as clearly as Mr. Cotton did," which was probably very true.[1]

Her condemnation was a matter of course, and at the end of two days the court banished her from the colony; but as it was winter she was committed to the temporary care of Mr. Joseph Welde, of Roxbury, brother of the Rev. Thomas Welde, who afterwards wrote a rancorous account of these difficulties, entitled *A Short Story*. While in his house, Mrs. Hutchinson was subjected to many exhortations by anxious elders, till her spirits sank under the trial and she made a retraction. Nevertheless, it was not as full as her tormentors desired, and the added penalty of dismissal from church was imposed. After her excommunication her spirits revived, "and she gloried in her condemnation and declared that it was the greatest happiness next to Christ that ever befell her."

In this affair Winthrop acted as prosecutor and judge. Before the spring had well set in he sent word to Mrs. Hutchinson to depart from the colony.

---

[1] Hutchinson, *Massachusetts Bay*, II., 423–447.

Accordingly, March 28, 1638, she went by water to her farm at Mount Wollaston (now Quincy), intending to join Mr. Wheelwright, who had gone to Piscataqua, in Maine, but she changed her mind and went by land to the settlement of Roger Williams at Providence, and thence to the island of Aquidneck, where she joined her husband and other friends.[1]

Such was the so-called Antinomian controversy in Massachusetts, and its ending had a far-reaching effect upon the fortunes of the colony. The suppression of Mrs. Hutchinson and her friends produced what Winthrop and the rest evidently desired —peace—a long peace. For fifty years the commonwealth was free from any great religious agitations; but this condition of quietude, being purchased at the price of free speech and free conscience, discouraged all literature except of a theological stamp, and confirmed the aristocratic character of the government. As one of its mouth-pieces, Rev. Samuel Stone, remarked, New England Congregationalism continued till the close of the century "a speaking aristocracy in the face of a silent democracy."[2] The intense practical character of the people saved the colony, which, despite the theocratic government, maintained a vigorous life in politics, business, and domestic economy.

[1] Winthrop, *New England*, I., 296–312.
[2] Adams, *Massachusetts: Its Historians and its History*, 57.

CHAPTER XIV

NARRAGANSETT AND CONNECTICUT SETTLE-
MENTS

(1635–1637)

THE island of Aquidneck, to which Mrs. Hutchinson retired, was secured from Canonicus and Miantonomoh, the sachems of the Narragansetts, through the good offices of Roger Williams, by John Clarke, William Coddington, and other leaders of her faction, a short time preceding her banishment, after a winter spent in Maine, where the climate proved too cold for them.[1] The place of settlement was at the northeastern corner of the island, and was known first by its Indian name of Pocasset and afterwards as Portsmouth. The first settlers, nineteen in number, constituted themselves a body politic and elected William Coddington as executive magistrate, with the title of chief judge, and William Aspinwall as secretary.[2] Other emigrants swelled the number, till in 1639 a new settlement at the southern part of the island, called Newport, resulted through the secession of a part of the settlers headed

[1] Clarke, *Ill Newes from New England* (Mass. Hist. Soc., *Collections*, 4th series, II., 1–113). [2] *R. I. Col. Records*, I., 52.

by Coddington. For more than a year the two settlements remained separate, but in March, 1640, they were formally united.[1] Settlers flocked to these parts, and in 1644 the Indian name of Aquidneck was changed to Rhode Island.[2]

Not less flourishing was Roger Williams's settlement of Providence on the main-land. In the summer of 1640 Patuxet was marked off as a separate township;[3] and in 1643 Samuel Gorton and others, fleeing from the wrath of Massachusetts, made a settlement called Shawomet, or Warwick, about twelve miles distant from Providence.

The tendency of these various towns was to combine in a commonwealth, but on account of their separate origin the process of union was slow. The source of most of their trouble in their infancy was the grasping policy of Massachusetts. Next to heretics in the bosom of the commonwealth heretic neighbors were especially abhorrent. When in 1640 the magistrates of Connecticut and New Haven addressed a joint letter to the general court of Massachusetts, and the citizens of Aquidneck ventured to join in it, Massachusetts arrogantly excluded the representation of Aquidneck from their reply as "men not fit to be capitulated withal by us either for themselves or for the people of the isle where

[1] R. I. Col. Records, I., 87, 100, 108.
[2] Ibid., 127. In 1614 the Dutch navigator Adrian Block gave to the country of Narragansett Bay the name of Rhode Island—the Red Island—because of the red clay in some portions of its shores.   [3] R. I. Col. Records, I., 27.

they inhabit."[1] And neither in 1644 nor in 1648 would Massachusetts listen to the appeal of the Rhode-Islanders to be admitted into the confederacy of the New England colonies.[2]

The desire of Massachusetts appeared to be to hold the heretics and their new country under a kind of personal and territorial vassalage, as was interestingly shown in the case of Mrs. Hutchinson and Samuel Gorton. Despite her banishment and excommunication the church at Boston seemed to consider it a duty to keep a paternal eye on Mrs. Hutchinson; and not long after her settlement at Portsmouth sent an embassy to interview her and obtain, if possible, a submission and profession of repentance.

The bearers of this message met with an apt reception and returned very much disconcerted. They found Mrs. Hutchinson, and declared that they came as messengers from the church of Boston, but she replied that she knew only the church of Christ and recognized no such church as "the church of Boston." Nevertheless, she continued to be annoyed with messages from Boston till, in order to be quiet and out of reach, she removed to a place very near Hell Gate in the Dutch settlement, and there, in 1643, she, with most of her family, perished in an Indian attack.[3]

[1] Winthrop, *New England*, II., 24; *Mass. Col. Records*, I., 305.
[2] *Plymouth Col. Records*, IX., 23, 110.
[3] Sparks, *American Biographies*, VI., 333, 352; Arnold, *Rhode Island*, I., 66, n.

The authority of Massachusetts over the banished was not confined to religious exhortations. Samuel Gorton, a great friend of Mrs. Hutchinson, was in many respects one of the most interesting characters in early New England history. This man had a most pertinacious regard for his private rights, and at Plymouth, Portsmouth, and Providence his career of trouble was very much the same. But he was not an ordinary law-breaker, and in Providence, in 1641, Gorton and his friends refused to submit to a distress ordained by the magistrates, for the reason that these magistrates, having no charter, had no better authority to make laws than any private person.[1]

The next year, 1642, thirteen citizens of Providence petitioned Boston for assistance and protection against him; and not long after, four of the petitioners submitted their persons and lands to the authority of Massachusetts.[2] Although to accept this submission was to step beyond their bounds under the Massachusetts charter, the authorities at Boston, in October, 1642, gave a formal notice of their intention to maintain the claim of the submissionists.[3] To this notice Gorton replied, November 20, 1642, in a letter full of abstruse theology and rancorous invective.

Nevertheless, he and his party left Patuxet and

---

[1] Sparks, *American Biographies*, V., 326–340.
[2] Winthrop, *New England*, II., 71.
[3] *Ibid.*, 102; *Mass. Col. Records*, II., 22.

removed to Shawomet, a tract beyond the limits of Providence, and purchased in January, 1643, from Miantonomoh, the great sachem of the Narragansetts.[1] Gorton's letter had secured for him the thorough hatred of the authorities in Massachusetts, and his removal by no means ended their interference. The right of Miantonomoh to make sale to Gorton was denied by two local sachems; and Massachusetts coming to their support, Gorton was formally summoned, in September, 1643, to appear before the court of Boston to answer the complaint of the sachems for trespass.[2] Gorton and his friends returned a contemptuous reply, and as he continued to deny the right of Massachusetts to interfere, the Boston government prepared to send an armed force against him.[3]

In the mean time, a terrible fate overtook the friend and ally of Gorton, Miantonomoh, at the hands of his neighbors in the west, the Mohegans, whose chief, Uncas, attacked one of Miantonomoh's subordinate chiefs; Miantonomoh accepted the war, was defeated, and captured by Uncas. Gorton interfered by letter to save his friend, and Uncas referred the question of Miantonomoh's fate to the federal commissioners at Boston. The elders were clamorous for the death penalty, but the commissioners admitting that "there was no sufficient ground for us

---

[1] *Simplicities Defence Against Seven-Headed Policy* (Force, *Tracts*, IV., No. vi.), 24.

[2] *Mass. Col. Records*, II., 40, 41.   [3] *Simplicities Defence.*

to put him to death," agreed to deliver the unhappy chieftain to Uncas, with permission to kill him as soon as he came within Uncas's jurisdiction. Accordingly, Miantonomoh was slaughtered by his enemy, who cut out a warm slice from his shoulder and declared it the sweetest morsel he had ever tasted and that it gave strength to his heart.[1] Thus fell Miantonomoh, the circumstances of whose death were "not at all creditable to the federal commissioners and their clerical advisers."[2]

Massachusetts sent out an armed force against the Gortonists, and after some resistance the leaders were captured and brought to Boston. Here Wilson and other ministers urged the death penalty upon the "blasphemous heretics." But the civil authorities were not prepared to go so far, and in October, 1643, adopted the alternative of imprisonment. In March, 1644, Gorton and his friends were liberated, but banished on pain of death from all places claimed to be within the jurisdiction of Massachusetts

They departed to Shawomet, but Governor Winthrop forbade them to stay there; and in April, 1644, Gorton and his friends once more sought refuge at Aquidneck.[3] Gorton, having contrived to reach England, returned in May, 1648, with an order

---

[1] Winthrop, *New England*, II., 157–162; *Acts of the Federal Commissioners*, I., 10–12.

[2] Fiske, *Beginnings of New England*, 171.

[3] *Simplicities Defence* (Force, *Tracts*, IV., No. vi.), 86; Winthrop, *New England*, II., 165, 188.

from the Parliamentary commissioners for plantations, directed to the authorities of Massachusetts, Plymouth, and Connecticut, to permit him and his friends to reside in peace at Warwick, which they were then permitted to do.[1] In 1652 Gorton became president of Providence and Warwick.[2]

In December, 1643, the agents of Massachusetts in England obtained from the Parliamentary commissioners for plantations a grant of all the mainland in Massachusetts Bay; and it appeared for the moment as if it were all over with the independence of the Rhode Island towns. Fortunately, Williams was in England at the time, and with indomitable energy he set to work to counteract the danger.

In less than three months he persuaded the same commissioners to issue, March 14, 1644, a second instrument[3] incorporating the towns of "Providence Plantations, in the Narragansett Bay in New England," and (in flat contradiction of the earlier grant to Massachusetts) giving them "the Tract of Land in the Continent of America called by the name of Narragansett Bay, bordering Northward and Northeast on the patent of the Massachusetts, East and Southeast on Plymouth Patent, South on the Ocean, and on the West and Northwest by the Indians called Nahigganeucks, alias Narregansets—

---

[1] Winthrop, *New England*, II., 387–390.
[2] *R. I. Col. Records*, I., 241.
[3] *Cal. of State Pap., Col.*, 1574–1660, p. 325.

the whole Tract extending about twenty-five English miles unto the Pequot River and Country."
The charter contained no mention of religion or
citizenship, though it gave the inhabitants full
power "to rule themselves and such others as shall
hereafter inhabit within any Part of the said Tract,
by such a Form of Civil Government, as by voluntary consent of all, or the greater Parte of them,
they shall find most suitable to their Estate and
Condition."

Williams returned to America in September,
1644. On account of the unfriendly disposition of
Massachusetts he was compelled, when leaving for
England, to take his departure from the Dutch port
of New Amsterdam. Now, like one vindicated in
name and character, he landed in Boston, and, protected by a letter[1] from "divers Lords and others
of the Parliament," passed unmolested through
Massachusetts, and reached Providence by the same
route which, as a homeless wanderer, he had pursued eight years before. It is said that at Seekonk
he was met by fourteen canoes filled with people,
who escorted him across the water to Providence
with shouts of triumph.[2]

Peace and union, however, did not at once flow
from the labors of Williams. The hostility of Massachusetts and Plymouth towards the Rhode-Islanders

---

[1] Winthrop, *New England*, II., 236.
[2] Richard Scott's letter, in Fox, *New England Fire Brand
Quenched*, App.

seemed at first increased; and the principle of self-government, to which the Rhode Island townships owed their existence, delayed their confederation. At last, in May, 1647, an assembly of freemen from the four towns of Portsmouth, Newport, Providence, and Warwick met at Portsmouth, and proceeded to make laws in the name of the whole body politic, incorporated under the charter. The first president was John Coggeshall; and Roger Williams and William Coddington were two of the first assistants.

Massachusetts, aided by the Plymouth colony, still continued her machinations, and an ally was found in Rhode Island itself in the person of William Coddington. In 1650 he went to England and obtained an order, dated April '3, 1651, for the severance of the island from the main-land settlements.[1] Fortunately, however, for the preservation of Rhode Island unity, an act of intemperate bigotry on the part of Massachusetts saved the state from Coddington's interference.

The sect called Anabaptists, or Baptists, opposed to infant baptism, made their appearance in New England soon after the banishment of Mrs. Hutchinson. Rhode Island became a stronghold for them, and in 1638 Roger Williams adopted their tenets and was rebaptized.[2] In 1644 a Baptist church was established at Newport.[3] The same year Massa-

---

[1] *Cal. of State Pap., Col.*, 1574–1660, p. 354.
[2] Winthrop, *New England*, I., 352.
[3] Palfrey, *New England*, II., 346.

chusetts passed a law decreeing banishment of
all professors of the new opinions.[1]   In October,
1650, three prominent Baptists, John Clarke, Oba-
diah Holmes, and John Crandall, visited Massachusetts, when they were seized, whipped, fined, imprisoned, and barely escaped with their lives.[2]

The alarm created in Rhode Island by these proceedings brought the towns once more into a common policy, and Clarke and Williams were sent to
England to undo the work of Coddington.   Aided
by the warm friendship of Sir Harry Vane, the efforts of the agents were crowned with success.   Coddington's commission was revoked by an order of
council in September, 1652, and the townships were
directed to unite under the charter of 1644.[3]   Coddington did not at once submit, and there was a
good deal of dissension in the Rhode Island towns
till June, 1654, when Williams returned from England.   Then Coddington yielded,[4] and, August 31,
commissioners from the four towns voted to restore the government constituted seven years before.   The consolidation of Rhode Island was perfected when, in 1658, Massachusetts released her
claims to jurisdiction there.[5]

Liberty of conscience as asserted by Roger Williams did not involve the abrogation of civil restraint,

---

[1] *Mass. Col. Records*, II., 85.
[2] Clarke, *Ill Newes from New England* (Mass. Hist. Soc., *Collections*, 4th series, II., 1–113).
[3] Backus, *New England*, I., 277.   [4] *R. I. Col. Records*, I., 328.
[5] *Mass. Col. Records*, IV., pt. i., 333.

and when one William Harris disturbed the peace in 1656, by asserting this doctrine in a pamphlet,[1] Williams, then governor, had a warrant issued for his apprehension. When, in 1658, Williams retired to private life the possibility of founding a state in which "religious freedom and civil order could stand together" was fully proved to the world.[2]

Besides the Indian power, as many as six independent jurisdictions existed originally in the present state of Connecticut. (1) The Dutch fort of "Good Hope," established in 1633, on the Connecticut River, had jurisdiction over a small area of country. (2) The Plymouth colony owned some territory on the Connecticut River and built a fort there soon after the Dutch came. (3) Next was the jurisdiction of Fort Saybrook, the sole evidence of possession on the part of the holders of a patent from the earl of Warwick, president of the Council for New England, who claimed to own the whole of Connecticut. (4) A much larger jurisdiction was that of the Connecticut River towns, settled in 1635–1636, contemporaneously with the banishment of Roger Williams. (5) New Haven was settled in 1638, in the height of the Antinomian difficulties. (6) A claim was advanced by the marquis of Hamilton for a tract of land running from the mouth of the Connecticut River to Narragansett Bay, as-

[1] R. I. Col. Records, I., 364.
[2] Doyle, English Colonies, II., 319.

signed to him in the division of 1635, but it did not become a disturbing factor till 1665.

The early relations between the Dutch and English colonies were, as we have seen, characterized by kindness and good-fellowship. The Dutch advised the Plymouth settlers to remove from their "present barren quarters," and commended to them the valley of the "Fresh River" (Connecticut), referring to it as a fine place both for plantation and trade.[1] Afterwards, some Mohegan Indians visiting Plymouth in 1631 made similar representations. Their chief, Uncas, an able, unscrupulous, and ambitious savage, made it his great ambition to attain the headship of his aggressive western neighbors, the Pequots. The only result had been to turn the resentment of the Pequots against himself; and he sought the protection of the Plymouth government by encouraging them to plant a settlement on the Connecticut in his own neighborhood.[2]

These persuasions had at length some effect, and in 1632 Edward Winslow, being sent in a bark to examine the river, reported the country as conforming in every respect to the account given of it by the Dutch and the Indians.[3] Meanwhile, the Indians, not liking the delay, visited Boston and tried to induce the authorities there to send out a colony, but, though Governor Winthrop received them politely,

[1] Bradford, *Plimoth Plantation*, 370, 371.
[2] Trumbull, *Connecticut*, I., 41.
[3] *Ibid.*, 31; Bradford, *Plimoth Plantation*, 371.

he dismissed them without the hoped-for assistance.[1]

In July, 1633, Bradford and Winslow made a special visit to Boston to discuss the plan of a joint trading-post, but they did not receive much encouragement. Winthrop and his council suggested various objections: the impediments to commerce due to the sand-bar at the mouth; the long continuance of ice in spring, and the multitude of Indians in the neighborhood. But it seems likely that these allegations were pretexts, since we read in Winthrop's *Journal* that in September, 1633, a bark was sent from Boston to Connecticut; and John Oldham, with three others, set out from Watertown overland to explore the river.[2]

Plymouth determined to wait no longer, and in October, 1633, sent a vessel, commanded by William Holmes, with workmen and the frame of a building for a trading-post. When they arrived in the river, they were surprised to find other Europeans in possession. The Dutch, aroused from their dream of security by the growth of the English settlement, made haste in the June previous to purchase from the Indians twenty acres where Hartford now stands, upon which they built a fort a short time after. When the vessel bearing the Plymouth traders reached this point in the river, the Dutch commander, John van Curler, commanded Holmes to stop and strike his flag. But Holmes, paying little

---

[1] Winthrop, *New England*, I., 62.   [2] *Ibid.*, 132, 162.

attention to the threats of the Dutchman, continued his voyage and established a rival post ten miles above, at a place now known as Windsor.[1]

Meanwhile, the ship which Winthrop sent to Connecticut went onward to New Netherland, where the captain notified Governor Van Twiller, in Winthrop's name, that the English had a royal grant to the territory about the Connecticut River. It returned to Boston in October, 1633, and brought a reply from Van Twiller that the Dutch had also a claim under a grant from their States-General of Holland.[2]   In December, 1633, Van Twiller heard of Holmes's trading-post and despatched an armed force of seventy men to expel the intruders. They appeared before the fort with colors flying, but finding that Holmes had received reinforcements, and that it would be impossible to dislodge him without bloodshed, they returned home without molesting him.[3]

The Plymouth settlers were destined to be dispossessed, not by the Dutch, but by their own countrymen. The people of Massachusetts were now fully aroused, and the news that came to Boston in the summer of 1634 that the small-pox had practically destroyed the Indians on the river increased "the hankering" after the coveted territory.[4] The people of Watertown, Dorchester, and Newtown

[1] Bradford, *Plimoth Plantation*, 373; Brodhead, *New York*, I., 241.   [2] Winthrop, *New England*, I., 133.
[3] Bradford, *Plimoth Plantation*, 373; Brodhead, *New York*, I., 242.   [4] Bradford, *Plimoth Plantation*, 388, 402.

(Cambridge) had long been restless under the Massachusetts authority, and were anxious for a change. Dorchester was the residence of Captain Israel Stoughton, and Watertown the residence of Richard Brown and John Oldham, all three of whom had been under the ban of the orthodox Puritan church. At Watertown also had sprung up the first decided opposition to the aristocratic claim of the court of assistants to lay taxes on the people. As for Newtown (now Cambridge), its inhabitants could not forget that, though selected in the first instance as the capital of the colony, it had afterwards been discarded for the town of Boston.

In all three towns there was a pressure for arable lands and more or less jealousy among the ministers. Some dissatisfaction also with the requirement in Massachusetts of church-membership for the suffrage may have been among the motives for seeking a new home. At the head of the movement was the Rev. Thomas Hooker, a graduate of Emmanuel College, Cambridge, who had lived in Holland, and while there had imbibed a greater share of liberality than was to be found among most of the clergy of Massachusetts. Cotton declared that democracy was "no fit government either for church or commonwealth," and the majority of the ministers agreed with him. Winthrop defended his view in a letter to Hooker on the ground that "the best part is always the least, and of that best part the wiser part is always the lesser." But Hooker replied that "in

matters which concern the common good a general
council, chosen by all, to transact business which
concerns all, I conceive most suitable to rule and
most safe for the relief of the whole."

Hooker arrived in the colony in September,
1633,[1] and in May, 1634, at the first annual general court after his arrival, his congregation at Newtown petitioned to be permitted to move to some
other quarters within the bounds of Massachusetts.[2]
The application was granted, and messengers were
sent to Agawam and Merrimac to look for a suitable
location.[3]   After this, when the epidemic on the
Connecticut became known, a petition to be permitted to move out of the Massachusetts jurisdiction was presented to the general court in September, 1634.   This raised a serious debate, and though
there can be little doubt that Winthrop and the
other leaders in Massachusetts shrewdly cherished
the idea of pre-empting in some way the trade of
the Connecticut, against both the Plymouth people
and the Dutch, an emigration such as was proposed
appeared too much like a desertion.   The fear of
the appointment by the crown of a governor-general
for New England was at its height, and so the application, though it met with favor from the majority of the deputies, was rejected by the court of
assistants.[4]

[1] Winthrop, *New England*, I., 129.
[2] *Mass. Col. Records*, I., 119.
[3] Winthrop, *New England*, I., 159.   [4] *Ibid.*, 167.

The popularity of the measure, however, increased mightily, and there is a tradition that in the winter of 1634–1635 some persons from Watertown went to Connecticut and managed to survive the winter in a few huts erected at Pyquag, afterwards Wethersfield.[1] The next spring the Watertown and Dorchester people imitated the Newtown congregation in applying to the general court for permission to remove. They were more successful, and were given liberty to go to any place, even outside of Massachusetts, provided they continued under the Massachusetts authority.[2]

Then began a lively movement, and Jonathan Brewster, in a letter written from the Plymouth fort at Windsor in July, 1635, tells of the daily arrival by land and water of small parties of these adventurous settlers. Their presence around the fort caused Brewster much uneasiness, since some began to cast covetous eyes upon the very spot which the Plymouth government had bought from the Mohegans and held against the Dutch.

As their numbers grew their confidence increased; and finally the men of Dorchester, headed by Roger Ludlow, one of the richest men in Massachusetts, pretending that the land was theirs as the "Lord's waste," upon which "the providence of God" had cast them, intruded themselves into the actual midst of the Plymouth people. The emigrants from

[1] Trumbull, *Connecticut*, I., 59.
[2] *Mass. Col. Records*, I., 146.

Plymouth protested, but were finally glad to accept a compromise, though, as Bradford remarks, "the unkindness was not soon forgotten." The Massachusetts settlers held on to fifteen-sixteenths of the land, while they magnanimously conceded to the Plymouth people one-sixteenth, in addition to their block-houses.[1]

The emigration in the summer of 1635 was preliminary to a much larger exodus in the fall. In October a company of about sixty men, women, and children, driving before them their cows, horses, and swine, set out by land and reached the Connecticut "after a tedious and difficult journey";[2] but the winter set in very early, and the vessels which were to bring their provisions by water not appearing, they were forced to leave their settlement for fear of famine. They were fortunate to find a ship frozen up in the river, which they freed from the ice and used to return to Boston. The other settlers who remained upon the river suffered very much, and were finally reduced to the necessity of eating acorns and ground-nuts, which they dug out of the snow. A great number of the cattle perished, and the Dorchester Company "lost near £2000 worth."[3]

These calamities were soon forgotten; and as soon as the first flowers of spring suggested the end of the dreary winter season, the Newtown people prepared

---

[1] Bradford, *Plimoth Plantation*, 402–406.
[2] Winthrop, *New England*, I., 204.   [3] *Ibid.*, 208, 219.

to move. Selling their lands on the Charles River to the congregation of Rev. Thomas Shepard, the whole body, in June, 1636, emigrated through the green woods, musical with birds and bright with flowers, under the leadership of their two eminent ministers, Thomas Hooker and Samuel Stone.[1] Among the lay members of the community were Stephen Hart, Thomas Bull, and Richard Lord.[2] A little later the churches of Dorchester and Watertown completed their removal, while a settlement was made by emigrants from Roxbury under William Pynchon at Agawam, afterwards Springfield, just north of the boundary between Massachusetts and Connecticut.[3]

At the beginning of the winter of 1636–1637 about eight hundred people were established in three townships below Springfield. These townships were first called after the towns from which their inhabitants removed — Newtown, Watertown, and Dorchester; but in February, 1637, their names were changed to Hartford, Wethersfield, and Windsor. The settlements well illustrate the general type of New England colonization. The emigration from Massachusetts was not of individuals, but of organized communities united in allegiance to a church and its pastor. Carrying provisions and supplies, erecting new villages, as communities they came from Eng-

---

[1] Winthrop, *New England*, I., 223.
[2] Trumbull, *Memorial History of Hartford County*,
[3] Palfrey, *New England*, I., 454.

land to Massachusetts, and in that character the people emigrated to Connecticut.

In the mean time, the silence of the Connecticut woods was broken by other visitors. The lands occupied by the Massachusetts settlers upon the Connecticut lay within a grant executed March 19, 1631, by the earl of Warwick, as president of the Council for New England for "all that part of New England in America which lies and extends itself from a river there called Narragansett River, the space of forty leagues upon a straight line near the seashore towards the southwest, west, and by south, or west, as the coast lieth towards Virginia, accounting three English miles to the league; and also all and singular the lands and hereditaments whatsoever, lying and being within the lands aforesaid, north and south in latitude and breadth, and in length and longitude of and within, all the breadth aforesaid, throughout the main-lands there, from the western ocean to the south sea." The grantees included Lord Say and Sele, Lord Brooke, and Sir Richard Saltonstall.[1]

Probably some report of the unauthorized colonies reached them and hastened Saltonstall to send out a party of twenty men in July, 1635, to plant a settlement on the Connecticut. But the Dorchester settlers treated them with even less consideration than they had the Plymouth men. They set upon them and drove them out of the river.[2] Then, in

[1] Trumbull, *Connecticut*, I., 495.
[2] Mass. Hist. Soc., *Collections*, 4th series, VI., 579.

October, 1635, John Winthrop, Jr., the eldest son of John Winthrop of Massachusetts, came from England with a commission to be governor of the "river Connecticut in New England" for the space of one year.[1]

He was, however, a governor in theory, and made but one substantial contribution to the permanent possession of Connecticut by the English. In November, 1635, he erected at the mouth of the river a fort called after Lord Say and Sele and Lord Brooke—Saybrook—which in the spring of 1636 he placed under the command of Lyon Gardiner, an expert military engineer, who had seen much service in the Netherlands.[2] Hardly had the English mounted two cannon on their slight fortification when a Dutch vessel sent from New Amsterdam on a sudden errand arrived in the river. Finding themselves anticipated, the Dutch returned home, and the scheme of cutting off the English settlements on the upper Connecticut from the rest of New England was frustrated.[3]

For a year the towns on the Connecticut, including Springfield, were governed by a commission issued by the general court of Massachusetts, in concert with John Winthrop, Jr., as a representative of the patentees.[4] When the year expired the

---

[1] Trumbull, *Connecticut*, I., 497.
[2] Winthrop, *New England*, I., 207.
[3] Brodhead, *New York*, I., 260.
[4] *Mass. Col. Records*, I., 170.

commission was not renewed, but a general court representing the three towns of Massachusetts and consisting of six assistants and nine delegates, three for each town, was held at Hartford in May, 1637. They became from this time a self-governing community under the name of Connecticut, and the union happened just in time to be of much service in repelling a great danger.

CHAPTER XV

FOUNDING OF CONNECTICUT AND NEW HAVEN
(1637–1652)

THE establishment of the new settlements on the Connecticut projected the whites into the immediate neighborhood of two powerful and war-like Indian nations—the Narragansetts in Rhode Island and the Pequots in Connecticut. With the first named there existed friendly relations, due to the politic conduct of Roger Williams, who always treated the Indians kindly. With the latter, conditions from the first were very threatening.

As early as the summer of 1633, Stone, a reckless ship-captain from Virginia, and eight of his companions, were slain in the Connecticut River by some Pequots. When called to account by Governor Winthrop of Massachusetts, the Indians justified themselves on the ground that Stone was the aggressor. Thereupon Winthrop desisted, and referred the matter to the Virginia authorities.[1] In 1634, when the settlements were forming on the Connecticut, a fresh irritation was caused by the course of the emigrants in negotiating for their

[1] Winthrop, *New England*, I., 146.

lands with the Mohegan chiefs instead of with the Pequots, the lords paramount of the soil.

The Pequots were greatly embarrassed at the time by threatened hostilities with the Narragansetts and the Dutch, and in November, 1634, they became reduced to the necessity of seeking the alliance of the Massachusetts colony. That authority inopportunely revived the question of Stone's death and required the Pequots to deliver annually a heavy tribute of wampum as the price of their forgiveness and protection.[1]   Had the object of the Massachusetts people been to promote bad feeling, no better method than this could have been adopted.

In July, 1636, John Oldham, who had been appointed collector of the tribute from the Pequots, was killed off Block Island by some of the Indians of the island who were subject to the Narragansett tribe.[2]   Although the Pequots had nothing whatever to do with this affair, the Massachusetts government, under Harry Vane, sent a force against them, commanded by John Endicott. After stopping at Block Island and destroying some Indian houses, he proceeded to the main-land to make war on the Pequots, but beyond burning some wigwams and seizing some corn he accomplished very little.

The action of Massachusetts was heartily con-

---

[1] Winthrop, *New England*, I., 176, 177.
[2] *Ibid.*, 225, 226; Gardiner, *Pequot Warres* (Mass. Hist. Soc., *Collections*, 3d series, III.), 131–160.

demned by the Plymouth colony and the settlers on
the Connecticut, and Gardiner, the commander of
the Saybrook fort, bluntly told Endicott that the
proceedings were outrageous and would serve only
to bring the Indians "like wasps about his ears."
His prediction came true, and during the winter
Gardiner and his few men at the mouth of the river
were repeatedly assailed by parties of Indians, who
boasted that "Englishmen were as easy to kill as
mosquitoes." [1]

Danger was now imminent, especially to the infant settlements up the river. For the moment it
seemed as if the English had brought upon themselves the united power of all the Indians of the
country. The Pequots sent messengers to patch
up peace with their enemies, the Narragansetts, and
tried to induce them to take up arms against the
English. They would have probably succeeded
but for the influence of Roger Williams with the
Narragansett chiefs. In this crisis the friendship of
Governor Vane for the banished champion of religious liberty was used to good effect. To gratify
the governor and his council at Boston, Williams,
at the risk of his life, sought the wigwams of Canonicus and Miantonomoh, and "broke to pieces the
Pequot negotiations and design." [2] Instead of accepting the overtures of the Pequots, the Narra-

---

[1] Gardiner, *Pequot Warrès;* Winthrop, *New England,* I., 231–
233, 238, 259.
[2] Mass. Hist. Soc., *Collections,* 1st series, I., 175.

gansetts sent Miantonomoh and the two sons of
Canonicus to Boston to make an alliance with the
whites.[1]

In the spring of 1637 the war burst with fury.
Wethersfield was first attacked at the instance of an
Indian who had sold his lands and could not obtain
the promised payment. In revenge he secretly instigated the Pequots to attack the place, and they
killed a woman, a child, and some men, besides some
cattle; and took captive two young women, who
were preserved by the squaw of Mononotto, a Pequot
sachem, and, through the Dutch, finally restored to
their friends.[2]

By May, 1637, when the first general court of
Connecticut convened at Hartford, upward of
thirty persons had fallen beneath the tomahawk.
The promptest measures were necessary; and without waiting for the assistance of Massachusetts, whose
indiscretion had brought on the war, ninety men
(nearly half the effective force of the colony) were
raised,[3] and placed under the command of Captain
John Mason, an officer who had served in the Netherlands under Sir Thomas Fairfax. The force sailed
down the river in three small vessels, and were wel-
comed at Fort Saybrook by Lieutenant Gardiner.

The Indian fort was situated in a swamp to the
east of the Connecticut on the Mystic River; but in-

---

[1] Winthrop, *New England*, I., 234–236.
[2] *Ibid.*, 267, 312; Mason, *Pequot War* (Mass. Hist. Soc., *Collections*, 2d series, VIII.), 132.   [3] *Conn. Col. Records*, I., 9.

stead of landing at the Pequot River, as he had been ordered, Mason completely deceived the Indian spies by sailing past it away from the intended prey. Near Point Judith, however, in the Narragansett country, Mason disembarked his men; and, accompanied by eighty Mohegans and two hundred Narragansetts, turned on his path and marched by land westward towards the Pequot country. So secretly and swiftly was this movement executed that the Indian fort was surrounded and approached within a few feet before the Indians took alarm.[1]

The victory of Mason was a massacre, the most complete in the annals of colonial history. The English threw firebrands among the wigwams, and in the flames men, women, and children were roasted to death. Captain Underhill, who was present, wrote that "there were about four hundred souls in this fort, and not above five of them escaped out of our hands." Only two white men were killed, though a number received arrow wounds.[2]

Mason, as he went to the Pequot harbor to meet his vessels, met a party of three hundred Indians half frantic with grief over the destruction of their countrymen, but contented himself with repelling their attack. Finally, he reached the ships, where

[1] Mason, *Pequot War* (Mass. Hist. Soc., *Collections*, 2d series, VIII.), 134–136.
[2] *Ibid.;* Underhill, *Pequot War* (Mass. Hist. Soc., *Collections*, 3d series, VI.), 25.

he found Captain Patrick and forty men come from Massachusetts to reinforce him. Placing his sick men on board to be taken back by water, Mason crossed the Pequot River and marched by land to Fort Saybrook, where they were "nobly entertained by Lieutenant Gardiner with many great guns," and there they rested the Sabbath. The next week they returned home.[1]

The remnant of the Pequots collected in another fort to the west of that destroyed by Mason. Attacked by red men and white men alike, most of them formed the desperate resolve of taking refuge with the Mohawks across the Hudson. They were pursued by Mason with forty soldiers, joined by one hundred and twenty from Massachusetts under Captain Israel Stoughton. A party of three hundred Indians were overtaken and attacked in a swamp near New Haven, and many were captured or put to death. Sassacus, the Pequot chief, of whom the Narragansetts had such a dread as to say of him, "Sassacus is all one God; no man can kill him," contrived to reach the Mohawks, but they cut off his head and sent it as a present to the English.[2]

The destruction of the Pequots as a nation was complete. All the captive men, women, and children were made slaves, some being kept in New England and others sent to the West Indies,[3] and

---

[1] Mason, *Pequot War* (Mass. Hist. Soc., *Collections*, 2d series, III.), 144.   [2] *Ibid.;* Winthrop, *New England*, I., 268, 278–281.
[3] Trumbull, *Connecticut*, I., 92.

there remained at large in Connecticut not over two hundred Pequots. September 21, 1638, a treaty was negotiated between the Connecticut delegates and the Narragansetts and Mohegans, by the terms of which the Pequot country became the property of the Connecticut towns, while one hundred Pequots were given to Uncas, and one hundred to Miantonomoh and Ninigret, his ally, to be incorporated with their tribes.[1]

So far as the whites of Connecticut were concerned the effect of the war was to remove all real danger from Indians for a period of forty years. Not till the Indians became trained in the use of fire-arms were they again matched against the whites on anything like equal terms. Among the Indian tribes, the result of the Pequot War was to elevate Uncas and his Mohegans into a position of rivals of Miantonomoh, and his Narragansetts, with the result of the overthrow and death of Miantonomoh. In the subsequent years war broke out several times, but by the intervention of the federal commissioners, who bolstered up Uncas, hostilities did not proceed.

On the conclusion of the Pequot War the freemen of the three towns upon the Connecticut convened at Hartford, January 14, 1639, and adopted "the Fundamental Orders," a constitution which has been justly pronounced the first written constitution framed by a community, through its own represent-

[1] Mason, *Pequot War* (Mass. Hist. Soc., *Collections*, 2d series, VIII.), 148.

atives, as a basis for government. This constitution contained no recognition whatever of any superior authority in England, and provided [1] that the freemen were to hold two general meetings a year, at one of which they were to elect the governor and assistants, who, with four deputies from each town, were to constitute a general court "to make laws or repeal them, to grant levies, to admit freemen, to dispose of lands undisposed of to several towns or persons, call the court or magistrate or any other person whatsoever into question for any misdemeanor, and to deal in any other matter that concerned the good of the commonwealth, except election of magistrates," which was "to be done by the whole body of freemen."

Till 1645 the deputies voted with the magistrates, but in that year the general court was divided into two branches as in Massachusetts. In one particular the constitution was more liberal than the unwritten constitution of Massachusetts: church-membership was not required as a condition of the suffrage, and yet in the administration of the government the theocracy was all - powerful. The settlers of Connecticut were Puritans of the strictest sect, and in the preamble of their constitution they avowed their purpose " to maintain and preserve the liberty and purity of the gospel of our Lord Jesus, which we now profess, as also the discipline of the churches, which, according to the truth of the said

[1] *Conn. Col. Records*, I., 20–25, 119.

gospel, is now practised among us." In 1656 the law of Connecticut required the applicant for the franchise to be of "a peaceable and honest conversation," and this was very apt to mean a church-member in practice.

No one but a church-member could be elected governor, and in choosing assistants the vote was taken upon each assistant in turn, and he had to be voted out before any nomination could be made.[1] In none of the colonies was the tenure of office more constant or persevering. In a period of about twenty years Haynes was governor eight times and deputy governor five times, Hopkins was governor six times and deputy governor five times, while John Winthrop, the younger, served eighteen years in the chief office.

The Connecticut government thus formed rapidly extended its jurisdiction. Although Springfield was conceded to Massachusetts the loss was made up by the accession, in 1639, of Fairfield and Stratford, west of New Haven, and, April, 1644, of Southampton, on Long Island, and about the same time of Farmington, near Hartford. In 1639 a town had been founded at Fort Saybrook by George Fenwick, who was one of the Connecticut patentees.[2] In the

[1] The same rule prevailed in Massachusetts. For the result, see Baldwin, *Early History of the Ballot in Connecticut* (Amer. Hist. Assoc., *Papers*, IV., 81; Perry, *Historical Collections of the American Colonial Church*, 21; Palfrey, *New England*, II., 10.

[2] Winthrop, *New England*, I., 368.

confusion which ensued in England Fenwick found himself isolated; and, assuming to himself the ownership of the fort and the neighboring town, he sold both to Connecticut in 1644, and promised to transfer the rest of the extensive territory granted to the patentees "if it ever came into his power to do so." [1] As the Connecticut government was entirely without any legal warrant from the government of England, this agreement of Fenwick's was deemed of much value, for it gave the colony a quasi-legal standing.

In 1649 East Hampton, on Long Island, was annexed to the colony, and in 1650 Norwalk was settled. In 1653 Mattabeseck, on the Connecticut, was named Middletown; and in 1658 Nameaug, at the mouth of the Pequot River, settled by John Winthrop, Jr., in 1646, became New London. In 1653 Connecticut had twelve towns and seven hundred and seventy-five persons were taxed in the colony.[2]

While Connecticut was thus establishing itself, another colony, called New Haven, controlled by the desire on the part of its leading men to create a state on a thoroughly theocratic model, grew up opposite to Long Island. The chief founder of the colony was John Davenport, who had been a noted minister in London, and with him were associated Theophilus Eaton, Edward Hopkins, and several

[1] Trumbull, *Connecticut*, I., 507–510.
[2] Palfrey, *New England*, II., 377.

other gentlemen of good estates and very religiously inclined. They reached Boston from England in July, 1637, when the Antinomian quarrel was at its height, and Davenport was a member of the synod which devoted most of its time to the settlement, or rather the aggravation, of the Antinomian difficulty.

Owing to Davenport's reputation and the wealth of his principal friends, the authorities of Massachusetts made every effort to retain them in that colony, and offered them their choice of a place for settlement. These persuasions failed, and after a nine months' stay Davenport and his followers moved away, nominally because they desired to divert the thoughts of those who were plotting for a general governor for New England, but really because there were too many Antinomians in Massachusetts, and the model republic desired by Davenport could never be brought about by accepting the position of a subordinate township under the Massachusetts jurisdiction.[1]

One of the results of the Pequot War was to make known the country west of Fort Saybrook, and in the fall of 1637 Theophilus Eaton and some others went on a trip to explore for themselves the coasts and lands in that direction. They were so much pleased with what they saw at "Quinnipiack" that in March, 1638, the whole company left Boston to take up their residence there, and called their new settlement New Haven. Soon after their arrival

[1] Winthrop, *New England*, I., 283, 312, 484.

they entered into a "plantation covenant," preliminary to a more formal engagement.[1] This agreement pledged the settlers to accept the teachings of Scripture both as a civil system and religious code.

Having no charter of any kind, they founded their rights to the soil on purchases from the Indians, of which they made two (November and December, 1638).[2] The next summer they proceeded to the solemn work of a permanent government. June 4, 1639, all the free planters met in a barn, and Mr. Davenport preached from the text, "Wisdom hath builded her home; she hath hewn out her seven pillars." He then proposed a series of resolutions which set forth the purpose of establishing a state to be conducted strictly according to the rules of Scripture. When these resolutions were adopted Davenport proposed two others designed to reduce to practice the theory thus formally approved. It was now declared that only church-members should have the right of citizenship, and that a committee of twelve should be appointed to choose seven others who were to be the constitution-makers.[3]

These articles were subscribed by one hundred and thirteen of the people, and after due time for reflection the twelve men chosen as above elected the "seven pillars," Theophilus Eaton, Esq., John Davenport, Robert Newman, Matthew Gilbert,

---

[1] *New Haven Col. Records*, I., 12.
[2] Trumbull, *Connecticut*, I., 98.
[3] *New Haven Col. Records*, I., 11-17.

Thomas Fugill, John Punderson, and Jeremiah Dixon, who proceeded in the same solemn and regular manner to reorganize the church and state. First they set up the church by associating with themselves nine others, and then after another interval, on October 25, 1639, a court was held at which the sixteen church-members proceeded to elect Theophilus Eaton as governor for a year and four other persons to aid him as "deputies," who were thereupon addressed by Davenport in what was called a charge.

Under the government thus formed a general court of the freemen was held every year for the election of governor and assistants, and to these officers was confided the entire administration of affairs. There was no body of statutes till many years later, and during this time the only restriction on the arbitrary authority of the judges was the rules of the Mosaic law. The body of the free burgesses was very cautiously enlarged from court to court.

Hardly had the people of New Haven settled themselves in their new government before two other towns, Guilford, seventeen miles north, and Milford, eleven miles south, sprang up in their neighborhood. Though practically independent, their constitution was modelled after that of New Haven.[1] Besides Guilford and Milford another town called Stamford, lying west of the Connecticut

[1] Trumbull, *Connecticut*, I., 107; Doyle, *English Colonies*, II., 196.

territory and loosely connected with New Haven, was also settled.[1] In the political isolation of these towns one sees the principle of church independence, as held by Davenport and his followers.

In April, 1643, apprehension from the Indians, the Dutch, and their neighbor Connecticut caused a union of these towns with New Haven. The new commonwealth was organized just in time to become a member of the greater confederation of the colonies founded in May, 1643. It was not, however, till October 27, 1643, that a general constitution was agreed upon.[2] It confined the suffrage to church-members and established three courts—the plantation court for small cases, consisting of "fitt and able" men in each town; the court of magistrates, consisting of the governor, deputy governor, and three assistants for weighty cases; and the general court, consisting of the magistrates and two deputies for each of the four towns which were to sit at New Haven twice a year, make the necessary laws for the confederation, and annually elect the magistrates. Trial by jury was dispensed with, because no such institution was found in the Mosaic law.

In 1649 Southold, on Long Island, and in 1651 Branford, on the main-land, were admitted as members of the New Haven confederacy; and in 1656 Greenwich was added. And the seven towns thus comprehended gave the colony of New Haven the utmost extent it ever obtained.

[1] *New Haven Col. Records*, I., 69.   [2] *Ibid.*, 112.

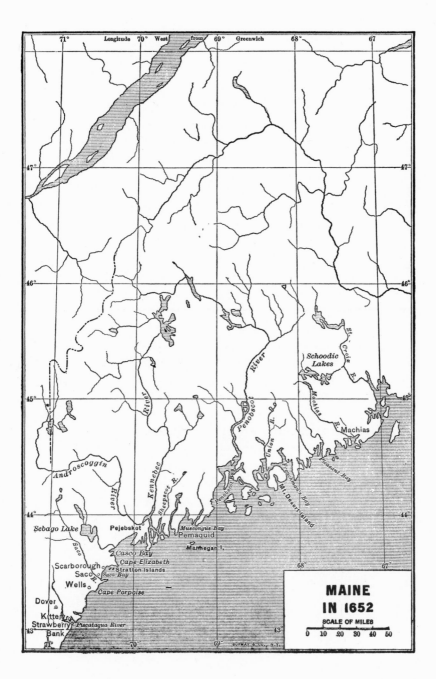

47°   47°

46°   46°

St. Croix R.

Schoodic
Lakes

45°   45°

River

Penobscot

Union R.

Machias R.

R. Machias

Androscoggin

River

Kennebec

River

Sheepscot R.

Damariscotta R.

Frenchman Bay

Mt. Desert Island

Pleasant Bay

Sebago Lake   44°
44°   Pejebskot   Muscongus Bay
                                              Pemaquid
                                              Manhegan I.
Saco R.
                    Casco Bay   68°   67°
Scarborough   Cape Elizabeth
Saco   Stratton Islands
                Saco Bay
Wells
Dover   Cape Porpoise
Kittery
Strawberry   Piscataqua River
Bank
43°   43°

MAINE
IN 1652

SCALE OF MILES

0   10   20   30   40   50

CHAPTER XVI

NEW HAMPSHIRE AND MAINE

(1653–1658)

AFTER the charter granted to the Council for
New England in 1620, Sir Ferdinando Gorges
and Captain John Mason procured, August 10, 1622,
a patent for "all that part of yᵉ maine land in New
England lying vpon yᵉ Sea Coast betwixt yᵉ rivers
of Merrimack & Sagadahock and to yᵉ furthest
heads of yᵉ said Rivers and soe forwards up into the
land westward untill threescore miles be finished
from yᵉ first entrance of the aforesaid rivers and
half way over that is to say to the midst of the said
two rivers wᶜʰ bounds and limitts the lands aforesaid togeather wᵗʰ all Islands and Isletts wᵗʰ in five
leagues distance of yᵉ premisses and abutting vpon
yᵉ same or any part or parcell thereoff." [1]

Mason was a London merchant who had seen service as governor of Newfoundland, and was, like
Gorges, "a man of action." His experience made
him interested in America, and his interest in America caused him to be elected a member of the Council
for New England, and ultimately its vice-president.[2]

[1] Maine Hist. Soc., *Collections*, 2d series, VII., 65–72.
[2] *Cal. of State Pap., Col.*, 1574–1660, p. 210.

266

The two leaders persuaded various merchants in England to join them in their colonial projects; and in the spring of 1623 they set up two settlements within the limits of the present state of New Hampshire, and some small stations at Saco Bay, Casco Bay, and Monhegan Island, in the present state of Maine.

Of the settlements in New Hampshire, one called Piscataqua, at the mouth of the river of that name, was formed by three Plymouth merchants, Colmer, Sherwell, and Pomeroy, who chose a Scotchman named David Thompson as their manager. They obtained a grant, October 16, 1622, for an island, and six thousand acres on the main, near the mouth of Piscataqua; and here Thompson located in the spring of 1623. He remained about three years, and in 1626 removed thence to an island in Boston harbor, where he lived as an independent settler.[1] The other plantation, called Cocheco, was established by two brothers, Edward and William Hilton, fish-mongers of London, and some Bristol merchants, and was situated on the south side of the Piscataqua about eight miles from the mouth of the river.[2]

November 7, 1629, Captain Mason obtained a patent[3] from the Council for New England for a tract extending sixty miles inland and lying between

---

[1] Mass. Hist. Soc., *Proceedings* (year 1876), 358.
[2] Belknap, *New Hampshire*, 20.
[3] Maine Hist. Soc., *Collections*, 2d series, VII., 96–98.

the Merrimac and Piscataqua rivers, being a part of
the territory granted to Gorges and himself in 1622.
He called it New Hampshire in honor of Hampshire,
in England, where he had an estate. Seven days
later the same grantors gave to a company of whom
Mason and Gorges were the most prominent merchants, a patent for the province of Laconia, describing it as "bordering on the great lake or lakes
or rivers called Iroquois, a nation of savage people
inhabiting into the landward between the rivers
Merrimac and Sagadahoc, lying near about forty-
four or forty-five degrees." And in 1631 Gorges,
Mason, and others obtained another grant for twenty
thousand acres, which included the settlement at the
mouth of the Piscataqua.

Under these grants Gorges and Mason spent upward of £3000[1] in making discoveries and establishing factories for salting fish and fur trading;
but as very little attention was paid to husbandry
at either of the settlements on the Piscataqua,
they dragged out for years a feeble and precarious
existence. At Piscataqua, Walter Neal was governor from 1630 to 1633 and Francis Williams
from 1634 to 1642, and the people were distinctly
favorable to the Anglican church. At Cocheco,
Captain Thomas Wiggin was governor in 1631; and
when, in 1633, the British merchants sold their
share in the plantation to Lord Say and Sele, Lord
Brooke, and two other partners, Wiggin remained

[1] Maine Hist. Soc., *Collections*, 2d series, VII., 98–107, 143–150.

governor, and the transfer was followed by the influx of Puritan settlers.[1]

After the Antinomian persecution in Massachusetts some of Mrs. Hutchinson's followers took
refuge at Cocheco, and prominent among them were
Captain John Underhill and Rev. John Wheelwright.
Underhill became governor of the town in 1638,
and his year of rule is noted for dissensions occasioned by the ambitious actions of several contentious, immoral ministers. Underhill was the
central figure in the disturbances, but at the next
election, in 1639, he was defeated and Roberts was
elected governor of Cocheco. Dissensions continued,
however, till in 1640 Francis Williams, governor of
Piscataqua, interfered with an armed force. Underhill returned to Boston, and by humbly professing repentance for his conduct he was again received into
the church there.[2] He then joined the Dutch, but
when Connecticut and New Haven were clamorous
for war with the Dutch in 1653 he plotted against
his new master, was imprisoned, and escaped to
Rhode Island,[3] where he received a commission to
prey on Dutch commerce.

Meanwhile, Mr. Wheelwright left Cocheco, and
in 1638 established southeast of it, at Squamscott
Falls, a small settlement which he and his fellow-
colonists called Exeter.[4]   In October, 1639, after

---

[1] Winthrop, *New England*, I., 137.
[2] *Ibid.*, I., 394, II., 33, 49, 76.
[3] *Plymouth Col. Records*, X., 31, 52, 426.
[4] Winthrop, *New England*, I., 349.

the manner of the Rhode Island towns, the inhabitants, thirty-five in number, entered a civil contract to "submit themselves to such godly and Christian lawes as are established in the realm of England to our best knowledge, and to all other such lawes which shall, upon good ground, be made and enacted among us according to God." This action was followed in 1641 by their neighbors at Cocheco, where the contract was subscribed by forty-one settlers; and about the same time, it is supposed, Piscataqua adopted the same system.[1]

This change of fishing and trading stations into regular townships was a marked political advance, but as yet each town was separate and independent. The next great step was their union under one government, which was hastened by the action of Massachusetts. In the assertion of her claim that her northern boundary was a due east and west line three miles north of the most northerly part of the Merrimac, Massachusetts as early as 1636 built a house upon certain salt marshes midway between the Merrimac and Piscataqua. Subsequently, when Mr. Wheelwright, in 1638, proposed to extend the township of Exeter in that direction, he was warned off by Governor Winthrop, and in 1641 Massachusetts settled at the place a colony of emigrants from Norfolk, in England, and called the town Hampton.

Massachusetts in a few years took an even more decided step. At Cocheco, or Dover, as it was now

---

[1] N. H. Hist. Soc., *Collections*, 1st series, I., 321, 324.

called, where the majority of the people were Non-conformists, the desire of support from Massachu-setts caused the policy of submission to receive the approval of both contending parties in town; and in 1639 the settlers made overtures to Massachu-setts for incorporation.[1] The settlers at Piscataqua, or Strawberry Bank (Portsmouth), being Anglicans, were opposed to incorporation, but submitted from stress of circumstances. After the death of Captain Mason, in 1635, his widow declined to keep up the industries established by him, and sent word to his servants at Strawberry Bank to shift for them-selves.[2]

Several years later Lord Say and Sele and Lord Brooke, who were the chief owners of Dover, obtained from Mason's merchant partners in England the title to Strawberry Bank, and being in sympathy with Massachusetts they offered, in 1641, to resign to her the jurisdiction of both places. The proposal was promptly accepted, and two commissioners, Sym-onds and Bradstreet, went from Massachusetts to arrange with the inhabitants the terms of incorpora-tion. The towns were guaranteed their liberties, allowed representation in the Massachusetts gen-eral court, and exempted from the requirements of the Massachusetts constitution that all voters and officers must be members of the Congregational church.[3]

[1] Winthrop, *New England*, I., 349, 384.
[2] *N. H. Col. Records*, I., 113.
[3] *Mass. Col. Records*, I., 332, 342, II., 29.

In 1643 Exeter followed the example of Dover and Strawberry Bank by accepting the protection of Massachusetts, but it thereby lost its founder. Being under sentence of banishment, Mr. Wheelwright withdrew to the territory of Sir Ferdinando Gorges, where, having obtained a patent, he founded the city of Welles. In 1644 he applied to Winthrop, and was permitted on a slight submission to take charge of the church at Hampton.[1] After several years he visited England, where he was a favorite of Cromwell. At the Restoration he returned and settled at Salisbury, in Massachusetts, where he died in 1679. He is perhaps the single bright light in the ecclesiastical history of early New Hampshire.[2]

The four towns—Dover, Strawberry Bank, Exeter, and Hampton, with Salisbury and Haverhill on the northern banks of the Merrimac — were, in 1643, made to constitute the county of Norfolk, one of the four counties into which Massachusetts was then divided.[3]

A similar fortune at a later date overtook the townships to the north of the Piscataqua. The origin of the name "Maine," applied to the regions of these settlements, has never been satisfactorily explained. Possibly it was a compliment to Henrietta Maria, the French wife of Charles I.; more probably the fishermen used it to distinguish the

[1] *Mass. Col. Records*, II., 67; Winthrop, *New England*, II., 195.
[2] Palfrey, *New England*, I., 594.
[3] *Mass. Col. Records*, II., 38.

continent from the islands. The term "Maine" first
occurs in the grant to Gorges and Mason, August 22,
1622, which embraced all the land between the
Merrimac and the Sagadahoc, or Kennebec. By
Mason's patent in 1629 the country west of the
Piscataqua was called New Hampshire, and after
that Maine was a name applied to the region between the Piscataqua and Kennebec. In more
modern times it was extended to the country beyond, as far as the St. Croix River.

Under Gorges' influence Christopher Levett made
a settlement in 1623 on an island in Saco Bay which
has been called "the first regular settlement in
Maine." [1]   The same year some Plymouth merchants planted a colony upon Monhegan Island,
which had been long a place of general resort for
fishermen.[2] And about the same time Gorges made
a settlement on the "maine" at Saco,[3] under the
management of Richard Vines. By two patents,
both dated February 12, 1630, this settlement was
divided into two parts—one to Vines and Oldham,
one to Lewis and Bonighton—each extending four
miles along by the sea-shore and eight miles along
the river-banks. These two tracts formed the township of Saco, a part of which now bears the name of
Biddeford. In 1625 the settlement of Pemaquid is

[1] Doyle, *English Colonies*, II., 215.
[2] Williamson, *Maine*, I., 226.
[3] Gorges, *Description of New England*, 79; Doyle, *English Colonies*, II., 215.

known to have occurred, but it was not patented till February 14, 1631, by the Bristol merchants Aldsworth and Elbridge. Next in order of settlement was probably the trading-post of the Plymouth colony at Kennebec, for which a patent was obtained in 1628.

Many other patents were issued by the Council for New England. Thus, March 13, 1630, John Beauchamp and Thomas Leverett obtained a grant of ten leagues square, between Muscongus and Penobscot Bay upon which they set up a factory for trading with the Indians; while the modern city of Scarboro, on Casco Bay, occupies a tract which was made the subject of two conflicting grants, one to Richard Bradshaw, November 4, and the other to Robert Trelawney and Moses Goodyear, December 1, 1631.[1]

Three other patents issued by the Council for New England, and having an important connection with subsequent history, remain to be mentioned. The first, December, 1631, granted twenty-four thousand acres ten miles distant from Piscataqua to Ferdinando Gorges (son and heir of John Gorges), Samuel Maverick, and several others. Many settlers came over, and the first manager was Colonel Norton, but in a short time he appeared to have been superseded by William Gorges, nephew of Sir Ferdinando Gorges.[2]

[1] Maine Hist. Soc., *Collections*, 2d series, VII., 125, 150, 160, 163; Doyle, *English Colonies*, II., 324.
[2] Gorges, *Description of New England*, 79.

After the division in 1635, by which his title between the Piscataqua and the Kennebec was af-
firmed, Sir Ferdinando Gorges erected the coast
from Cape Elizabeth, a few miles north of Saco, as
far as Kennebec, into a district called New Somerset-
shire.[1] Two years later Gorges obtained from King
Charles a royal charter constituting him proprietor of the "province or county of Maine," with all
the rights of a count palatine.[2] The provisions of
this charter are more curious than important. The
territory granted, which included Agamenticus, was
embraced between the Piscataqua and Kennebec,
and extended inland one hundred and twenty miles.
The lord proprietor had the right to divide his province into counties, appoint all officers, and to exe-
cute martial law. But while his rights were thus
extensive, the liberties of the people were preserved
by a provision for a popular assembly to join with
him in making laws.

The charter certainly was out of keeping with
the conditions of a distant empire inhabited only by
red savages and a few white fishermen; but Gorges'
elaborate plan for regulating the government seemed
even more far-fetched. He proposed to have not only
a lieutenant-governor, but a chancellor, a marshal, a
treasurer, an admiral, a master of ordnance, and a
secretary, and they were to act as a council of state.[3]

---

[1] Winthrop, *New England*, I., 276.
[2] Maine Hist. Soc., *Collections*, 2d series, VII., 222–243.
[3] Gorges, *Description of New England*, 83.

To this wild realm in Norumbega, Thomas Gorges, "a sober and well-disposed young man," nephew of the lord proprietor, was commissioned in 1640 to be the first governor, and stayed three years in the colony.[1]   Agamenticus (now York) was only a small hamlet, but the lord proprietor honored it in March, 1652, by naming it Gorgeana, after himself, and incorporating it as a city.   The charter of this first city of the United States is a historical curiosity, since for a population of about two hundred and fifty inhabitants it provided a territory covering twenty-one square miles and a body of nearly forty officials.[2]

The second of the three important patents led to the absorption of Maine by the government of Massachusetts.   The claim of Massachusetts to jurisdiction over the settlements in New Hampshire as readily applied to Maine; and, in addition, the patent granted in June, 1632, by the Council for New England, to George Way and Thomas Purchas, gave a tract of land along the river "Bishopscot" or "Pejepscot," better known as the Androscoggin.[3]   In 1639 Massachusetts, by buying this property, secured her first hold on the land within Gorges' patent.[4]   The revival in 1643 of another patent, believed to have been abandoned, but with rights conflicting with the patent of Gorges, both

[1] Winthrop, *New England*, II., 11.
[2] Hazard, *State Papers*, I., 470.
[3] *Cal. of State Pap., Col.*, 1574–1660, p. 152.
[4] *Mass. Col. Records*, I., 272.

prompted and excused the interference of Massachusetts.

The third great patent was a grant made by the Council for New England, in June, 1630, for a tract extending from Cape Porpoise to Cape Elizabeth, and hence taking in Gorges' settlement at Saco.[1] This patent was known as the Lygonian, or " Plough patent," the latter commemorating the name of the vessel which brought over the first settlers, who after a short time gave up the settlement and went to Boston in July, 1631. For twelve years the patent was neglected, but in 1643 the rights of the original patentees were purchased by Alexander Rigby, a prominent member of Parliament.[2] He sent over as his agent George Cleves, but when he arrived in America in 1644 his assumption of authority under the Plough patent was naturally resisted by the government of Sir Ferdinando Gorges.

Cleves set up his government at Casco, and Vines, his rival, organized his at Saco. When Cleves sent his friend Tucker to Vines with a proposal to settle the controversy, Vines arrested the envoy and threw him into prison. Both parties appealed to the government of Massachusetts, who gave them advice to remain quiet. The contention continued, however, and at last the Massachusetts court of assistants, in June, 1646, consented to refer the case to a jury. Then it appeared that there were six or

---

[1] Maine Hist. Soc., *Collections*, 2d series, VII., 133–136.
[2] Winthrop, *New England*, I., 69, II., 186.

eight patentees in the original Plough patent, and Mr. Rigby's agent could only show an assignment from two. On the other hand, Vines could not produce the royal patent of Sir Ferdinando Gorges, which was in England, and had only a copy attested by witnesses. On account of these defects the jury declined to bring in a verdict.

Cleves had better fortune with the parliamentary commissioners for foreign plantations, to whom he carried the dispute, since before this tribunal the veteran Gorges, who had taken the king's side, had little chance to be heard. In March, 1646, they decided in favor of Rigby, and made the Kennebunk River the boundary-line between the two rival proprietors, thus reducing Gorges' dominions in Maine to only three towns—Gorgeana, Welles, and Kittery, which had grown up at the mouth of the Piscataqua opposite to Strawberry Bank.[1]

The year following this decision Gorges died, and the province of Maine was left practically without a head. The settlers wrote to his heirs for instruction, but owing to the confusion of the times received no reply.[2] In this state of doubt and suspense the general court was, in 1649, convoked at Welles, when Edward Godfrey was elected governor. Then another address was prepared and transmitted to England, but it met with no better fortune than the first. Accordingly, in July, 1649, the settlers

---

[1] Winthrop, *New England*, II., 186, 313, 390.
[2] Maine Hist. Soc., *Collections*, 2d series, VII., 266, 267.

of the three townships met at Gorgeana and declared themselves a body politic. Edward Godfrey was re-elected governor, and a council of five members were chosen to assist him in the discharge of his duties.[1]

In this state of affairs, deserted by their friends in England, the Maine settlements looked an inviting prey to Massachusetts. In October, 1651, three commissioners were appointed to proceed to Kittery to convey the warning of Massachusetts "against any further proceeding by virtue of their combination or any other interest whatsoever." [2]   Godfrey declined to submit, and in behalf of the general court of the colony addressed a letter, December 5, 1651, to the Council of State of Great Britain praying a confirmation of the government which the settlers had erected. Cleves, at the head of the Rigby colony, made common cause with Godfrey and carried the petition to England, but he met with no success. The death of Rigby rendered Cleves's influence of no avail against the Massachusetts agent, Edward Winslow, who showed that Cleves's mission had originated among American royalists.[3]

This opposition, in fact, served only to hasten the action of Massachusetts. In May, 1652, surveyors were appointed by the general court who traced the stream of the Merrimac as far north as the par-

---

[1] Maine Hist. Soc., *Collections*, 2d series, VII., 266, 267 ; Williamson, *Maine*, I., 326.   [2] *Mass. Col. Records*, IV., pt. i., 70.
[3] Williamson, *Maine*, I., 336.

allel of 43° 40′ 12″.[1] Then, despite the protests of Godfrey, commissioners were again sent to Kittery, where they opened a court, November 15, and shortly after received the submission of the inhabitants.[2] They next proceeded to Gorgeana, where the like result followed, Governor Godfrey reluctantly submitting with the rest. Gorgeana was made a town under the Massachusetts jurisdiction, by the name of York, and all the country claimed by Massachusetts beyond the Piscataqua was made into a county of the same name.[3]

Next year, 1653, commissioners were sent to Welles, the remaining town in the Gorges jurisdiction, to summon to obedience the inhabitants there and at Saco and Cape Porpoise, in the Lygonian patent, and the conditions made resistance unlikely. Disregarding the Rigby claims,[4] the settlers in southern Maine accepted the overture of the Massachusetts commissioners. Accordingly, Welles, Saco, and Cape Porpoise followed the example of Kittery and Gorgeana, and came under the government of Massachusetts.

The inhabitants north of Saco about Casco Bay remained independent for several years after. Cleves and other leading inhabitants would not submit, and they tried to secure the interference of

[1] Maine Hist. Soc., *Collections*, 2d series, VII., 273.
[2] *Ibid.*, 274; *Mass. Col. Records*, IV., pt. i., 122–126.
[3] *Mass. Col. Records*, IV., pt. i., 129.
[4] Williamson, *Maine*, I., 340, 341.

Cromwell. When they failed in this attempt, the people of Casco Bay, in 1658, recognized the authority of Massachusetts. It was at this time that the plantations at Black Point, at Spurwink, and Blue Point were united and received the name of Scarboro and those at Casco Bay received that of Falmouth.[1]

Whatever judgment we may pass on the motives of Massachusetts in thus enlarging her borders to the farthest limits of settled territory north of Plymouth, it must be acknowledged that her course inured to the benefit of all parties concerned. The unruly settlements of the north received in time an orderly government, while each successive addition of territory weakened the power of the religious aristocracy in Massachusetts by welcoming into the body politic a new factor of population.

[1] *Mass. Col. Records*, IV., pt. i., 157–165, 359–360.

CHAPTER XVII

COLONIAL NEIGHBORS

(1643–1652)

ALTHOUGH the successive English colonies—
Virginia, Maryland, Plymouth, Massachusetts,
Rhode Island, Connecticut, New Haven, New Hampshire, and Maine—each sprang from separate impulses, we have seen how one depended upon another and how inextricably their history is connected each with the other. Even the widely separated southern and northern groups had intercourse and some transmigration. Thus the history of each colony is a strand in the history of England in America.

In the same way the history of each colony and of the colonies taken together is interwoven with that of colonies of other European nations — the Spaniards, French, and Dutch—planted at first distant from the English settlements, but gradually expanding into dangerous proximity. It was from a desire to protect themselves against the danger of attack by their foreign neighbors and to press their territorial claims that the New England group of English colonies afforded the example of the first American confederation.

Danger to the English colonization came first from the Spaniards, who claimed a monopoly of the whole of North America by virtue of discovery, the bull of Pope Alexander VI., and prior settlement. When Sir Francis Drake returned from his expedition in 1580 the Spanish authorities in demanding the return of the treasure which he took from their colonies in South America vigorously asserted their pre-emptive rights to the continent. But the English government made this famous reply—"that prescription without possession availed nothing, and that every nation had a right by the law of nature to freely navigate those seas and transport colonies to those parts where the Spaniards do not inhabit." [1]

The most northerly settlement of the Spaniards in 1580 was St. Augustine, in Florida, for, though in 1524 Vasquez de Ayllon had planted a settlement called San Miguel on James River, starvation, disease, and Indian tomahawk soon destroyed it. After the defeat of the Spanish Armada and the subsequent terrible punishment inflicted on the Spanish marine England was less disposed than ever to listen to the claims of Spain.[2] Reduced in power, the Spaniards substituted intrigue for warlike measures, and while they entangled King James in its web and hastened a change in the form of government for Virginia, they did not inflict any permanent injury upon the colony.

[1] Brown, *Genesis of the United States*, I., 8.
[2] Bourne, *Spain in America*, chap. x.

In 1624 England declared war against Spain, and English emigrants invaded the West Indies and planted colonies at Barbadoes, St. Christopher, Nevis, Montserrat, and other islands adjoining the Spanish settlements. Till the New England Confederation the chief scene of collision with the Spanish was the West Indies. In 1635 the Spanish attacked and drove the English from the Tortugas, and Wormeley, the governor, and many of the inhabitants took refuge in Virginia.[1]

Because of their proximity the danger from the French colonies was far more real. Small fishing-vessels from Biscay, Brittany, and Normandy were in the habit of visiting the coast of Newfoundland and adjacent waters from as early as 1504. Jean Denys, of Honfleur, visited the Gulf of St. Lawrence in 1506, and in 1508 Thomas Aubert sailed eighty leagues up the St. Lawrence River.[2] In 1518 Baron de Lery attempted to establish a colony on Sable Island, and left there some cattle and hogs, which multiplied and proved of advantage to later adventurers. Then followed the great voyage of John Verrazzano, who, in 1524, in a search for the East Indies, sailed up the coast from thirty-four to fifty-four degrees. In 1534 Jacques Cartier visited Newfoundland and advanced up the river St. Lawrence till he reached the western part of Anticosti Island. The next year Cartier came again and

---

[1] *Cal. of State Pap., Col.*, 1574–1660, pp. 75, 85, 98.
[2] Charlevoix, *New France* (Shea's ed.), I., 106.

ascended the great river many miles, visiting Sta-
daconé (Quebec) and Hochelaga (Montreal). At
Quebec he encamped with his men, and, after a
winter rendered frightful by the cold and the rav-
ages of the scurvy, he returned in the spring to St.
Malo.[1]

No further attempt was made till a short peace
ended the third desperate struggle between Charles
V. and Francis I. In 1540 King Francis created
Francis de la Roque, Sieur de Roberval, lord of
Norumbega and viceroy of "Canada, Hochelaga,
Saguenay, Newfoundland, Bell Isle, Carpunt, Labra-
dor, Great Bay, and Baccalaos"; and Cartier was
made "captain-general." The expedition sailed
in two divisions, Cartier commanding the first, which
left St. Malo May 23, 1541. Again he passed a winter of gloom and suffering on the St. Lawrence, and
in June of the following year set out to return.

On the coast of Newfoundland he met Roberval,
who had charge of the second division of the ships
and two hundred colonists. The viceroy ordered
him to return, but Cartier slipped past him at night
and left Roberval to hold the country the best he
could. Undismayed, Roberval pursued his way,
entered the St. Lawrence, and established his colony
at Quebec. He sent Jean Alefonse to explore
Norumbega, a term applied to the coast of Maine,
Nova Scotia, and Newfoundland; and he himself

---

[1] Hakluyt, *Voyages*, III., 250–297; Charlevoix, *New France*
(Shea's ed.), I., 129–131; cf. Bourne, *Spain in America*, chap. x.

explored the river Saguenay. Lescarbot tells us
that in the course of 1543 the king sent out Cartier,
who brought home the wretched survivors of the
company.

Then for nearly fifteen years the civil wars in
France prevented any further effort at settlement
on the St. Lawrence. Scores of French vessels,
however, visited the region of the northwest for fish
and furs, and as soon as the civil wars were ended
the work of colonization was taken up anew. Failure as of old attended the first experiments. In
1598 Marquis de la Roche landed forty convicts at
Sable Island, but after seven years the few survivors
received a pardon and returned home. In 1600
Chauvin and Pontgravé promised to establish a colony on the St. Lawrence, and obtained from King
Henry IV. a grant of the fur trade, but Chauvin
died and the undertaking came to an end.[1]

In 1603 the first systematic effort to found French
colonies in America was made. A company was
formed at the head of which was Aymar de Chastes,
governor of Dieppe, who sent over Samuel Champlain. He visited the St. Lawrence, and after care-
ful exploration returned to France with a valuable
cargo of furs. On his arrival he found De Chastes
dead, but Pierre du Guast, Sieur de Monts, a patriotic Huguenot, took up the unfinished work. He
received from Henry IV. a patent [2] "to represent

---

[1] Parkman, *Pioneers of France in the New World*, 213, 218.
[2] Maine Hist. Soc., *Collections*, 2d series, VII., 2–6.

our person as lieutenant-general in the country of Acadia from the fortieth to the forty-sixth degree," with governmental authority, and the exclusive privileges of traffic with the Indians.

April 7, 1604, De Monts, accompanied by Champlain, sailed from Havre de Grace, and May 1 came in sight of Sable Island. They sailed up the Bay of Fundy and entered a harbor on the north coast of Nova Scotia. Poutrincourt, one of the leading men, was so pleased with the region that he obtained a grant of it from De Monts, and named it Port Royal (now Annapolis). After further exploration De Monts planted his settlement on the Isle of St. Croix, at the mouth of the St. Croix River, where he passed the winter; but half the emigrants died from exposure and scurvy, and in the spring the colony was transferred to Port Royal. After three years spent in the country, during which time the coast was explored thoroughly by Champlain and Poutrincourt as far as Nausett Harbor, the Acadian emigrants went back to France, which they reached in October, 1607.

The design was not abandoned. Poutrincourt returned in 1610 and re-established his colony at Port Royal, which he placed in charge of his son. In 1611 two Jesuit priests, Biard and Masse, came over, under the patronage of Madame de Guercheville, and in 1613 they planted a Jesuit station at Mount Desert Island, on the coast of Maine.[1]

[1] Charlevoix, *New France* (Shea's ed.), I., 247–263.

Champlain did not return to Port Royal, but was employed in another direction. In April, 1608, De Monts sent out Champlain and Pontgravé to establish a colony on the St. Lawrence and traffic with the Indians of that region. Of this expedition Champlain was constituted lieutenant-governor, and he was successful in planting a settlement at Quebec in July, 1608. It was a mere trading-post, and after twenty years it did not number over one hundred persons. But Champlain looked to the time when Canada should be a prosperous province of France, and he was tireless and persistent. Aided by several devout friars of the Franciscan order, he labored hard to Christianize the Indians and visited lakes Champlain, Nipissing, Huron, and Ontario. While he made the fur trade of great value to the merchant company in France, he committed the fatal mistake of mixing up with Indian quarrels. Between the Five Nations of New York and the Hurons and their allies, the Algonquins of the St. Lawrence, perpetual war prevailed, and Champlain by taking sides against the former incurred for the French the lasting hatred of those powerful Indians.

The progress of the colony was not satisfactory to Champlain or to the authorities in France, and in 1627 Cardinal Richelieu dissolved the company which had charge of affairs, and instituted a new one with himself at its head. In the spring of 1628 he despatched to Canada four armed vessels and eighteen transports laden with emigrants, stores, and cannon, but war had broken out between the English and French the year before, and on their way the fleet was intercepted and the ships and goods confiscated.

The English had not recognized the claims of the French to any part of the North American continent, and the very year that the Jesuit station was planted at Mount Desert Island Samuel Argall came twice from Virginia and burned the houses of the intruding French at all of their settlements in Acadia: Mount Desert Island, Isle de Croix, and Port Royal. The French rebuilt Port Royal, and at the death of Poutrincourt's son Biencourt, about the year 1623, his possessions and claims fell to his friend and companion Claude de la Tour.

Meanwhile, in 1621, Sir William Alexander obtained a grant from King James for New Scotland, being that part of Acadia now comprising the provinces of Nova Scotia and New Brunswick;[1] and he sent over from time to time a few Scotch emigrants. De la Tour and the French submitted, and English rule seemed firmly established in Acadia when war was declared in 1628. In February, 1629, Alexander received a patent for St. Lawrence River and "fifty leagues of bounds on both sides thereof," and on both sides of its tributary lakes and rivers as far as the Gulf of California.[2]

After the failure of the expedition sent by Cardinal Richelieu, Alexander and his partners despatched

[1] Maine Hist. Soc., *Collections.* 2d series, VII., 57.   [2] *Ibid.*, 82.

an English fleet commanded by David Kirke, which appeared before Quebec in July, 1629. Champlain and his small garrison were compelled to surrender, and all New France fell under English power. Unfortunately for Alexander and Kirke, war between the two nations had ceased, and the articles of peace provided that all conquests made subsequent to April 24, 1629, should be restored to the former owner. This insured the loss of Quebec and was the forerunner of other misfortunes. In 1632 a treaty was made at St. Germain by which, despite the protest of Sir William Alexander and a memorial from the Scottish Parliament, King Charles consented "to give up and restore all the places occupied in New France, Acadia, and Canada" by his subjects.[1]

In 1632 Champlain returned to his government at Quebec, and with him arrived a number of zealous Jesuit priests, who began that adventurous career of exploration which, after Champlain's death in 1635, connected the fame of their order with the great lakes and the Mississippi. The king of France appointed Chevalier Razilly governor of Acadia, who designated as his lieutenants Claude de la Tour's son Charles, for the portion west of St. Croix; and Charles de Menou, Sieur d'Aulnay Charmisé, for the portion to the east.[2] They claimed dominion for France as far as Cape Cod.

Subsequently the two rivals quarrelled, and in

[1] *Cal. of State Pap., Col.*, 1574–1660, pp. 119, 130.
[2] Hannay, *Acadia*, 140.

1641 D'Aulnay obtained an order from the king deposing De la Tour, but the latter refused obedience and sent an envoy to Boston in November, 1641, to solicit aid. This envoy was kindly treated, and some of the Puritan merchants despatched a pinnace to trade with De la Tour; but they met with D'Aulnay at Pemaquid, who threatened to make prize of any vessel which he caught engaged in the fur trade in Acadia.[1]

The Dutch claim to America was comparatively recent, as it was not until 1597 that voyages were undertaken from Holland to the continent. In 1602 the Dutch East India Company was chartered, and in 1609 sent out Henry Hudson, an Englishman by birth, to seek a way to India by the northeast. After sailing to Nova Zembla, where fogs and fields of ice closed against him the strait of Veigatz, he changed his course for Newfoundland and coasted southward to Chesapeake Bay. Returning on his path he entered the Hudson in September, 1609, and stayed four weeks exploring the river and trafficking with the natives.[2]

The reports brought by him to Europe of a newly discovered country abounding in fur-bearing animals created much interest, and in 1612 some merchants in Holland sent Christiansen and Blok to the island of Manhattan, where they built a little fort, which, it is stated, Argall attacked in 1613. Losing

---

[1] Winthrop, *New England*, II., 106, 109.
[2] Purchas, *Pilgrimes*, III., 581–596.

his ship by fire, Blok built a yacht of sixteen tons at Manhattan, and with this small craft was the first explorer (1614) of the Connecticut River. He also visited Narragansett Bay, and gave to its shores the name of Roode Eiland (now Rhode Island).

After his return home the merchants obtained from the States-General a charter for three years' monopoly of the trade of New Netherland, as the present New York was now first formally called. It was defined as extending between New France and Virginia, from the fortieth to the forty-fifth degree of north latitude.[1] After this New Netherland continued to be resorted to by Dutch traders, though no regular settlement was formed for some years.

In 1619 Thomas Dermer visited the Hudson and brought news to England of the operations of the Dutch and the value of the fur trade. Thereupon Captain Samuel Argall, with many English planters, prepared to make a settlement on the Hudson, and when the Dutch government, in June, 1621, chartered the Dutch West India Company, the English court, on Argall's complaint, protested against Dutch intrusion within what was considered the limits of Virginia. The States-General at first evaded a reply, but finally declared that they had never authorized any settlement on the Hudson.[2] The charter,[3] in fact, gave the company only an ex-

---

[1] Brodhead, *New York*, I., 57–62.
[2] *N. Y. Docs. Rel. to Col. Hist.*, III., 6–8.
[3] Maine Hist. Soc., *Collections*, 2d series, VII., 53–56.

clusive right to trade for twenty-four years on the coasts of Africa and America.

Nevertheless, the company proceeded to send over, in 1622, a number of French Walloons, who constituted the first Dutch colony in America. One party, under the command of Captain Cornelius Jacobson May, the first Dutch governor, sailed to the South, or Delaware River, where, four miles below the present Philadelphia, they erected a fort called Nassau; and another party under Adrian Joris went up the Hudson, and on the site of Albany built Fort Orange. Peter Minuit succeeded May in 1626, and bought from the Indians the whole of Manhattan Island, and organized a government with an advisory council.

The population of New Netherland was only two hundred, and though trade was brisk there was little agriculture. The company met this difficulty by obtaining a new charter and seeking to promote emigration by dividing up the country among some great patroons: Samuel Godyn, Killiaen van Rens-salaer, Michael Pauw, David Pieterson de Vries, and other rich men. In 1631 De Vries settled Swaanen-dael, on the South River, as the Dutch called the Delaware; but in a few months the Indians attacked the place and massacred the settlers.[1] Soon the patroons became rivals of the West India Company in the fur trade, and in 1632 Minuit, who favored them, was recalled and Wouter van Twiller was

[1] N. Y. Hist. Soc., *Collections*, 2d series, III., 16, 22.

made governor. His accession marks the first real clash between the rival claims of the Dutch and English.[1]

In 1632 Lord Baltimore obtained a patent for Maryland which included all the south side of Delaware Bay and river; and a month later Sir Edmund Plowden obtained a grant from the English king for "Long Isle and also forty leagues square of the adjoining continent," including the very site of Manhattan.[2] In April, 1633, Jacob Eelkens, in command of an English vessel, forced his way past Fort Amsterdam, on Manhattan Island, and traded with the Indians, until the incompetent Van Twiller at length stripped him of his goods and drove him from the river.[3] The same year Van Twiller, as we have seen, planted a fort near the site of the present city of Hartford, which served as the seed of future troubles.

In 1634 Captain Thomas Young visited the Delaware and lorded it over the Dutch vessels which he found in the river.[4] Then in 1635, while settlers from Massachusetts poured into Connecticut, and the Council for New England, preliminary to its dissolution, assigned Long Island, despite the Dutch claim, to Sir William Alexander, men came from Virginia to Delaware Bay and seized Fort Nassau, then abandoned by the Dutch; but Van Twiller

[1] Brodhead, *New York*, I., 222.
[2] *Cal. of State Pap., Col.*, 1574–1660, p. 154.
[3] Brodhead, *New York*, I., 230.
[4] Mass. Hist. Soc., *Collections*, 4th series, IX., 125–128

soon drove them away.[1]   Thus step by step English
progress encroached upon the territories of the Dutch.

In 1638 Van Twiller was recalled and William
Kieft was sent over.   He had to deal with Swedes as
well as English, for in 1626 King Gustavus Adolphus
was persuaded by Usselinx, an Amsterdam merchant, to form the Swedish West India Company,
and after his death Oxenstierna, his prime-minister,
renewed the scheme.   In 1638 he sent out a Swedish
expedition under Peter Minuit, the late governor of
New Netherland, who established a fort on the Delaware near the present Wilmington, and called it
"Christina," and the Swedes paid no attention to
the protest of Governor Kieft.[2]

In 1640 a party of English settlers from New
Haven obtained deeds to the soil on Long Island
from Farrett, agent of Sir William Alexander, and
settled at Southold; and another party from Massachusetts, more daring still, settled at Schouts Bay,
almost opposite to Manhattan.   When a force of
Dutch troops was sent against them they retired to
the east end of the island and settled Southampton.
A more adventuresome proceeding was attempted
in 1641 when another party from New Haven took
the Dutch in the flank by settling on the Delaware.
Dutch and Swedes united to drive the intruders away.
As if these were not troubles enough, Kieft, in 1642,
provoked war with the Indians all along the Hudson.

---

[1] N. Y. Hist. Soc., *Collections*, 2d series, III., 77.
[2] Winsor, *Narr. and Crit. Hist.*, IV., 443–452.

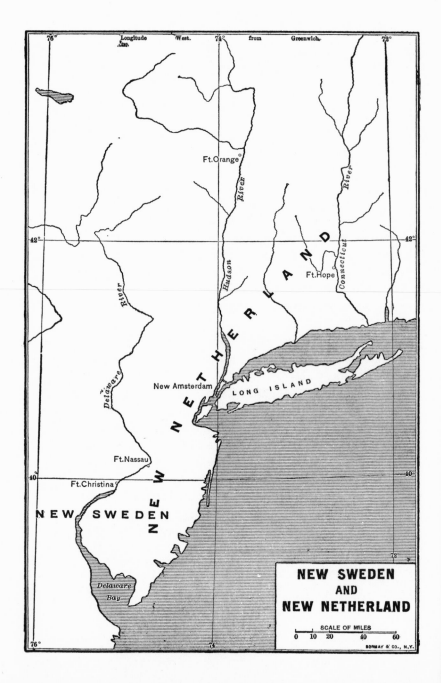

NEW SWEDEN
AND
NEW NETHERLAND

SCALE OF MILES
0 10 20   40   60

BORMAY & CO., N.Y.

CHAPTER XVIII

THE NEW ENGLAND CONFEDERATION
(1643–1654)

THESE Dutch settlements brought about a political union of the New England colonies, although the first cause of the New England confederation was the Indian tribes who lay between the Dutch and the English. In August, 1637, during the war with the Pequots, some of the Connecticut magistrates and ministers suggested to the authorities at Boston the expediency of such a measure. The next year Massachusetts submitted a plan of union, but Connecticut demurred because it permitted a mere majority of the federal commissioners to decide questions. Thereupon Massachusetts injected the boundary question into the discussions, and proposed an article not relished by Connecticut, that the Pequot River should be the line between the two jurisdictions.[1] Thus the matter lay in an unsettled state till the next year, when jealousy of the Dutch stimulated renewed action.

In 1639 John Haynes, of Connecticut, and Rev. Thomas Hooker came to Boston, and again the plan

[1] Winthrop, *New England*, I., 283, 342–344.

of a confederation was discussed, but Plymouth and Massachusetts quarrelled over their boundary-line, and the desirable event was once more postponed. Nearly three more years passed, and the founding of a confederacy was still delayed. Then, at a general court held at Boston, September 27, 1642, letters from Connecticut were read "certifying us that the Indians all over the country had combined themselves to cut off all the English."

At this time the war between De la Tour and D'Aulnay was at its height, and the Dutch complaints added to the general alarm. Thus the Connecticut proposition for a league received a more favorable consideration and was referred to a committee "to consider" after the court. At the next general court which met in Boston, May 10, 1643, a compact of confederation in writing was duly signed by commissioners from Plymouth, Massachusetts, Connecticut, and New Haven.[1] The settlement of Gorges and Mason at Piscataqua and the plantations about Narragansett Bay were denied admission into the confederacy—the former "because they ran a different course from us both in their ministry and administration,"[2] and the latter because they were regarded as "tumultuous" and "schismatic."

After a preamble setting forth that "we live encompassed with people of several nations and strange

---

[1] Winthrop, *New England*, II., 95, 99, 102, 121–127.
[2] *Ibid.*, 121.

languages," that "the savages have of late combined
themselves against us," and that "the sad distractions" in England prevent the hope of advice and
protection," the document states that the contract-
ing parties' object was to maintain "a firm and
perpetual league of friendship and amity, for offence
and defence, mutual advice and succor upon all
just occasions both for preserving and propagating
the truth and liberties of the gospel, and for their
own mutual safety and walfare." It then declared
the name of the new confederation to be "the United
Colonies of New England," and in ten articles set
out the organization and powers of the federal
government. The management was placed in the
hands of eight commissioners, two for each colony,
"all in church-fellowship with us," who were to
hold an annual meeting in each of the colonies by
rotation, and to have power by a vote of six "to
determine all affairs of war or peace, leagues, aids,
charges, and number of men for war, division of
spoils, or whatever is gotten by conquest," the admission of new confederates, etc. All public charges
were to be paid by contributions levied on the colonies proportioned to the number of inhabitants
in each colony between sixteen and sixty; and for
this purpose a census was to be taken at stated
times by the commissioners. In domestic affairs the
federal government was not to interfere, but each
colony was guaranteed the integrity of its territory
and local jurisdiction.

Two defects were apparent in this constitution:
the federal government had no authority to act directly upon individuals, and thus it had no coercive
power; the equal number of votes allowed the members of the confederation in the federal council was
a standing contradiction of the measure of contribution to the burdens of government. The confederacy contained a population of about twenty-
three thousand five hundred souls, of which number
fifteen thousand may be assigned to Massachusetts,
three thousand each to Connecticut and Plymouth,
and two thousand five hundred to New Haven.
Massachusetts, with two out of eight commissioners,
possessed a population greater than that of the other
three colonies combined.

There was really no Indian combination in 1643
against the colonists, but the rivalry between the
Narragansetts and the Mohegans gave grounds for
uneasiness. After the death of Miantonomoh, under
the circumstances already related, the fear of an
Indian attack was temporarily removed. But the
Narragansetts were grief-stricken over the loss of
their chieftain and thought only of revenge upon the
hated Uncas and his Indians, at whose door they
laid all the blame. To give opportunity for intended
operations, they made Gorton and others inter-
mediaries for a complete cession of their country to
the king of England in April, 1644. Then, when
summoned by the general court of Massachusetts
to Boston, Canonicus and Pessacus, the two leading

chiefs, pleaded the king's jurisdiction and declined to appear.[1] Two envoys sent by the general court in May, 1644, to the wigwam of Canonicus, were compelled to stay out in the rain for two hours before being admitted, and Pessacus, instead of giving them satisfaction, persisted in his threat of hostilities against Uncas, agreeing only not to attack Uncas "till after next planting-time," nor then till after due notice given to the English.[2]

The truce did not restrain the Narragansetts, and in the spring of 1645 they attacked the Mohegans and defeated them, and thereupon the federal commissioners, in July, 1645, met at Boston, and upon the refusal of the Narragansetts to make peace with Uncas they made preparations for war. A force of three hundred men was raised, one hundred and ninety from Massachusetts, forty each from Plymouth and Connecticut, and thirty from New Haven.

Upon the question of appointment of a commander-in-chief colonial independence came in conflict with federal supremacy. In 1637 Massachusetts was the champion of the principle that all questions should be decided by a simple majority vote of the commissioners; but now the Massachusetts general court asserted that no appointment of a commander should be valid without their confirmation. The federal commissioners stood stoutly for their rights, and the issue was evaded for a time by

---

[1] *Simplicities Defence* (Force, *Tracts*, IV., No. vi., 93).
[2] Winthrop, *New England*, II., 203, 243, 301, 463.

the appointment of Major Gibbons, who was a citizen of Massachusetts.

The report of these warlike preparations brought the Narragansetts to terms; but uneasiness still continued, and the subsequent years, though free from bloodshed, were full of rumors and reports of hostilities, compelling frequently the interference of the commissioners in behalf of their friend Uncas. In all these troubles[1] the question is not so much the propriety of the particular measures of the federal commissioners as their conduct in making the confederation a party to the disputes of the Indians among themselves. The time finally came when Uncas, "the friend of the white man," was regarded by his former admirers as a hopeless marplot and intriguer.

More commendable were the services of the federal commissioners with the Indians in another particular. One of the professed designs of the charter of Massachusetts was to Christianize the heathen savages, but more than twelve years elapsed after the coming of Winthrop and his colonists before New England was the scene of anything like missionary work. Then the first mission was established in 1643 by Thomas Mayhew at the island of Martha's Vineyard, which was not included in any of the New England governments and was under the jurisdiction of Sir William Alexander. In 1651 Mayhew reported that one hundred and ninety-nine men,

---

[1] *Plymouth Col. Records*, IX., 32-49.

women, and children of Martha's Vineyard and Nantucket were "worshippers of the great and ever living God."

His example was followed by John Eliot, the minister of Roxbury, in Massachusetts, who learned to speak the Indian tongue, and in 1646 preached to the Indians near Watertown. The Massachusetts general court a week later endorsed the purposes of Eliot by enacting that the church should take care to send two ministers among the Indians every year to make known to them by the help of an interpreter "the heavenly counsel of God." In four years two colonies of Indians were established, one at Nonantum and the other at Concord. But the converts were still under the influence of their sagamores, who were hostile to Eliot's schemes, and in 1651 he removed his Indians to Natick, on the Charles River, where they might be free from all heathenish subjection.

In the mean time, the intelligence of what was taking place was communicated to Edward Winslow, the agent of the colony in England. He brought the matter to the attention of Parliament, and July 19, 1649, an ordinance was passed incorporating "the society for the promoting and propagating of the gospel of Jesus Christ in New England." This society selected the federal commissioners as the managers of the fund which flowed into them from persons charitably inclined, and in seven years the sums which were remitted to New England amounted to more than £1700. The commissioners laid out the money in paying Eliot and Mayhew and other teachers, in printing catechisms in the Indian language, and providing the Indian converts with implements of labor. By 1674 the number of these "praying Indians," as they were called, was estimated at four thousand.[1]

The commissioners also rendered many services in the domestic affairs of the colonies. In order to secure the claim which she had advanced in 1637 to the Pequot River as her southern boundary, Massachusetts in 1644 authorized John Winthrop, Jr., to plant a colony on Pequot Bay at a spot called Nameaug, now New London.[2] The Connecticut government protested against the authority of Massachusetts, and in 1647 the commissioners decided that "the jurisdiction of the plantation doth and ought to belong to Connecticut." [3] This decision, however, only settled the ownership of a particular place, and the exact southern and northern boundaries of Connecticut remained for several years a matter of contention.

In another matter of internal interest the influence of the confederacy was manifested. Among other considerations for the cession of the Saybrook fort, Fenwick was promised the proceeds for the

[1] Palfrey, *New England*, II., 187–198, 332–341, III., 141; Hutchinson, *Massachusetts Bay*, I., 153.

[2] Winthrop, *New England*, II., 325.

[3] Palfrey, *New England*, II., 234.

term of ten years of a duty on all corn, biscuit,
beaver, and cattle exported from the Connecticut
River.[1] March 4, 1645, the general court of Connecticut passed an act to carry out their promise;
but as the law affected the trade of Springfield on
the upper waters of the Connecticut River as much
as that of the Connecticut towns, Springfield protested, and appealed to the protection of Massachusetts. Thereupon the general court of that colony
lodged a vigorous complaint with the federal commissioners, and the cause was patiently heard by
them at two separate meetings. Massachusetts had,
doubtless, the right on her side, but the Connecticut
contention rested on what was international usage
at the time.

The result of the deliberation of the commissioners
was a decision in July, 1647, in favor of Connecticut.
This was far from satisfying Massachusetts, and she
reopened the question in September, 1648. To
enforce her arguments, she offered certain amendments to the confederation, which, if adopted, would
have shorn the commissioners of pretty nearly all
their authority. But the commissioners stood firm,
and declared that "they found not sufficient cause
to reverse what was done last year."[2]

Feeling on both sides had now become quite embittered. At a special meeting of the federal commissioners in July, 1649, Massachusetts renewed her

[1] Trumbull, *Connecticut*, I., 508.
[2] *Ibid.*, 165, 166; Palfrey, *New England*, II., 240–249.

objections, and during the discussions her commissioners produced an order,[1] passed two months before by their general court, which, reciting the decision against Springfield, laid a tax upon all articles imported to Boston from any one of the other three confederate colonies, or exported to them from "any part of the Bay." This proceeding was justly interpreted by the federal commissioners to mean not only a retaliation upon Connecticut for the Saybrook tax, but a punishment upon the other two colonies—Plymouth and New Haven—for taking her side in the court of the confederation.

The commissioners acted with dignified firmness, and forwarded to Massachusetts a remonstrance in which they pointedly desired "to be spared in all further agitations concerning Springfield."[2] Massachusetts reluctantly yielded and the next year repealed her impost,[3] while Connecticut continued to tax the trade of Springfield till the ten years expired. Whether the tax imposed by Connecticut was right or not, Massachusetts had, nevertheless, gone dangerously near to nullification in these proceedings.

Not less interesting is the history of the dealings of the commissioners with the French and Dutch. Encouraged by the favor which had been extended to him in Massachusetts, De la Tour arrived in person

---

[1] *Mass. Col. Records*, III., 152.
[2] *Plymouth Col. Records*, IX., 158.
[3] *Mass. Col. Records*, IV., pt. i., 11.

in Boston, June 12, 1643, to crave assistance against D'Aulnay, his rival. As, notwithstanding the French king's order of the previous year, he showed a commission from the vice-admiral of France which styled him as lieutenant-general of Acadia, Governor Winthrop, influenced by the merchants of Boston, whose cupidity was excited by the valuable fur trade of Acadia, permitted him to hire both men and shipping in Massachusetts. When his preparations were completed he sailed away, accompanied by a fleet of four ships and a pinnace, the property of two intimate friends of the governor—Major Gibbons and Captain Hawkins—the latter of whom went along in charge of the Puritan contingent.[1]

In permitting this expedition Winthrop not only violated the articles of confederation and the laws of neutrality, but exposed himself to the reproach of Endicott and some of the more straitlaced elders, that he consorted with "idolators" and "antichrists," as Puritans chose to call Roman Catholics. It seems that Winthrop and his Boston friends did not intend to do more than to restore De la Tour to St. Johns, which D'Aulnay was then besieging. But the original wrong had its natural result. When D'Aulnay saw his rival's formidable fleet approaching he promptly raised the blockade and made haste to get under the protection of his stronghold at Port Royal. De la Tour followed and attacked, and, though he failed to dislodge his enemy, with

[1] Winthrop, *New England*, II., 128, 130, 153.

the assistance of the Boston men he killed several of D'Aulnay's soldiers, burned his mill, and did much other damage.

After this, while D'Aulnay went to France to get fresh orders from the king against his rival, De la Tour came to Massachusetts in May, 1644, in hopes of again interesting the Puritans there in his fortunes. But John Endicott had been elected governor in the place of Winthrop, and all the cheer De la Tour could get in return for permitting free-trade was the promise of a letter addressed to D'Aulnay urging peace with De la Tour and protesting against the capture of Massachusetts' trading vessels.[1]

In September, 1644, the federal commissioners met at Hartford, and showed dislike of the conduct of ex-Governor Winthrop by passing a resolution to the effect that "no jurisdiction within this confederation shall permit any voluntaries to go forth in a warlike way against any people whatever without order and direction of the commissioners of the other jurisdictions." In the mean while, D'Aulnay came back from France with fresh orders from the king for the arrest of De la Tour, and in October, 1644, sent to Boston an envoy with the new credentials. The Massachusetts authorities were reluctant to abandon De la Tour, but seeing no alternative they made a treaty for free-trade, subject to confirmation by the federal commissioners.[2]

---

[1] Winthrop, *New England*, II., 163, 180, 219, 220.
[2] *Plymouth Col. Records*, IX., 59.

Still the ties that bound the Boston merchants
to De la Tour were not wholly dissolved even now.
They gave an asylum to De la Tour's wife at Boston, and sent her with supplies to his fort at Port
Royal; and when the fort succumbed under D'Aulnay's attack they fitted her husband out with a
ship and truck for trading. At last De la Tour's
dealings thoroughly opened their eyes. When the
ship came to Cape Sable, De la Tour and his Frenchmen suddenly arose against the English crew, put
them out in the woods, and seized and appropriated
the vessel and cargo. Prominent among those who
had lent money and influence to De la Tour was
Major Edward Gibbons, who lost upward of £2500.

D'Aulnay retaliated and took a ship belonging to
Massachusetts, and in September, 1646, a new treaty
was made with him by envoys representing the confederacy. The English made a formal acknowledg-
ment of error, and the French accepted in full satisfaction a present to D'Aulnay of a sedan - chair,
which had been sent as a present by the viceroy of
Mexico to his sister, but was captured in the West
Indies by Cromwell and given by him to Governor
Winthrop.[1]

In 1648 the colony of Massachusetts applied to the
French officials at Quebec for a reciprocity of trade.
As the Iroquois had proved very destructive to the
French and their Algonquin and Huron allies, the
French governor caught at the plan of granting the

[1] Winthrop, *New England*, II., 244, 335.

desired privileges in return for military aid. Accordingly, in 1650, the French governor, D'Aillebout, sent the Jesuit father Druillettes, who had acted as missionary among the Algonquins of Maine, as envoy to Boston to negotiate a treaty.[1] But Massachusetts did not repeat the error of former times, and would do nothing without consent of the federal commissioners. To them, therefore, the matter was referred, with the result that the commissioners declined to involve the confederacy in a war with the Iroquois by authorizing any assistance to be given the French privately or officially.[2]

In the relations with the Dutch the temperate and conservative force in the confederacy was Massachusetts, who took steady ground for peace and opposed hostile measures. In doing so, however, she went the whole length of nullification and almost broke up the confederacy. William Kieft, the governor of New Netherland (1637–1647), seemed to recognize at once the significance of the confederacy as well as the importance of making friends with Massachusetts; and in July, 1643, before the commissioners had time to hold their first meeting, he wrote a letter of congratulations to Governor Winthrop, which he loaded, however, with complaints against Connecticut for intruding upon the land of the Dutch fort at Hartford. Governor

[1] Parkman, *Jesuits*, 327–335.
[2] Hutchinson, *Massachusetts Bay*, I., 156–158.

Winthrop in reply assured Kieft that the influence of Massachusetts would be on the side of peace, for that "the ground of difference being only a small parcel of land " was a matter of too small value to cause a breach between two people so nearly related as the Dutch and English.

When the federal commissioners met in September they showed a hostile spirit, and addressed vehement letters to the Swedish and Dutch on account of their "foul injuries" offered the New Haven settlers on the Delaware. In March, 1644, letters came from the Swedes and Dutch full of expressions of regard for the English and "particularly for Massachusetts." They promised to refrain from interfering with visitors who should bring authority from the commissioners, which so encouraged some Boston merchants that they sent to the Delaware a pinnace to search for a great lake reported to be its source. But when they arrived at the Delaware, the Swedish and Dutch governors, while telling the captain that he might go up the river as far as he chose, prohibited him from any trafficking with the Indians, which caused the return of the pinnace to Boston. After this the war which Kieft provoked with the Indians so occupied the Dutch that for two years they had no time to give attention to their English neighbors. So hard pressed were they that, instead of making further reclamations on New Haven, they earnestly but unsuccessfully solicited her aid. After great losses to both the Dutch and the Indians the Mohawks intervened as arbitrators, and brought about a peace in September, 1645.[1]

In 1646 the men of New Haven set up a trading-house near the mouth of the Housatonic, and thereupon Kieft wrote to the commissioners, who met at New Haven in April, 1646, a blustering letter of which the following is a good sample: "We protest against all you commissioners met at the Red Mount (New Haven) as against breakers of the common league, and also infringers of the rights of the lords, the states, our superiors, in that you have dared, without our express and especial consent, to hold your general meeting within the limits of New Netherland." [2]   At the close of Kieft's administration in 1647 the whole province of New Netherland could furnish not more than three hundred fighting-men and contained a population of not more than two thousand.   Compared with the population of New England these figures seem insignificant enough, and render highly improbable the story popular with some New England historians that the Dutch were enlisted in a great scheme of uprooting the English colonies.

In 1647 Peter Stuyvesant was sent over as governor.   He had the sense to see that the real safety of the Dutch consisted not in bluster, but in settling a line between the possessions of the two nations as soon as possible.   The charter of the West India

---

[1] Winthrop, *New England*, II., 155, 157, 169, 189, 193, 229; Brodhead, *New York*, I., 409.   [2] Trumbull, *Connecticut*, I., 158.

Company called for the territory between forty and forty-five degrees north latitude, but to assert the full extent of the patent would have been to claim the jurisdiction of Massachusetts. Accordingly, Stuyvesant, soon after his arrival, addressed a letter to Governor Winthrop, asserting the Dutch claim to all the land between the Connecticut and Delaware and proposing a conference. But it is evident that in claiming the Connecticut he was actuated more by a hope of deterring the further aggressions of English settlers than otherwise. The federal commissioners returned a polite reply, but showed no anxiety to come to an accommodation. Soon after a fresh quarrel broke out with New Haven, and in March, 1648, Stuyvesant wrote to the governor of Massachusetts offering to submit to him and the governor of Plymouth the matter in dispute. He then wrote home for instructions, and as diplomatic relations between England and Holland were suspended, the West India Company bade him make such terms as he could with his English neighbors.[1]

Accordingly, in September, 1650, Stuyvesant visited Hartford while the federal commissioners were in session there. The discussions were carried on in writing, and Stuyvesant dated his letter at "New Netherland." The federal commissioners declined to receive this letter, and Stuyvesant changed the

---

[1] Winthrop, *New England*, II., 382, 395; Brodhead, *New York*, I, 499.

address to "Connecticut." This proving satisfactory to the commissioners, Stuyvesant set out his
territorial claim and the imputed wrongs suffered by
the Dutch from the English, and the federal commissioners rejoined in a similar manner. Then Stuyvesant proposed to refer the question in dispute to
four arbitrators, all Englishmen, two to be appointed
by himself and two by the federal commissioners.

The offer was accepted, and after a full hearing
by these arbitrators, Thomas Willet, George Baxter,
Simon Bradstreet, and Thomas Prince, declined to
decide upon the wrongs complained of by either
party and rendered an award upon the territorial
question only. They decided that the Dutch should
retain their fort on the Connecticut, and that the
boundary should begin at a point on the west side of
Greenwich Bay, about four miles from Stamford,
and run due north twenty miles. From that point
it should be extended as the Dutch and New Haven
might agree, provided that the line should not come
nearer the Hudson River than ten miles. The
English obtained most of Long Island besides, for
in that quarter the line was declared to be a meridian drawn through the westernmost part of Oyster
Bay.[1] If these terms subjected Stuyvesant to
severe criticism at New Amsterdam, it was really a
stroke of statesmanship to obtain, even at a sacrifice,
what was for the first time an international barrier
to English intrusion.

[1] Trumbull, *Connecticut*, I., 189-192.

The southern flank of New Netherland was left unprotected, and in 1651 New Haven once more endeavored to plant a colony on the Delaware. The failure of the former attempt bore heavily upon the wealthy merchants of the town, and they had ill luck in another adventure. In January, 1646, they sent an agent to England to solicit a charter from the English government. The ship in which he sailed carried seventy other prominent citizens of the place and a cargo valued at £5000. A great storm ensued after the ship's departure and she was lost at sea.[1] So disheartening was this misfortune that many at New Haven entertained the idea of removing to the West Indies or Ireland.

Now, in 1651, under a commission from Governor Eaton, fifty men from New Haven prepared to sail for the Delaware.[2] Their ship touched at New Amsterdam, and Stuyvesant arrested both passengers and officers, and only released them on their promise to return home. The adventurers appealed to the commissioners, and these officials wrote a letter to Stuyvesant protesting against his course.[3]

Next year war broke out between Holland and England, and the war spirit spread to this side of the ocean. Rumors got afloat that the Dutch and Indians had conspired against the English, and Connecticut and New Haven became hysterical for war;

---

[1] Winthrop, *New England*, II., 325, 337.
[2] Trumbull, *Connecticut*, I., 196.
[3] *Plymouth Col. Records*, IX., 210-215.

while Rhode Island commissioned John Underhill, lately escaped from the Dutch, to take all Dutch vessels he could find.[1] Stuyvesant indignantly denied the charge of conspiring with the Indians, and proposed to refer the examination of the facts to any impartial tribunal. Nevertheless, all the old complaints were revived.

In 1652 the federal commissioners resolved on hostilities,[2] but the Massachusetts general court, which had all along taken a position in favor of peace, refused to be bound by a vote of six commissioners representing Plymouth, Connecticut, and New Haven.[3] On the other hand, the commissioners of the three smaller colonies protested against the conduct of the court of Massachusetts as violating the confederation.[4] New Haven and Connecticut took measures to wage war on their own account,[5] and in April, 1654, Connecticut sequestered the Dutch fort at Hartford.[6]

When, in June, 1654, a fleet despatched by Cromwell, in response to appeals made to him, appeared in Boston harbor, Connecticut and New Haven were overjoyed, and proceeded with alacrity to make arrangements for an attack on the hated Dutch. Massachusetts refused to raise troops, although she gave her citizens privilege to enlist if they chose.

[1] *R. I. Col. Records*, I., 266.
[2] *Plymouth Col. Records*, X., 102.
[3] *Mass. Col. Records*, III., 311.
[4] *New Haven Col. Records*, II., 36.   [5] *Ibid.*, 37
[6] *Conn. Col. Records*, I., 254.

Yet her policy of peace prevailed in the end, for before the preparations described could be completed a stop was put to them by the news that a treaty of peace had been signed between England and Holland April 5, 1654.[1]

Massachusetts had successfully nullified the plain provisions of the articles, and for a time it looked as if the dissolution of the confederacy would be the consequence. New Haven voted at first not to choose commissioners, but finally decided to do so,[2] and meetings of the commissioners went on apparently as before. Nevertheless, the effect of the action of Massachusetts was far-reaching—from that time the respective colonies diverged more and more, till the hope of a permanent intercolonial bond vanished.

[1] Trumbull, *Connecticut*, I., 219, 220.
[2] *New Haven Col. Records*, II., 111.

CHAPTER XIX

EARLY NEW ENGLAND LIFE
(1624–1652)

DURING the civil war in England the sympathies of Massachusetts, of course, were with Parliament. New England ministers were invited to attend the Westminster assembly of divines held in September, 1642, and several of them returned to England. The most prominent was Rev. Hugh Peter, who was instrumental in procuring the decapitation of Charles I., and paid for the offence, on the restoration of Charles II., with his own life. In 1643 Parliament passed an act [1] freeing all commodities carried between England and New England from the payment of "any custom, subsidy, taxation, imposition, or other duty."

The transfer of the supreme authority to the Parliament, though hailed with enthusiasm in New England, increased, if anything, her confidence. In the summer of 1644 a ship bearing a commission from the Parliament attacked and captured in the harbor of Boston another ship friendly to the king; Massachusetts showed her displeasure by addressing

[1] N. H. Hist. Soc., *Collections*, I., 323–326.

a strong protest to Parliament. Not long after another vessel of Parliament attacked a ship belonging to persons from Dartmouth in sympathy with the king. This time Winthrop turned the guns of the battery upon the parliamentary captain and made him pay a barrel of powder for his insolence.[1]

The same summary action was adopted in regard to the growing demand for a freer suffrage. In May, 1646, an able and respectful petition was presented to the general court for the removal of the civil disabilities of all members of the churches of England and Scotland, signed by William Vassall, Samuel Maverick, Dr. Robert Child, and four other prominent Presbyterians. The petition was pronounced seditious and scandalous, and the petitioners were roundly fined. When Child set out for England with his grievances, he was arrested and his baggage searched. Then, to the horror of the rulers of Massachusetts, there was discovered a petition addressed to Parliament, suggesting that Presbyterianism should be established in New England and that a general governor should be sent over. The signers, brought before the court, were fined more heavily than before and imprisoned for six months. At length Vassall and his friends contrived to reach England, expecting to receive the aid of the Presbyterian party in Parliament; but misfortune overtook them there as in Massachusetts, for the In-

---

[1] Winthrop, *New England*, II., 222-224, 228, 238-240.

dependents were now in control and no help could be obtained from them.[1]

The agitation in England in favor of Presbyterianism, and the petition of Vassall and his friends in Massachusetts, induced the general court in May, 1646, to invite the clergy to meet at Cambridge, "there to discuss, dispute, and clear up, by the word of God, such questions of church government and discipline as they should think needful and meet," until "one form of government and discipline" should be determined upon. The "synod" met September 1, 1646, and after remaining in session fourteen days they adjourned. In August, 1648, after the downfall of Presbyterianism in England, another meeting was held, and a plan of church government was agreed upon, by which order and unity were introduced among members theoretically independent.[2]

By a unanimous vote the synod adopted "a platform" approving the confession of faith of the Westminster divines, except as to those parts which favored the Presbyterian discipline. The bond of union was found in the right of excluding an offending church from fellowship and of calling in the civil power for the suppression of idolatry, blasphemy, heresy, etc. The platform recognized the prerogative of occasional synods to give advice and admoni-

---

[1] *New England's Jonas Cast Up at London* (Force, *Tracts*, IV., No. iii.); Winthrop, *New England*, II., 319, 340, 358, 391.
[2] Winthrop, *New England*, II., 329, 330, 402.

tion to churches in their collective capacity, but general officers and permanent assemblies, like those of the Presbyterian and Anglican churches, armed with coercive power to act upon individuals, were disclaimed.[1]

Nevertheless, by the organization thus effected, the benumbing influence of the Calvinistic faith upon the intellectual life of New England was fully established, and the deaths of John Winthrop and John Cotton, which happened not long after, were the forerunners of what Charles Francis Adams styles the "glacial period of Massachusetts."[2] Both Winthrop and Cotton were believers in aristocracy in state and church, but the bigotry of Winthrop was relieved by his splendid business capacity and that of Cotton by his comparative gentleness and tenderness of heart.

"Their places were taken by two as arrant fanatics as ever breathed"[3]—John Endicott, who was governor for thirteen out of fifteen years following Winthrop's death, and John Norton, an able and upright but narrow and intolerant clergyman. The persecuting spirit which had never been absent in Massachusetts reached, under these leaders, its climax in the wholesale hanging of Quakers and witches.

In the year of Cotton's death (1652), which was

---

[1] Mather, *Magnalia*, book V.
[2] Adams, *Massachusetts, its Historians and its History*, 59.
[3] Fiske, *Beginnings of New England*, 179.

the year that Virginia surrendered to the Parliamentary commissioners and the authority of the English Parliament was recognized throughout English America, the population of New England could not have been far short of fifty thousand. For the settlements along the sea the usual mode of communication was by water, but there was a road along the whole coast of Massachusetts. In the interior of the colony, as Johnson boasted, "the wild and uncouth woods were filled with frequented ways, and the large rivers were overlaid with bridges, passable both for horse and foot." [1]

All the conditions of New England tended to compress population into small areas and to force the energies of the people into trade. Ship-building was an early industry, and New England ships vied with the ships of Holland and England in visiting distant countries for commerce.[2] Manufacturing found early encouragement, and in 1639 a number of clothiers from Yorkshire set up a fulling-mill at Rowley.[3] A glass factory was established at Salem in 1641,[4] and iron works at Lynn in 1643,[5] under the management of Joseph Jenks. The keenness of the New-Englander in bargains and business became famous.

In Massachusetts the town was the unit of repre-

---

[1] Johnson, *Wonder Working Providence*, book III., chap. i.
[2] Weeden, *Econ. and Soc. Hist. of New England*, I., 143.
[3] Palfrey, *New England*, II., 53.
[4] *Mass. Col. Records*, I., 344.
[5] Weeden, *Econ. and Soc. Hist. of New England*, I., 174.

sentation and taxation, and in local matters it governed itself. The first town government appears to have been that of Dorchester, where the inhabitants agreed, October 8, 1633, to hold a weekly meeting "to settle and sett down such orders as may tend to the general good."[1] Not long after a similar meeting was held in Watertown, and the system speedily spread to the other towns. The plan of appointing a body of "townsmen," or selectmen, to sit between meetings of the towns began in February, 1635, in Charlestown.[2]

The town-meeting had a great variety of business. It elected the town officers and the deputies to the general court and made ordinances regarding the common fields and pastures, the management of the village herds, roadways, boundary-lines, fences, and many other things. Qualified to share in the deliberations were all freemen and "admitted inhabitants of honest and good conversation" rated at £20 (equivalent to about $500 to-day).[3]

In the prevalence of the town system popular education was rendered possible, and a great epoch in the history of social progress was reached when Massachusetts recognized the support of education as a proper function of government. Boston had a school with some sort of public encouragement in 1635,[4] and in 1642, before schools were required by

[1] Clapp, *Dorchester*, 32.   [2] Frothingham, *Charlestown*, 51.
[3] Howard, *Local Constitutional History*, I., 66.
[4] Palfrey, *New England*, II., 47.

law, it was enjoined upon the selectmen to "take account from time to time of parents and masters of the ability of the children to read and understand the principles of religion and the capital lawes of the country." [1]   In November, 1647, a general educational law required every town having fifty householders or more to appoint some one to teach children how to read and write, and every town having one hundred householders or more to establish a "grammar (Latin) school" to instruct youth "so far as may be fitted for the university." [2]

In 1636 the Massachusetts assembly agreed to give £400 towards "a schoole or Colledge," [3] to be built at Newtown (Cambridge). In 1638 John Harvard died within a year after his arrival, and left his library and "one-half his estate, it being in all about £700, for the erecting of the College." In recognition of this kindly act the general court fitly gave his name to the institution,[4] the first founded in the United States.

In 1650 Connecticut copied the Massachusetts law of 1647, and a clause declared that the grammar - schools were to prepare boys for college. The results, however, in practice did not come up to the excellence of the laws, and while in some towns in both Massachusetts and Connecticut a public rate was levied for education, more generally the parents had to pay the teachers, and they were

[1] *Mass. Col. Records*, II., 9.
[2] *Ibid.*, 203.   [3] *Ibid.*, I., 183.   [4] *Ibid.*, 253.

hard to secure. When obtained they taught but two or three months during the year.[1] Bad spelling and wretched writing were features of the age from which New England was not exempt. Real learning was confined, after all, to the ministers and the richer classes in the New England colonies, pretty much as in the mother-country. In Plymouth and Rhode Island, where the hard conditions of life rendered any legal system of education impracticable, illiteracy was frequent. The class of ignorant people most often met with in New England were fishermen and the small farmers of the inland townships.

Scarcity of money was felt in New England as in Virginia, and resort was had to the use of wampum as a substitute,[2] and corn, cattle, and other commodities were made legal tenders in payment of debts.[3] In 1652 a mint was established at Boston, and a law was passed providing for the coinage of all bullion, plate, and Spanish coin into "twelvepenny, sixpenny, and threepenny pieces." The master of the mint was John Hull, and the shillings coined by him were called "Pine-Tree Shillings," because they bore on one side the legend "Massachusetts" encircling a tree.[4]

[1] Weeden, *Econ. and Soc. Hist. of New England*, I., 282, II., 861.
[2] Weeden, *Indian Money as a Factor in New England Colonization* (*Johns Hopkins University Studies*, II., Nos. viii., ix.).
[3] *Mass. Col. Records*, I., 110; *Conn. Col. Records*, I., 8.
[4] *Mass. Col. Records*, IV., pt. i., 84, 118.

Marriage was a mere civil contract, and the burials took place without funeral service or sermon. Stern laws were made against card - playing, long hair, drinking healths, and wearing certain articles, such as gold and silver girdles, hat-bands, belts, ruffs, and beaver hats. There were no Christmas festivals and no saints' days nor recognized saints, though special feasts and thanksgiving days were frequent.[1] The penal legislation of New England was harsh and severe, and in Massachusetts and Connecticut there were fifteen crimes punishable with death, while the law took hold also of innumerable petty offences. In addition the magistrates had a discretionary authority, and they often punished persons on mere suspicion.

There can be no doubt that the ideal of the educated Puritan was lofty and high, and that society in New England was remarkably free from the ordinary frivolities and immoralities of mankind; but it would seem that human nature exacted a severe retaliation for the undue suppression of its weaknesses. There are in the works of Bradford and Winthrop, as well as in the records of the colonies, evidence which shows that the streams of wickedness in New England were "dammed" and not dried up. At intervals the impure waters broke over the obstacles in their way, till the record of crime caused the good Bradford "to fear and tremble at the consideration of our corrupt natures." [2]

---

[1] Howe, *Puritan Republic*, 102, 110, 111.
[2] Bradford, *Plimoth Plantation*, 459.

The conveniences of town life gave opportunities for literature not enjoyed by the Virginians, and, though his religion cut the Puritan almost entirely off from the finer fields of poetry and arts, New England in the period of which we have been considering was strong in history and theology. Thus the works of Bradford and Winthrop and of Hooker and Cotton compare favorably with the best productions of their contemporaries in England, and contrast with the later writers of Cotton Mather's "glacial period," when, under the influence of the theocracy, "a lawless and merciless fury for the odd, the disorderly, the grotesque, the violent, strained analogies, unexpected images, pedantics, indelicacies, freaks of allusion, and monstrosities of phrase" were the traits of New England literature.[1]

[1] Tyler, *American Literature*, II., 87.

CHAPTER XX

CRITICAL ESSAY ON AUTHORITIES

BIBLIOGRAPHICAL AIDS

FOUR special bibliographies of American history are serviceable upon the field of this volume. First, most searching and most voluminous, is Justin Winsor, *Narrative and Critical History of America* (8 vols., 1888–1889). Mr. Winsor has added to the study of the era of colonization by the writers of his co-operative work the vast wealth of his own bibliographical knowledge. The part of Winsor applicable to this volume is found in vol. III., in which most of the printed contemporary material is enumerated. The second bibliography is the *Cambridge Modern History*, VII. (1903); pages 757–765 include a brief list of selected titles conveniently classified. J. N. Larned, *Literature of American History, a Bibliographical Guide* (1902), has brief critical estimates of the authorities upon colonial history. Channing and Hart, *Guide to the Study of American History* (1896), contains accounts of state and local histories (§ 23), books of travel (§ 24), biography (§ 25), colonial records (§ 29), proceedings of learned societies (§ 31), also a series of consecutive topics with specific references (§§ 92–98, 100, 101, 109–124). For the field of the present volume a short road to the abundant sources of material is through the footnotes of the principal secondary works enumerated below. The critical chapters in *The American Nation*, vols. III.

and V., contain appreciations of many authorities which also bear on the field of vol. IV.

GENERAL SECONDARY WORKS

The "Foundation" period, from 1574 to 1652, is naturally one of the most interesting in the annals of the American colonies. The most important general historians are George Bancroft, *History of the United States* (rev. ed., 6 vols., 1883–1885); J. A. Doyle, *English Colonies in America* (3 vols., 1882–1887); Richard Hildreth, *History of the United States* (6 vols., 1849–1852); George Chalmers, *Political Annals of the American Colonies* (1780); Justin Winsor, *Narrative and Critical History of America* (8 vols., 1888–1889); John Fiske, *Discovery of America* (2 vols., 1892), *Old Virginia and Her Neighbors* (1900), *Beginnings of New England* (1898), *Dutch and Quaker Colonies in America, New France and New England* (1902).

Among these writers three have conspicuous merit— Doyle, Winsor, and Fiske. Doyle's volumes manifest a high degree of philosophic perception and are accurate in statement and broad in conclusions. Of his books the volumes on the Puritan colonies are distinctly of a higher order than his volume on the southern colonies. The chief merit of Winsor's work is the critical chapters and parts of narrative chapters, which are invaluable. John Fiske is not wanting in the qualities of a great historian— breadth of mind and accuracy of statement; but his great charm is in his style and his power of vivifying events long forgotten. He has probably come nearer than any one else to writing real history so as to produce a popular effect.

COLLECTIONS OF SOURCES

The main contemporary collectors of materials for the history of the early voyages to America were Richard Eden, Richard Hakluyt, and Samuel Purchas. Eden's

Decades of the New World or West Indies (7 vols., 1555) consists of abstracts of the works of foreign writers—Peter Martyr, Oviedo, Gomara, Ramusio, Ziegler, Pigafetta, Munster, Bastaldus, Vespucius, and others. Richard Hakluyt first published *Divers Voyages* (1582; reprinted by the Hakluyt Society) and then his *Principal Voyages* (3 vols., folio, 1589; reissued 1600). Samuel Purchas's first volume appeared in 1613 under the title, *Purchas: His Pilgrimage of the World, or Religions Observed in all Ages and Places Discovered, from the Creation unto this Present.* The four subsequent volumes were published in 1623 under the title, *Hakluytius Posthumous, or, Purchas: His Pilgrimes.*

Among these three compilers Hakluyt enjoys pre-eminence, and the Hakluyt Society has supplemented his labors by publishing in full some of the narratives which Hakluyt, for reasons of accuracy or want of space, abbreviated. *The Historie of Travaile into Virginia*, by William Strachey, secretary to Lord Delaware, was published by the Hakluyt Society in 1848, and this book contains excellent accounts of the expeditions sent by Sir Walter Raleigh to Roanoke, the voyages of Bartholomew Gosnold and George Weymouth, and the settlement made under its charter by the Plymouth Company at Sagadahoc, or Kennebec.

The only official collection of documentary materials that covers the entire period is the *Calendar of State Papers, Colonial Series, America and West Indies*, 1574–1696 (9 vols., 1860–1903). George Sainsbury, the editor, was a master at catching the salient points of a manuscript. Many of his abstracts have elsewhere been published in full.

The principal private collectors are E. Hazard, *State Papers* (2 vols., 1792–1794); Peter Force, *Tracts* (4 vols., 1836–1846); Alexander Brown, *Genesis of the United States* (2 vols., 1891); Albert Bushnell Hart, *American History Told by Contemporaries* (4 vols., 1898–1902); Maryland Historical Society, *Archives of Maryland;* and the series called *Documents Relating to the Colonial History of New York*, edited by John Romeyn Brodhead. Two convenient volumes embodying many early writings are Stedman and Hutchinson, *Library of American Literature*, I. (1888); Moses Coit Tyler, *History of American Literature During the Colonial Time, 1607–1676*, I. (1897).

VIRGINIA

The standard authorities for the history of Virginia are Robert Beverley, *History of Virginia* (1722) (extends to Spotswood's administration); William Stith, *History of Virginia* (1747) (period of the London Company); John D. Burk, *History of Virginia* (4 vols., 1805); R. R. Howison, *History of Virginia* (2 vols., 1846); Charles Campbell, *History of the Colony and Ancient Dominion of Virginia* (1847); and John Fiske, *Old Virginia and Her Neighbors* (1900). For the period Stith is by far the most important. His work covers the duration of the London Company, and as he had access to manuscripts now destroyed the history has the value of an original document. As president of William and Mary College Stith was an accomplished scholar, and his work, pervaded with a broad, philosophic spirit, ranks perhaps first among colonial histories. As a mere collection of facts upon the whole colonial history of Virginia Campbell's work is the most useful. The greatest collection of original material bearing upon the first ten years of the colony's history is in Alexander Brown, *Genesis of the United States* (2 vols., 1890). This remarkable work contains an introductory sketch of what has been done by Englishmen prior to 1606 in the way of discovery and colonization, and a catalogue of charters, letters, and pamphlets (many of them republished at length) through which the events attending the first foundation of an English colony in the New World are developed in order of time. Dr. Brown's other works, *The First Republic in America* (1898), and *English Politics in America* (1901) make excellent companion pieces to the *Genesis*, though the author has made a great mistake in not supporting his text with foot-notes and references.

Among the contemporary writers, John Smith, *Works* (1884), edited by Edward Arber, is a compilation rather than a history, and in spite of its partisan coloring contains much that is valuable regarding Virginia affairs from 1607 to 1629. For matters from 1619–1624 we have the sure guide of the London Company's *Journal*, in Virginia Historical Society, *Collections*, new series, VII. After that time the main dependence, apart from the *Calendar of State Papers*, is Hening, *Statutes at Large of Virginia* (13 vols., 1823). The leading incidents in Virginia connected with Lord Baltimore's colony of Maryland and the Puritan persecution are set forth by J. H. Latané, *Early Relations of Maryland and Virginia* (*Johns Hopkins University Studies*, XIII., Nos. iii., iv.) Many documents illustrative of this period may be read in Force, *Tracts*, and Hazard, *State Papers;* Virginia history is illuminated by many original documents printed in the *Virginia Magazine of History and Biography* (11 vols., 1893–1903); and the *William and Mary College Quarterly* (12 vols., 1892–1903). The works of Edward D. Neill are also of a documentary nature and of much value. Those which bear upon Virginia are *The Virginia Company* (1868), *Virginia Carolorum* (1886), *Virginia Vestusta* (1885), and *Virginia and Virginiola* (1878). Many tracts are cited in the foot-notes.

MARYLAND

The standard authorities for the history of Maryland are J. V. L. McMahon, *Historical View of the Government of Maryland* (1831); John Leeds Bozman, *History of Maryland* (2 vols., 1837, covering the period of 1634 to 1658); James McSherry, *History of Maryland* (1849); J. T. Scharf, *History of Maryland* (3 vols., 1879); William Hand Browne, *History of Maryland* (1893), and *George and Cecilius Calvert* (1893); Edward D. Neill, *Founders of Maryland* (1876), and *Terra Mariæ* (1867). Of these Bozman's work is an invaluable magazine of information, being, in fact, as much a calendar of documents as a continuous narrative. William Hand Browne's books show great familiarity with the story of Maryland and its founders, but his treatment of the subject is marked by strong bias and partisanship in favor of Lord Baltimore and his government. Neill's books, on the other hand, argue strongly in favor of the Puritan influence on the history of Maryland. There are many interesting pamphlets relating to Maryland in the series of *Johns Hopkins University Studies*, such as Edward Ingle, *Parish Institutions of Maryland*, I., No. vi.; John Hensley Johnson, *Old Maryland Manors*, I., No. vii.; Lewis W. Wilhelm, *Maryland Local Institutions*, III., Nos. v., vi., vii.; D. R. Randall, *The Puritan Colony at Annapolis, Maryland*, IV., No. vi.; J. H. Latané, *Early Relations of Virginia and Maryland*, XIII., Nos. iii., iv., and Bernard C. Steiner, *The Beginnings of Maryland*.

The documentary material of Maryland is very extensive, as the State has been fortunate in preserving most of its colonial records. *The Archives of Maryland* (23 vols., 1889–1903), published by the Maryland Historical Society, is composed of the proceedings of the council, legislature, and provincial court. The *Fund Publications* of the society (36 nos. in 4 vols., 1867–1900), are also valuable in this respect, and contain among other things *The Calvert Papers* (*Fund Publications*, No. 34). A complete list of all these publications can be found in the annual report of the society for 1902.

For the controversy between Lord Baltimore and the Puritans the chief authorities are Winthrop, *History of New England* (2 vols., 1790–1853); *Lord Baltimore's Case Concerning the Province of Maryland* (1653); *Virginia and Maryland, or Lord Baltimore's Case Uncased and Answered* (Force, *Tracts*, II., No. ix.); Leonard Strong, *Babylon's Fall in Maryland, a Fair Warning to Lord Baltimore;* John Langford, *A Just and Clere Reputation of Babylon's Fall* (1655); John Hammond, *Leah and Rachel* (Force,

Tracts, III., No. xiv.); *Hammond versus Heamans, or an Answer to an Audacious Prophet;* Heamans, *Brief Narrative of the Late Bloody Designs Against the Protestants.* The battle of the Severn is described in the letters of Luke Barber and Mrs. Stone, published in Bozman, *Maryland,* II., 688.

PLYMOUTH AND MASSACHUSETTS

The standard authorities for the history of these two colonies are Thomas Hutchinson, *History of the Colony of Massachusetts Bay* (3 vols., 1795–1828); John G. Palfrey, *History of New England* (3 vols., 1858–1890); J. S. Barry, *History of Massachusetts* (3 vols., 1855–1857). Very lively and interesting are Charles Francis Adams, *Massachusetts: Its Historians and Its History* (1893); *Three Episodes of the History of Massachusetts* (2 vols., 1895). The best account of Plymouth is J. E. Goodwin, *The Pilgrim Republic* (1888).

The chief original authority for the early history of the Puritan colony of New Plymouth is William Bradford, *Plimoth Plantation* (several eds.); and for Massachusetts, John Winthrop, *History of New England* (several eds.), which is, however, a journal rather than a history. Edward Arber, *Story of the Pilgrim Fathers as Told by Themselves* (1897), is a collection of ill-arranged sources. The documentary sources are numerous. Hazard prints many documents bearing upon the early history of Massachusetts, and much valuable matter is found in the *Records of Plymouth* (12 vols., 1855–1859), and the *Records of Massachusetts Bay* (5 vols., 1853–1854). Then there are the published records of numerous towns, which throw much light upon the political, social, and economic condition of the colonies. The publications of the Massachusetts Historical Society and of the New England Historic-Genealogical Society contain much original matter and many interesting articles upon the early history of both Plymouth and Massachusetts. Special tracts and documents are referred to in the foot-notes to chaps. ix.–xiii., above.

The general histories are J. N. Arnold, *History of the State of Rhode Island and Providence Plantation* (2 vols., 1878), and Irving B. Richman, *Rhode Island, Its Making and Meaning* (2 vols., 1902). The chief original authorities for the early history of Rhode Island are John Winthrop, *History of New England*, and the *Colonial Records*, beginning in 1636. The publications of the Rhode Island Historical Society consist of *Collections* (9 vols.), *Proceedings* (21 numbers), and *Publications* (8 vols.). In all of these important material for history is preserved. The Narragansett Club, *Publications* (6 vols.), contain Roger Williams's letters; and there is some important matter in S. S. Rider, *Rhode Island Historical Tracts* (1877–1895), in the *Narragansett Historical Register* (9 vols.), and the *Newport Historical Reports* (4 vols.).

For Connecticut the standard authority is Benjamin Trumbull, *History of Connecticut* (2 vols., 1818). Other general histories are by Theodore Dwight, G. H. Hollister, and W. H. Carpenter. Original material is found in the *Colonial Records*, edited by J. H. Trumbull and C. J. Hoadly; Winthrop, *History of New England;* Connecticut Historical Society, *Proceedings*, which contain Hooker's famous letter to Winthrop; and Massachusetts Historical Society, *Collections*.

For New Haven the reader should consult Edward E. Atwater, *History of New Haven* (1881); Charles H. Levermore, *Republic of New Haven* (1886); and the publications of the New Haven Historical Society and the *Records of the Colony of New Haven*, in which the documentary material is chiefly printed. In connection with this volume the records of Hartford and of Southold are important. Special authorities are cited in chaps. xiv., xv. above.

NEW HAMPSHIRE AND MAINE

The standard authority for the history of New Hampshire is Jeremy Belknap, *History of New Hampshire* (3 vols., 1784–1813); and that for Maine is William D. Williamson, *History of Maine* (2 vols., 1832). Documents illustrating the history of New Hampshire can be found in the *New Hampshire Provincial and State Papers* and in John Scribner Jenness, *Transcripts of Original Documents in the English Archives Relating to the Early History of the State of New Hampshire* (1876).

Important papers occur in the ten volumes of *Collections* published by the New Hampshire Historical Society. For Maine the reader is referred to the *Collections* of the Massachusetts Historical Society and those of the Maine Historical Society. Important original material may be found in *York Deeds* (11 vols., 1642–1726).

For the early history of both colonies John Winthrop, *History of New England*, is the principal original authority. The narrative of Gorges has some value in connection with both colonies. Special tracts and documents are treated in chap. xvi., above.

DUTCH COLONY OF NEW NETHERLAND

The standard authorities for the early history of this colony are E. B. O'Callaghan, *History of New Netherland* (2 vols., 1855), and John Romeyn Brodhead, *History of the State of New York* (2 vols., 1872). The voyage of Henry Hudson is told in Purchas; and the *Documents Relating to the History of New York* (15 vols., 1856–1861) collected by John Romeyn Brodhead shed light on the early Dutch trading-post at New Amsterdam. The first mention by the English of the Dutch on the Hudson is made in a work republished in the *Collections* of the Massachusetts Historical Society (2d series, IX., 1–25), in which it is stated that an English sea-captain, Dermer, "met on his voyage from [Virginia to New England] with certain Hollanders who had a trade in Hudson River some years before that time, 1619."

For the relations of the Dutch with the English the main authorities are William Bradford, *Plimoth Plantation;* John Winthrop, *History of New England;* the "Proceedings of the Federal Commissioners," published in *Plymouth Colony Records*, IX., X., and *New Haven Records*, and Hazard, *State Papers*, II.; and Peter de Vries, *Journal* (N. Y. Hist. Soc., *Collections*, 2d series, III.).

NEW SWEDEN

The founding of New Sweden is probably best told in Benjamin Ferris, *History of the Original Settlements on the Delaware* (1846), extracted from works already published in English, and is interesting and valuable as identifying and describing many of the places mentioned. Winthrop and the records of the federal commissioners set out pretty fully the relations with the English colonies.

NEW FRANCE AND ACADIA

A series of chapters in Winsor, *Narrative and Critical History of America* (vol. IV., chaps. i.–iv.) tell the story of the founding of the French dominion in America. The chief original authorities are Richard Hakluyt, *Voyages;* Samuel de Champlain, *Les Voyages;* Marc Lescarbot, *Histoire de la Nouvelle France;* and the *Jesuit Relations.*

For relations with the English the chief original authority is Winthrop. Among the late French writers the pre-eminence is accorded to the Jesuit father Pierre François Xavier de Charlevoix, *Histoire de la Nouvelle France.*

RIVALRY WITH SPAIN

The rivalry of England with Spain, which is the greatest underlying principle of English colonization, is depicted fully in Hakluyt, *Discourses on Western Planting*, written at Raleigh's request and shown to Queen Elizabeth; first printed in 1877 by Dr. Charles Deane in the Maine Hist. Soc., *Collections* (2d series, II.). The lives of Gilbert and Raleigh were manifestations of this spirit of rivalry, and Edward Edwards, *Life of Sir Walter Raleigh* (2 vols., 1868), contains the fullest and best account extant of the two half-brothers. In an excellent little work, *Thomas Hariot and His Associates* (1900), developed by Henry Stevens chiefly from dormant material, we have a most entertaining and interesting account of Thomas Hariot, Sir Humphrey Gilbert, Sir Walter Raleigh, Jacques Le Moyne, Captain John White, and other noble spirits associated in the colonization of America. Compare the critical chapter of E. G. Bourne, *Spain in America* (*The American Nation*, III.).

RELIGIOUS INFLUENCES

Religious influences entered largely into the settlement and development of the different colonies in America. The chief authorities on the subject are James Carwithen, *History of the Church of England* (1849); Daniel Neal, *History of the Puritans* (1844); Anderson, *History of the Church of England in the Colonies* (2 vols., 2d ed., 1856); William Stevens Perry, *History of the American Episcopal Church* (2 vols., 1885); Francis Lister Hawks, *Contributions to the Ecclesiastical History of the United States* (2 vols., 1836–1839). William Meade, *Old Churches in Virginia* (2 vols., 1857), tells much about the early church in Virginia. In the *Johns Hopkins University Studies* are Paul E. Lauer, *Church and State in New England*, X., Nos. ii., iii.; and George Petrie, *Church and State in Maryland*, X., No. iv.

SOCIAL AND ECONOMIC CONDITIONS

For Virginia the economic side has been fully presented by Philip A. Bruce in his *Economic History of Virginia in the Seventeenth Century* (2 vols., 1896). The social side during the period of the present volume has not been

thoroughly covered by any modern writer. For Maryland
no detailed statement can be found, but much valuable
information is contained in Newton D. Mereness, *Maryland as a Proprietary Province* (1901). For New England
the social and economic status is fully presented by William
B. Weeden, *Economic and Social History of New England*
(2 vols., 1891). John G. Palfrey, *History of New England*
(4 vols.), has also several valuable chapters on the subject.
Edward Eggleston, *Beginners of a Nation* (1897) and
Transit of Civilization (1900) deal very appreciatively with
social elements and conditions.

INDEX

341

80, 106; improved ministry, 110.

Claiborne, William, Kent Island settlement, 95, 134; and Harvey, 96; commissioner, 111, 112; opposes Baltimore's charter, 121; career, 121; denies Baltimore's authority, 135; arrest ordered, 136; appeals to king, 136, 137; conflict on island, 136; treachery of Evelin, 137; island seized 138; attainted, 138; claim invalidated, 138; property confiscated, 138; return to Kent Island, 142; ascendency in Maryland, 147.

Cocheco. *See* Dover.

Coddington, William, in Rhode Island, 229, 237; royal commission, 237, 238.

Colonies, English, Gilbert's charter, 15; immunities, 16; Gilbert's attempts, 16 – 21; debt to Raleigh, 32; Gosnold and Gilbert's attempt, 34; joint - stock companies, 36; royal administration, 96, 206; connected history, 282; bibliography, 329 – 331; bibliography on religious influences, 338; bibliography on social and economic conditions, 338. *See also* colonies and companies by name.

Colonies, French. *See* Acadia, Canada.

Colonies, Spanish, influence on Spain, 4; and Hawkins, 9, 10; Drake's attacks, 11, 12; Cavendish plunders, 13; bibliography on English relations, 337.

Commission for Foreign Plantations, 96, 206.

Communism in Virginia, 59, 73, 77, 79; in Plymouth, 167.

Conant, Roger, in Massachusetts, 170, 171, 183.

Congregationalism, beginnings, 154; established in Massachusetts, 190, 196, 201, 202, 210; disclaimed, 194, 197; Massachusetts clergy, 200, 205; opposition, 211, 212; Antinomian controversy, 219–228; in Connecticut, 258; in New Haven, 263; Cambridge platform, 320; effect, 321. *See also* Pilgrims.

Connecticut, elements, 239; Plymouth's interest, 240–242, 245; Dutch in, 241, 249, 310, 316; migration from Massachusetts, 242–247; settled by organized communities, 247; Saltonstall's settlement, 248; Saybrook, 249; union of settlements, 250; Pequot War, 251–257; Fundamental Orders, 257–259; suffrage, 258; theocracy, 258; tenure of office, 259; growth, 259, 260; acquires Fenwick patent, 260; population (1653), 260; Massachusetts boundary, 304; river tolls, 304–306; bibliography, 335. *See also* New England.

Constitutions, Connecticut (1639), 257–259.

Cotton, John, in Massachusetts, 205; character, 218, 243, 321; and Antinomianism, 220, 223, 226, 227; death, 321.

Council in Maryland, 129. *See also* Assistants.

Council for New England, charter, 152; territory, 152; patent to Plymouth, 164; grant to Weston, 166; fishing monopoly endangered, 167; temporary activity, 168; division, 168, 185; discouraged, 169; grant to Massachusetts, 184; conflicting grants, 185, redivision, 207; resigns charter, 207; grants